Managers Divided

Wiley Series in Information Systems

Managers Divided

Organisation Politics and Information Technology Management

DAVID KNIGHTS
FERGUS MURRAY
Manchester School of Management, UMIST,
Manchester, UK

JOHN WILEY & SONS
Chichester • New York • Brisbane • Toronto • Singapore

Copyright ©️ 1994 by John Wiley & Sons Ltd,
Baffins Lane, Chichester,
West Sussex PO19 1UD, England

National Chichester 01243 779777
International (+44) 1243 779777

Other Wiley Editorial Offices

John Wiley & Sons, Inc., 605 Third Avenue,
New York, NY 10158-0012, USA

Jacaranda Wiley Ltd, G.P.O. Box 859, Brisbane,
Queensland 4001, Australia

John Wiley & Sons (Canada) Ltd, 22 Worcester Road,
Rexdale, Ontario M9W 1L1, Canada

John Wiley & Sons (SEA) Pte Ltd, 37 Jalan Pemimpin #05-04,
Block B, Union Industrial Building, Singapore 2057

Library of Congress Cataloging-in-Publication Data

British Library Cataloguing in Publication Data

A catalogue record for this book is available from the British Library

ISBN 0-471-935867

Typeset in 10/12pt Palatino from author's disks by Production Technology Department,
John Wiley & Sons Ltd, Chichester
Printed and bound in Great Britain by Biddles Ltd, Guildford, Surrey

Contents

Series Preface

The information systems community has grown considerably since 1984, when we first started the Wiley Series in Information Systems. We are pleased to be part of the growth of the field, and believe that the series books have played an important role in the intellectual development of the discipline. The primary objective of the series is to publish scholarly works which reflect the best of research in the information systems community.

PREVIOUS VOLUMES IN THE SERIES

Watkins & Eliot: *Expert Systems in Business and Finance—Issues and Applications*

Lacity & Hirschheim: *Information Systems Outsourcing—Myths, Metaphors and Realities*

Österle, Brenner & Hilbers: *Total Information Systems Management—A European Approach*

Ciborra & Jelassi: *Strategic Information Systems*

THE PRESENT VOLUME

As the information systems field matures, there is an increased need to carry the results of its growing body of research into practice. Therefore the series is also concerned with publishing research results that speak to important needs in the development and management of information systems, and we are broadening our editorial mission to recognize more explicitly the need for research to inform the practice and management of information systems. This is not so much a dramatic altering of direction as a change in emphasis. The present volume, *Managers Divided: Organisation Politics and Information Technology Management*, by David Knights and Fergus Murray, is a fine example of this new balance in our editorial emphasis.

Managers Divided: Organisation Politics and Information Technology Management, by David Knights and Fergus Murray, is an especially good example of our desire to showcase empirical research that speaks to the practical concerns of management and also extends our theoretical understanding of the development and deployment of information technology. Concerning practice, it presents a detailed discussion of the organisational processes surrounding the attempt to transform the organisation with information technology that will be useful to thoughtful practitioners engaged in the management of information systems. For our academic audience, the book informs these observations with a sophisticated social theory analysis and makes an important scholarly contribution to our understanding of power, gender and information technology.

RUDY HIRSCHHEIM   DICK BOLAND
University of Houston,   *Case Western Reserve University,*
Texas   *Ohio*

Preface

This book owes its origins to our good fortune in being selected by the ESRC to study the management and organisation dimensions of IT in their Programme on Information and Communication Technology (PICT). More specifically, we should thank Professor Bill Melody, Sally Wyatt and Paschal Preston for having faith in our team at the Manchester School of Management to pursue this important eight-year programme.

As a result of this funding, the Centre for Research on Organisations, Management and Technical Change (CROMTEC) was formed in the Manchester School of Management at UMIST and we thank all our colleagues there for the support and stimulation they have given us. Particular mention should be made of Rod Coombs who has managed the PICT research overall and Hugh Willmott who was involved with David Knights in studying the case study of Pensco prior to this particular project. Fergus Murray took over the empirical study focusing on systems development management and, while the authorship of this book is collaborative, he produced the bulk of the fieldwork and the first draft of a majority of the chapters.

A further stimulation and support for this book, given its focus, has been the Financial Services Research Centre in the School of Management at UMIST. It has provided the context for continuous debate in this field and here Glenn Morgan and Andrew Sturdy should be thanked for their contribution.

Of even more importance, we thank those practitioners in our two case studies Effessco and Pensco and others that were interviewed, who gave of their time and energy, unwittingly perhaps, in ways that have contributed to the completion of this book.

Finally, we thank Alison Smith for typing numerous drafts of the text.

Introduction

Many writers, journalists, politicians, management consultants and would-be gurus have claimed that effective (information) technology management is the key to business success in the increasingly competitive global economies of the millennium. Organisations in the future, it is argued, will stand or fall in relation to how speedily, efficiently and interactively they develop and process information and IT systems, deploying the most sophisticated and up-to-date computing facilities. Systems development, then, is clearly at the forefront of corporate management as we approach the twenty-first century, though its promise and potential is far from realised.

But how is systems development currently understood? Often it is viewed as mere technical links in a chain of human 'progress'. In short, and with few notable exceptions, systems development is perceived in terms of the same unilinear logic as the computer programs that form its anatomical base. In so far as systems development is contextualised within the organisations in which it is created and sustained, either implicit or explicit assumptions concerning consensually held values regarding the 'progress' of technology, and the goals and benefits it supports, are taken for granted. In this book, we adopt a very different approach by locating systems development practices within the context of organisational politics that involve conflict and competition about both the goals of organisations and their means of attainment.

Our approach differs from the technical literature on systems development in identifying and seeking to theorise the social, political and hence problematic nature of systems and software development in contemporary society. Unlike the technical literature that tends to restrict the examination of the social and political side of software development to the sphere of user–developer relations or human–computer interactions, we place it at the centre of our analysis.

It may be thought that our approach parallels much of the sociological and organisational literature that perceives technology as a significant force for change in society, and which polarises around the issue of 'progress' whether seen as 'positive' or 'negative'. On the 'negative' side, the 'doom and gloom' merchants peddle a crisis of increasing control and surveillance as the likely outcome of the revolutionary advances in information technology. At the other more positive extreme, the visionaries predict a new world order in which the drudgery of work would be eradicated as factories and offices become automated, computer controlled environments and business is managed/operated through electronic communication and information networks. Neither the pessimists nor the optimists have seen their nightmares or dreams realised, though some would argue that it is still early days in what they see as the IT revolution.

Between these two controversies, less grandiose research work has been conducted with the aim of opening up the 'black box' of new technology to a more detailed investigation and seeking empirically grounded understanding of management and organisational conditions, contexts and consequences of IT use and development. We see this book contributing to the literature but focusing specifically on how social and political definitions of, and impositions upon, reality enter each and every stage of IT production from design to ultimate use and back again.

Theoretically the book draws upon, criticises and develops a range of literature classified along two separate dimensions: the local/global focus of technology research, on one side, and the degree to which organisational politics is seen as disruptive but eradicable or simply inescapable, on the other. While acknowledging different contributions and insights stemming from a number of perspectives, our own research favours an approach that analyses power and politics as inescapable features of organisations. It seeks to study the use and development of IT in that political context through detailed and localised studies of management practice that are understood to be influenced by, and have consequences for, broader socio-political and economic, organisational, technological and what we term security conditions. It is largely through the social interpretation, construction or reconstruction of these conditions and what they mean for the organisation that specific political alliances are mobilised and particular information systems are made possible. For purposes of shorthand, therefore, we call these 'conditions of possibility' when they are introduced in Chapter 2 and elaborated in subsequent chapters.

As a way of illustrating these ideas, we explore the socio-political contexts, relations and interconnections between organisational practice and software development through longitudinal empirical case study research in the financial sector. This sector was chosen for a number of reasons. First, one of the authors had practical as well as prior research experience in this sector. Second, the technological innovation literature had for some time been focused exclusively on the manufacturing sector, and yet, the development of IT was having more impact in the service and particularly the financial sector because of its information-intensive character. Indeed insurance and banking were some of the earliest and most widespread users of IT. Third, the financial services sector has not only experienced dramatic change as a result of the IT revolution but throughout the period of our research was undergoing the most radical upheaval in its history. This was a function of regulatory changes and the partial privatisation of state pensions—the latter of which was the stimulus for the development of a new information system in our central case study company. These turbulent conditions were seen as creating considerable challenges to the effective and efficient management of IT in the financial sector and our research demonstrates this to have been the case.

Finally, and perhaps of equal importance was the quality of our access to companies in this sector and, in particular, to an insurance company where in a previous study (Knights and Willmott, 1993) we had been given *carte blanche* to interview at any level in the organisation, attend and tape record committee proceedings (including the equivalent of board meetings), visit branches, read documents and sit in on training sessions and corporate conferences and rallies. This company, given the pseudonym Pensco, clearly figures significantly in this study of an information system designed to support government-induced new pensions contracts. The system was traced from genesis to final launch through a detailed examination of the trials and tribulations of its development.

The intensive fieldwork offers a thick description of software practices that are firmly located in the specific and general conditions that render particular technology developments possible. As such, the organisation is seen as more than an isolated island cut off from society and history. Instead, organisations are analysed as part and parcel, or condition and consequence, of a broader set of structured social and political relations.

Systems development has often been regarded as a technical activity bracketed off from organisational and social life. It has been theorised as a privileged sphere of activity that is powerful yet uncomfortably on the edge of modern organisations. In the past, there may have been some historical justification for this view but not any longer. The development and use of information systems are now a strategic, operational and prosaic feature of organisational reality. And whether they like it or not, IS specialists are being edged further and further towards the centre of organisational life.

Assumptions regarding the 'technical' and 'different' character of systems development have played a large part in guiding software debates over the last 20 years. Although there are exceptions, this debate within the IT community has focused on a search for 'solutions to a changing range of software development problems'. In recent years this has most prominently taken the guise of a search for a more rigorous, engineering-like development methodology.

Evidence from our research suggests that this technicist approach of software engineers and practitioners is misguided and unlikely to secure an understanding of their problems, let alone ameliorate or resolve them. This is because the development of software cannot be isolated from the social world into a technical enclave. Software activity is a social activity and is shaped and constructed through, and plays back upon, the web of social relations and knowledge that constitute the dynamic of contemporary organisations and society. This social character of software work is, of course, recognised to an extent by writers on software practices and methods. But, as we have already suggested, this recognition is usually restricted to that part of systems development which involves, for example, securing user requirements or 'selling' the system to reluctant users. While, at one level, this could be seen as a political focus, we treat politics as much more than user resistance to systems.

By politics we mean the very stuff, the marrow of organisational process; by politics we mean managerial and staff concerns to secure careers, to avoid blame, to create success and to establish stable identities within competitive labour markets and organisational hierarchies where the resources that donate relative success are necessarily limited.

Politics is placed at the heart of the analysis in the work presented here because we believe that contemporary society, and the organisations that constitute it, are structured around and through the concern of individuals to secure a symbolic and material sense of themselves in historically particular conditions of uncertainty and competition. That is, as individuals we are involved in a challenge to secure employment, job security, promotion, status, affirmation and physical and mental well-being while we seek to minimise anxiety, blame, abuse and punishment. Unfortunately, we undertake this challenge of contemporary life in conditions of structured inequality that are not of our own choosing. Rather this challenge is played out in highly constrained conditions where factors such as class, gender, race and the social organisation of production and knowledge often appear to take the form of immovable givens.

Clearly, systems development and IS specialists do not stand outside these concerns and conditions of possibility. Yet it has often been assumed that this was the case and that the technical activities of the IS specialist acted as a talisman to ward off social relations and the politics of organisational life inherent in them. This book sets out fundamentally to challenge this notion of IS activities and the discourse of 'progressive technology' that raises the technologist above the hurly burly of everyday life.

The main part of this study consists of a theoretical and empirical examination of the politics of systems development. In the first part of the book we review existing literature and introduce our theoretical approach to systems development. This is supplemented by a consideration of the growing complexity of IT management issues; and the changing outlines and organisation of the IS profession; and the rise to dominance of a 'user relations' problem within contemporary systems development. In the second part of the book, we develop an in-depth, longitudinal case study of a major systems project. This examines the building of a major system from the early decisions concerning its desirability and design through to its launch and initial assessment. In presenting this material we focus on different aspects of the organisational politics of software development. These include the social construction of successful systems; inter-managerial competition around and within software development; the importance of organisational conditions of technological possibility; and the politics of the IS division itself. Such a detailed examination of a single systems development project within an organisational and sectoral setting with which we are thoroughly acquainted has allowed us to focus on the intricate and complex ways in which politics invades, supports and at times subverts different stages of the systems development process. By way of concluding this introduction, we now provide a brief synopsis of each of the chapters.

Throughout history, technological change has been a constant concern of organisational analysis, industrial sociology and labour process theory. In Chapter 1 we review some of the dominant trends in this literature on technological change in the context of a classificatory model in which we have attempted to locate the various approaches in accordance with the scope or scale of their study, on one dimension, and their attitude towards power and politics, on the other. In this discussion we provide a critical account of the literature which has a bearing on the politics of information technology management and, in so doing, hint at the broad parameters of our own perspective that is to be elaborated in Chapter 2. Here we generate an analysis of technology and information systems that understands politics as a central and pervasive feature of organisational life through which they are developed and stimulate change. The struggles and conflict that constitute politics and which are the flipside of managerial co-operation and collaboration, it is argued, are channelled by well-worn rules and routines and played out around career issues, involving particular individual and group preoccupations with subjective status and security. In Chapter 2, we introduce a framework for analysing technological change and systems development that is firmly rooted in the particular organisational and sectoral conditions of that change. However, this framework also allows and encourages an understanding of the linkages between the individual organisation under consideration and its broader or more global social and technological contexts.

While politics is a pervasive aspect of organisational life, the intensity and form this politics takes varies over time according to different conditions. Thus in Chapter 3 we outline broad parameters of political intensity due to factors such as the rapidity of organisational change, the institutionalisation of political routines and practices, and the degree of uncertainty facing decision-makers and those charged with implementing decisions taken elsewhere. The central part of Chapter 3, then, examines the increasing complexity of IT management issues in the 1980s and 1990s as the spread and scope of IT applications expanded. The chapter closes by examining managerial attempts to conquer and control this uncertainty through the implementation of IT strategies.

In Chapter 4 we turn to consider the occupational organisation, position and career paths of IS specialists as central actors in the systems development process. Thus we examine the UK labour market position of IS specialists, managerial attempts to solve the software crisis through the intensification of IS labour, and the broad outlines of, an albeit changing, IS culture. The second part of the chapter focuses on the changing relationship between IS specialists and their users over the last 30 years and charts the conditions that have led to what is currently called a 'user relations' phase of systems development. This is characterised by the increasing power and IT knowledge of users and the introduction of IS systems into increasingly market-sensitive applications within and between organisations.

A more detailed examination of the user relations problematic forms the basis of Chapter 5. The first part of the chapter outlines some of the formal changes that have occurred in the battle over the direction and control of IS divisions before looking at different ways of facilitating user involvement. This draws on empirical material drawn from the UK financial services industry. The second section of the chapter examines the detailed negotiation of user relations drawing on empirical material from one of our case study companies, an insurance subsidiary of a UK bank here called Effessco. This highlights some of the ambiguities of the concept of user relations focusing in particular on issues of control, resistance and identity in conditions of increased competition and uncertainty.

In Chapters 4 and 5 we begin to raise issues concerning gender relations in IT management and systems development. In Chapter 6 these become a central focus as we investigate the importance of a particular macho masculinity as a condition of much systems development. In so doing we briefly examine symbiotic relations between technology and masculinity and their definition of each other. We then analyse the importance of these relations in the development of business application software through further material drawn from our Effessco case study.

The second part of the book is constituted by Chapters 7 to 11. These are based on in-depth case study material of a major systems project undertaken at a UK life insurance company, here called Pensco. In Chapter 7 we introduce Pensco, a rather traditional company that has undergone rapid changes in a fast changing marketplace, before outlining the chronology of the major system development project we charted in the latter years of the 1980s. This system, which was designed to assist the sale and administration of a new range of pensions products was particularly market sensitive, vital for the company's future, and involved inputs from a wide variety of users. It thus combined rapid organisational change with a high degree of uncertainty and generated a particularly visible and intense politics in the organisation.

Having introduced the pension system development we go on, in Chapter 8, to look at the ways in which the 'finished' systems were evaluated within the company. Here we describe the different presentations and assessments of the systems made by a variety of organisational actors, from the clerical staff using the systems to the senior management team who were keen to impress on the marketplace and their directors the success of Pensco's pensions products and systems. In this chapter we argue that systems are not mere technical achievements but effectively socially constructed by those involved in their making. That is to say, their meaning and significance are artfully accomplished by those whose careers are at stake when evaluations of outcomes as successful or otherwise have to be made. But this artful accomplishment of reality, we argue, is neither straightforward nor devoid of tensions, conflicts and contradictions. Indeed throughout the development of the pensions system in Pensco, constructions of reality regarding its direction, meaning and significance were in continuous turmoil as different groups competed for pre-eminence through the management practices and procedures by which the system was in process of being designed and implemented.

While senior management were united in their desire to paint a success-ful picture of the pensions project to an external audience, there were also clear divisions between IS, customer services and marketing managers and functions. Chapter 9 considers these centrifugal forces of inter-managerial competition. Here we show how tensions and conflicts surrounding insta-bility and change at Pensco found their expression through the systems development project. We do this by examining the politics of career and resource competition as a medium and outcome of IS practices.

In Chapter 10 we examine the organisational conditions whereby particular technological developments relating to the pensions project at Pensco became possible. Here we look at both the state of Pensco's IT systems and the organisation and history of IS staff and managers in the company. From this investigation, we argue that Pensco was in a very poor position to implement its ambitious pensions systems. From this we draw two points: firstly, that reflection on organisational conditions of technological possibility is an essential prerequisite of major IS deci-sions; and, secondly, that these conditions of possibility cannot simply be read off from the organisation. Rather, like all organisational phe-nomena, these conditions of possibility are mobilised through the inter-action, conflict, and suppression of competing constructions of those conditions. At Pensco, senior IS managers arrived at a particularly optimistic and benign interpretation of their existing systems and IS staff infrastructures. We conclude the chapter by speculating on why this interpretation came to dominate the pensions project.

While Chapters 7 to 9 were concerned with relations between the IS division and the various user divisions, in Chapter 11 we focus on the politics of the IS division itself. Here we argue that the work of manage-ment concerns not only the control and co-ordination of subordinates, negotiations with other managers, and planning and strategy. Also a vital, if often unrecognised, aspect of managerial 'work' includes the constitution of meaning concerning the 'self' or identity and the acti-vities and structures that make up the organisation. Thus, we examine the ways in which the IS chief attempted to control the constitution of meaning within his division and pensions project such that this reflected favourably on him as a competent and state-of-the-art IS manager. Drawing on debates from the literature on the social construction of technology, we examine the way in which the IS AGM deployed the rhetoric of user relations, here mobilised as 'marketing-led IT use', and proliferating user demands as a means to discipline his staff and increase IS specialist productivity.

Finally, in Chapter 12 we provide an overall discussion of our findings and their implications for research in IS, in particular, and organisation studies, more generally.

1
Organisational Politics and Theories of Technological Change

INTRODUCTION

In this chapter we examine a selective but diverse range of social research on technological change. This extends from the well-worn fields of technological determinism to the more recent developments of social construction analyses and social shaping accounts of technological innovation and use.

Our purpose in reviewing this literature is two-fold. Firstly, the review enables us to focus upon certain key topics that inform the chapters of this book. Secondly, it indicates our critical use of, and departure from, the prevailing literature in regard to the political process perspective to technological change that is developed in Chapter 2. In addition, there is an intention to provide for the general reader an idea of the different perspectives that can be deployed in seeking to account for technological change.

As indicated in the introduction, our intention in this book is to provide a theoretically innovative and empirically grounded account of Information Technology management, which particularly focuses on the process of systems development. In so doing we argue, firstly, that the process of systems development is socially constructed and, secondly, that this occurs through a 'contested terrain' (Edwards, 1979) of organisational politics.

When looking at the technical change literature, therefore, some central concerns for us are the way in which different studies account for change, the role and definition they accord power in this change process, and the manner in which they accommodate or ignore issues of conflict and competition.

This involves examining various studies of technological change and identifying their theoretical positioning. One way of understanding the diverse range of positions taken by the technological change literature is to classify studies in accordance with their location within a two-dimensional model based upon research and methodological focus, on the one hand, and position with respect to politics, on the other (see Figure 1.1). In terms of research focus, it is possible to separate the more global (macro) from localised (micro) studies. In the main, global studies tend to rely on systemic or structural factors to explain the pace and direction of change whether by appeal to technological innovation or class and gender interests. Studies that focus on micro processes are less able to abstract away or ignore the complexities, contingencies and specificities of given cases and tend to produce vivid and dense descriptions of technological and organisational change—but always at the risk of losing their analytical power.

The distinction between global and local needs qualification. This is because almost all studies combine elements of both the global and the local; even the most narrowly focused study of a technological innovation must place it in the context of technology history and the contemporary socio-economic environment. Likewise, the plausibility of macro studies of the impact of technology on modern society is dependent to some degree on the use of specific localised

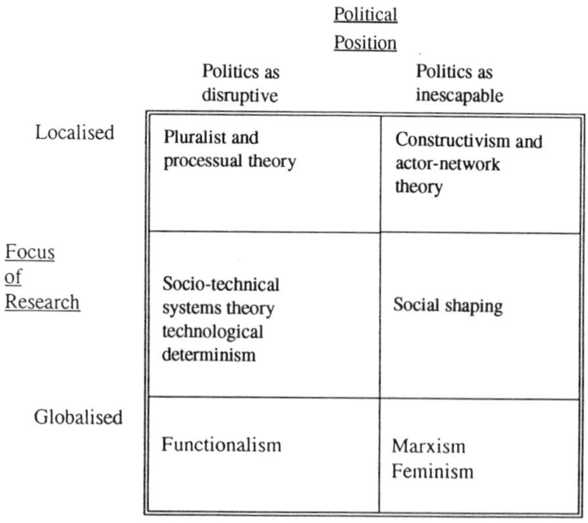

	Political Position	
	Politics as disruptive	Politics as inescapable
Localised	Pluralist and processual theory	Constructivism and actor-network theory
Focus of Research	Socio-technical systems theory technological determinism	Social shaping
Globalised	Functionalism	Marxism Feminism

Figure 1.1 *A Classification of Theoretical Approaches to Technological Change*

examples that illustrate the general argument. Consequently, locating studies on the global/local dimension is merely one of emphasis. This is less so with regard to the political dimension. Here authors will tend to see politics in one of two ways: either as disruptive of the 'smooth' and 'rational' management of an organisation or as an inescapable 'fact' of organisational life.

While a two-dimensional classification clearly does violence to the complexity of research, locating studies within particular perspectives so as to locate them within the classifactory scheme further duplicates such violence. Nonetheless, as long as it is recognised that the scheme and any single position within it may be challenged and reconstructed, then it can be seen as a means of simplifying a complex terrain and drawing attention to contrasts between different research approaches. In this sense, the framework we present in this chapter is an heuristic device. We will shortly proceed to examine the different perspectives in detail but before doing so, let us look at the model in broad terms.

We first look at the perspectives that see politics as disruptive and abnormal. These perspectives have traditionally drawn upon Durkheimian (1947) social theory. Social organisation, for Durkheim, is a delicate moral order that may easily break down into anomic disorder and disintegration should 'egoistic' self-interest fuel behaviour in violation of the 'scientific' understanding of society as an interdependent objective reality.

The functionalist paradigm that followed in Durkheim's footsteps and has dominated twentieth-century sociology and organisation theory (see Gouldner, 1976) has also been the most prominent perspective in the systems development literature (see Lyytinen, 1993) whether global (i.e. the macro-society) or local (i.e. micro-organisational) in its scope of analysis. Either implicitly or explicitly, it has informed both theorists and practitioners of systems in such a way as to render them immune to problems of organisational politics. This is because the overarching assumptions underlying systems development have been that problems, such as they exist, are *technical*, not social or organisational, in nature. As a consequence, organisations are treated like machines: once the technology is functioning properly, the organisation is presumed to transmit its content unproblematically like a car body responding to the energy under its bonnet. Organisationally, systems development theory and practice has assumed a consensus on the values of technology—namely, that it is a progressive and inevitable development that should not be questioned. In so far as an intellectual orientation is adopted at all, systems development tends to subscribe to one or other version of technological determinism where technology is the instrument of change rather than its product. Because value-consensus underlies the functionalist paradigm, in normal circumstances conflict or resistance to the progress of technology does not occur. But where there is evidence of political conflict, it is presumed to be pathological or deviant and must be purged much like a virus in a piece of computer software, lest it contaminate the whole system.

When examined at a global level of analysis, the functionalist assumptions of value-consensus with regard to technology and systems development are comparatively easy to maintain since, predominantly, the focus is on large-scale outcomes in which any political conflicts or disruptions have eventually been 'smoothed away' and, in any case, are unrecorded and therefore no longer accessible. One of the criticisms of functionalism in general, however, was its failure to examine the more detailed micro events that might be said to constitute the whole whether this be a society, an organisation or a technological system. When researchers began to study development at the more local level of a particular organisation, the assumption of value-consensus underlying the functional paradigm could no longer be taken for granted. The evidence of conflict and power struggles was impossible to deny and the view that technology had a central determining force on an organisation and its sociopolitical life had to be questioned.

One outcome of this questioning was a new perspective that eventually was called 'processual theory' on the basis of its concern with, and focus upon, the socio-political processes within which and whereby technology systems were developed. Yet despite the focus upon power, status and career struggles underlying the development and use of new technologies, the overarching view remained that these struggles were in some way disruptive of the smooth running and rational development of systems. In short, politics remained somehow an, albeit temporally inescapable, pathological or foreign body to be eradicated if 'normal' service was to be resumed. Although the crudity of absolute consensus underlying global functionalism has been dismissed, there remains here the fundamental Durkheimian belief that rational organisation involves individuals and groups working together interdependently in pursuit of a commonly agreed set of organisational and system goals. Processual theory does not deny the self-interested and often informal political struggles and conflict over scarcely valued material and symbolic goods, but they are seen as disruptive of the rational and coherent development of systems and the attainment of organisational goals. In short, if not actually pathological, political conflict is still seen as an aberration that can and should be contained or removed.

On the other side of this classificatory model we have both global and local approaches that see political struggles and conflict as inherent and central features of all organisational and social life. Global perspectives subscribing to this view fall into two camps: Marxists who identify political conflicts as deriving from the polarisation of class interests and feminists who see such conflicts as largely a product of the domination of men over women within patriarchal structures of social relations. Although sometimes both Marxism and feminism have fallen into functionalist ways of thinking, they have always seen politics and conflict as inescapable in the absence of class or gender equality. Within such frameworks, technology or systems development is viewed as a reflection or outcome of these class or gender relations and is seen to serve primarily the interests of the bourgeoisie or men.

As with all areas of the model, there are various degrees of sophistication from the basic set of premises. So, for example, a recent version on this side of the model is the social shaping of technology (MacKenzie and Wajcman, 1985; Wajcman, 1991), where a central concern has been to reverse the strong influence of technological determinism in technology studies. MacKenzie and Wajcman (1985, p3) first stress the human element within technology itself in that the physical objects constituting it are meaningless outside of human activity and knowledge associated with them. But this physical–human combination is then seen to be created, designed and developed and thus ultimately shaped by, or even a function of, distinct sets of human or social interests of which class, gender and race or ethnicity are the most prevalent. While there is considerable diversity within this literature, it shares in common the view that technology and its development is not neutral and, therefore, must be political to some greater or lesser extent.

So far the social shaping literature has tended to remain global in many of its pronouncements although, like all the perspectives outlined here, the boundaries between global/local dimensions are blurred and shifting. And clearly there is important research (e.g. Cockburn, 1983, 1985; Noble, 1977, 1984) which has drawn upon detailed localised case studies where the authors, though not explicitly declaring themselves to follow a social shaping approach, subscribe to the same sort of understandings. Also there are connections between the social shaping approach and social constructionism and actor-network theory (e.g. Bijker et al, 1987; Law et al, 1993), although the latter see technology and the social as much more intimately interrelated than do the social shapers and concentrate their work on localised contexts in which the social and the technical mutually define one another.

In developing an organisational politics of technology and systems development, we make critical use of a broad range of the following perspectives which we now proceed to review in rather more detail. We do not, however, examine global functionalist perspectives further except in so far as their assumptions have continued to inform technological determinism and even 'processual theory'. This is largely because the focus of this book is not on 'grand theories' of the technological society but on the socio-political and organisational context of particular technology developments and implementations.

In conducting this review, however, we are particularly interested in the way in which different accounts of technological and organisational change address the related issues of power and politics.

THEORIES OF TECHNOLOGICAL CHANGE

Technological Determinism

Theories of technological determinism developed out of classical, rationalist and positivist approaches to management. Their primary concern was to measure the correlation between organisational performance and organisational structure with regard to different production technologies. In the organisation theory field, technological determinists have argued that different production technologies determine different organisational structures and behaviours independent of local context (Sayles, 1958; Woodward, 1958).

Woodward (1958) and Woodward et al (1965, 1970) were equally concerned to establish the best organisational design and structure related to specific types of technology. It was in this sense an (albeit limited) precursor of the contingency approach (Hickson et al, 1971) to management and organisational behaviour. Classifying industry broadly into unit/batch, mass and process forms of production, Woodward and her colleagues found that output performance and conflict behaviour were correlated with definite levels of authority, spans of control and ratios of managers to staff but variable as to the specific kinds of technology in use. In short, there was a structural norm for each type of technology which produced the best record on output and the fewest problems in terms of industrial conflict. Sayles (1958) found that levels of conflict varied consistently with the type of technology being utilised and that mass production was most likely to be associated with worker militancy. Following this kind of approach and drawing upon a wide range of studies, Blauner (1964) concluded that the type of technology largely determined levels of job dissatisfaction or what he termed alienation and that, again, mass production workers were the most alienated. He also anticipated that the advent of process technologies in industries such as the petrochemicals sector signalled the end of worker alienation and conflict (cf. Nichols and Armstrong's, 1976, critical response to this thesis).

These technological constraint theorists clearly challenged the plausibility of the then dominant classical administrative theory, with its insistence on 'correct' organisational design or 'one best way' (Daft, 1989) as well as much of the increasingly populist human relations literature. For if performance could be correlated with specific organisational structures largely determined by type of production technology, then neither universal administrative structures nor the intricacies of informal relations, interpersonal behaviour and leadership styles were as significant to management as classical and human relations theory respectively claimed.

However, it could be said that the classification of technology into unit/batch, mass and process production was too simple and their distinctiveness given too much weight independently of the interpretative procedures of practitioners. The classification has clearly become obsolete by further developments in computing and information technology. Other criticisms relate to the inadmissibility of assuming a cause from a correlation, the tendency to examine production plants independently of their environmental or socio-political context and the general problem of selecting out technology as the more significant determinant of organisational structure and behaviour.

In the field of innovation studies technological determinists have argued that technologies develop within paradigms and along trajectories according to a logic which resides within these technologies themselves (Dosi, 1982; Nelson and Winter, 1977). In other words, the direction and pace of particular technologies is accounted for by technical forces alone independent of economic or social conditions. Such analyses have been criticised for ignoring these social and economic contexts and the possibility that so-called 'natural' technological trajectories were in fact *self-fulfilling prophesies* rather than the unrolling of an indisputable technological logic (MacKenzie, 1990). That is, that technologists' expectations of the course of a given technological innovation are in themselves an important influence on the course of that innovation. As MacKenzie says. 'Persistent patterns of technological change are persistent in part because technologists and others, believe they will be persistent' (1991, p.10). He cites the example of the 10-fold increase every five years that is now expected of computer calculation speeds. Far from being a 'natural trajectory' this persistent increase in calculation speed is achieved, at least in part, because computer developers believe this is the increase in calculation speed they must achieve if their products are to be competitive.

Although much challenged by recent research, technological determinism still holds considerable attraction, if in often attenuated ways. A number of studies of technology (e.g. Sabel, 1982; Piore and Sabel, 1984; Zuboff, 1988) have based their rather optimistic forecasts of organisational health and democratisation on the supposedly innate characteristics of IT. Zuboff's *In the Age of the Smart Machine* (1988) has been particularly popular despite continuing in a technological determinist tradition that has been severely questioned elsewhere (Noble, 1977; Wilkinson, 1983; MacKenzie and Wajcman, 1985; Knights and Willmott, 1988).

The central thesis of Zuboff's research is that IT has the potential to transform organisational structures and processes in a 'progressive' and 'liberating' manner. As such, IT promises to democratise work and make enterprises more effective, flexible and adaptable. In particular, Zuboff focuses on IT's so-called 'informating' capacity which increasingly renders work a more abstract and 'intellective' activity requiring constant learning and skill sharing.

According to Zuboff, the informated organisation will differ radically from its pre-IT counterpart. It will shift from hierarchical towards concentric structures, the strait-jacket of managerial 'imperative control' will be replaced by equality, and the distinction between managerial and non-managerial labour will be eradicated in favour of collaborating 'co-workers'. These staggering changes will create the constantly 'learning organisation' able to react flexibly and quickly to rapidly changing market opportunities.

Zuboff's work is almost Utopian in its optimism and bears some resemblance to Sabel (1982) who also endows IT with a liberating potential. But whereas Sabel and Piore locate the possibility of realising this potential in the break-up of mass-markets consequent upon a proliferation of differentiated consumer demands, Zuboff seems to believe that IT will bring about these changes itself, if only management can let go of its obsolete and dysfunctional obsession with control. Thus, for example, she rhetorically asks:

> If we unleash the *autonomous informating effects* of this new technology, can it transform the conception of managerial authority and thus, the social structures sustained by that conception? (Zuboff, 1988, p.217, emphasis added)

This talk of 'unleashing IT's autonomous informating effects' is a clear and bold reiteration of technological determinism. And at other points Zuboff talks about IT's inherent informating capacity that 'invites learning', apparently autonomously and by itself independent of human volition (ibid., pp.306–7)

If IT then is providing the driving force for the realisation of the informated organisation, it is management as presently constituted which stands in its way. Yet Zuboff does not give us much idea as to how managers will be persuaded to let go their authority and control at a time when competition between managers is intensifying (see, for example, Scase and Goffee, 1989). Instead, she rather lamely argues that the informated organisation will not tolerate 'unilateral authority', although it is questionable if any organisation actually functions through unilateral authority alone, and that informaters will 'have to pay careful attention to developing a constitutional infrastructure that legitimises public debate and mutual influence' (Zuboff, 1988, p.406). This talk of 'public debate and mutual influence' appears to be a somewhat modified version of her earlier claim that IT would promise 'equality' in organisations.

Despite the acclaim accorded to Zuboff's work, it seems underlain by a naive thesis that accords an inherently progressive role to IT and the promise of less hierarchical and unequal, yet more dynamic and innovative, organisations capable of continuous learning and adaptability. Of perhaps greater interest is the case study material in Zuboff's research. This carefully explores the ways in which IT has been predominantly used to increase managerial surveillance and control of labour processes and the problems created for management by the multiplication of organisational information and data flows. In this it focuses on the increasing importance of electronic data and accessible information in organisations. As such, Zuboff adds her voice to the literature on the transformation of work into 'knowledge work' (e.g. Poster, 1990) in which the principal concern is the 'creation of meaning' (Zuboff, 1988, p.349).

While Zuboff adds a new dimension to literature on the meaning of work and the work of meaning construction, she exaggerates the role of IT as an autonomous change agent. Clearly, IT can and does change the way in which meaning is created, in that in the informated organisation, organisational activity is increasingly represented through real-time, abstract data flows that are much more speedily communicated and reconstructed. It therefore intensifies the flux and flow of meaning but this is more likely to reinforce hierarchical power than undermine it. For in building information systems, concepts of 'profit', 'costs', 'assets', 'turnover', etc., become represented as unproblematic and quantified reifications through which organisational relations come to be defined (Coombs, 1993). Short of challenging the whole information system—a near impossibility either for reasons of limited technical competence or simply because it embodies such 'powerful' organisational resources—the possibility of resisting or reconstructing particular concepts and practices becomes increasingly difficult. Information systems are clearly not neutral with respect to management control, as Zuboff appears to intimate.

In sum, technological determinists treat technology and its so-called effects as objectively real attributing to it an autonomous organising force. Consequently, they largely ignore issues of power and politics in technological change. Where Zuboff does relate to these issues, she simply assumes managerial power to be a dysfunctional impediment to the realisation of the transformative potential or determinative effects of IT. In terms of our classification (see Figure 1.1), while the focus of technological determinists encompasses both local and global aspects of research, organisational politics is on the whole seen as a disruptive element that needs to be eradicated.

Socio-technical Approaches

Arising out of the ashes of the early crude versions of technological determinism the socio-technical perspective (Trist et al, 1963; Miller and Rice, 1967; Rice, 1963) identified work groups and social relations as important mediators of technological possibilities. In short, the positive effects of technology on production were seen as dependent upon social factors and group behaviour. The underlying preoccupation of the socio-technical theorists, however, was to match social, technical and environmental demands for purposes of increasing economic productivity. Consequently, its managerial focus precluded any serious examination of politics and power in the processes of technological change.

Early socio-technical work often assumed that particular types of technology, albeit mediated by specific social and informal relations, were the primary factor in determining organisational form (Trist et al, 1963). This was later modified and socio-technical work in the IT field has taken as its primary concern the resolution of the tension between human needs, often imputed from psychoanalytic theory or industrial psychology, and organisational forms in technological change processes. Mumford (Mumford and Ward, 1968; Mumford, 1979) has been the primary protagonist of socio-technical approaches in the IT community. Her work has looked at means of resolving socio-technical conflicts in work group and task redesign brought about by computerisation. This has been guided by the socio-technical school's prescriptive bent to promote the twin goals of human well-being (largely in the form of job satisfaction) and organisational productive efficiency.

The socio-technical approach has made a substantial contribution to the IT literature. In particular, it stresses the importance of variations in organisational contexts of IT applications and the need to take account of organisation members' social and work needs in the process of systems design. This has led to the advocacy of various forms of user involvement in systems design. However, because of an albeit worker-participative managerialism, socio-technical approaches have largely ignored issues of power and politics in organisations. Nor do they attempt to theorise the relationship between organisations and their broader socio-economic context. Thus, their prescriptions for user involvement are unrealistic at best, and misleading at worst, in that they do not reckon with the conflict and contests surrounding structured inequality within and outside the workplace (see, for example, Mumford and Henshall, 1979).

In their focus on achieving an efficient 'fit' between computer systems and what they perceive to be political and cultural organisational contexts, Willcocks and Mason (1987) reflect a continuity with the legacy of socio-technical paradigms. By contrast, however, they place politics at the centre of their analysis of computerisation. Their notion of politics is grounded in a resource dependency perspective (Pfeffer and Salancik, 1978; Pfeffer, 1981) that identifies power as residing in those actors who mobilise or secure the most difficult material or symbolic resources (e.g. money, prestige, expertise) upon which the organisation depends (Pfeffer, 1981, p.101). In general, Willcocks and Mason's analysis combines a modified socio-technical approach with a contingency theory of organisations and a resource- dependency theory of power.

Advancing the interventionist approach of Mumford and her colleagues, Willcocks and Mason supply IS managers and staff with techniques that will enable them to analyse and mobilise organisational politics in pursuit of managerial purpose. As such they unashamedly promote IS specialists as change agents, seeming to believe that IS personnel do not have an agenda of their own other than one of implementing successful systems. This is a problematic and perhaps even dangerous assumption, illustrating the weakness of a political analysis drawn from resource-dependency theory in which hierarchy is taken for granted.

Their work then privileges the technologist as change agent and technology as the primary source of organisational change. It is steeped in a conception of management as rational and IS managers, in particular, as wholly benign. In promoting the sectional interests of IS specialists, they are blind to the contradictions and tensions of organisational life in market contexts and how these make the 'rational' objectives of any one group difficult to achieve. Their research 'cries out' for a broader analysis of markets, socio-economic power and the political nature of managerial labour. Like technological determinism, then, socio-technical approaches avoid the implications of their recognition that politics is a factor in technological and organisational change. Unless politics can be mobilised in favour of managerial goals, it is viewed as disruptive.

The 'fall out' from socio-technical approaches pushed research in one of two directions: in the direction of a full blown systems theory or towards processual or pluralist approaches. As we have already indicated, systems approaches to technological change have dominated the literature not least because of an attraction to the functionalist paradigm in which assumptions of value-consensus remove all social or political contention, leaving problems of IS development to be exclusively the domain of the 'technical'. Since there is little or no consideration whatever of power and politics in systems theory conceptions of IS development, it has not informed the analysis in the book other than negatively to look elsewhere for research inspiration. Consequently we now turn directly to an examination of the processual approach.

Processual and Pluralist Approaches

Processual Approaches

While broader issues of power and inequality are neglected, the politics of management is a central focus of processual theory albeit, as we suggest in our classification, defined as a disruption to, or constraint on, rational and strategic planning.

Where Mumford's work tended to shy away from organisational politics, one of her doctoral students—Pettigrew (1973)—produced an important study of the politics of organisational decision-making focused empirically on early computing applications. Its major achievement was to apply sociological conceptions of power and politics to an empirical analysis of organisational decision-making. This sounds a straightforward enough task but up until that time few such studies had been conducted. Nor have many more been added to the literature since (cf. Noble, 1977; Wilkinson, 1983; Scarborough and Corbett, 1992). Furthermore, the study had a particular relevance for the IS field in that it examined major IT-related decision-making processes.

In his 1973 study Pettigrew was concerned to establish two basic and interrelated motors of organisational politics. The first of these concerned the, by then, increasingly commonplace notion of the organisation as a political system divided into sub-units vying for a share of a limited pool of resources. Although comparatively widely known, following the success of March (1965) and Cyert and March's (1963) work, a political conception of decision-making still presented a major challenge to the dominant functionalist paradigm (e.g. Selznick, 1949; Miller and Rice, 1967) wherein it was assumed that normative consensus prevailed with respect to organisational means and goals.

Pettigrew developed his second motor of organisational politics by drawing on the work of Mills (1956), Dalton (1959), Burns and Stalker (1961). These authors had identified the politics of career and self-advancement as a major dynamic in organisational reproduction and change. Mills (1956) drew attention to the process whereby in seeking to advance their careers, individuals would place great emphasis on constructing and selling the right kind of organisational 'personality'. Career advancement would regularly involve, for example, displaying oneself as an 'organisational man' [*sic*] (Whyte, 1961) or, as is commonly the case, demonstrating commitment 'beyond the call of duty'—a phenomenon described by some (e.g. Cockburn, 1991; Collinson et al, 1990) as indirectly discriminating and certainly an aspect of a dominantly masculine managerial culture (see Kerfoot and Knights, 1993; Collinson and Hearn, forthcoming). By contrast, Dalton (1959) concentrated on the particular informal career strategies pursued by individuals behind the façade of formal organisational structures and procedures, and Burns (1969) argued that the career and political objectives and activities of individuals in organisations were often at odds with the officially defined organisational goals.

This bringing together of the two literatures on sub-unit competition and career and political dynamics was important in linking broader organisational struggles and conflict with the individual jockeying for position and deal-making that Pettigrew was able to observe in his own empirical study. Extending this work, he attempted:

> to explain processually the relationship between the strategies pursued by various interested parties and the final decisional outcome. Such an analysis involves tracing out the generation of demands and the mobilisation of support for those demands, (Pettigrew, 1973, p.22).

There is considerable overlap between these and our own concerns to trace out the generation of demands, their mobilisation and moderation, and the way in which 'decisional outcomes' differ from initial objectives and strategies. But we seek to go further by examining how, once they have been officially 'taken', decisions are often subject to a continual reworking in the process of their implementation and later evaluation.

Pettigrew clearly had to address the issue of power once he began to place political processes at the heart of his analysis. This he did by lining up with those challenging the dominant Parsonian (1951) notion of consensually derived and maintained authority (e.g. Giddens, 1968) and at least questioning the well-established division between a legitimate and consensual authority and a political power based on conflict over the distribution of resources.

For Pettigrew power was a social relationship rather than the attribute of a person. As the ability of one person to get another to do what she or he would not otherwise do (Dahl, 1957), this theory of power carried a strong notion of dependency, interdependency and reciprocity within it. This was because for all but the most brutal power relations to work, the dominant and submissive partner must agree about the rules of the mutual expectations they have of each other.

In *The Politics of Organisational Decision-Making*, Pettigrew (1973) was particularly interested in the relationship between organisational subordinates and their hierarchical superiors, particularly where the former possessed an expertise on which their executive managers were dependent. Through the strategic or tactical use of this expertise, subordinates could reverse the power relation turning executive dominance into executive dependence.

Experts were in a position to exercise power because they could control the access to, and the accumulation of, specialist information. At the same time sociological research and contingency theory in organisation studies suggested that actors who could control uncertainty in organisations were also likely to accrue considerable power (Hickson et al, 1971). Experts appeared, or would claim to possess the ability, particularly in periods of rapid scientific or technological change, to understand and predict the future course of this change.

The power exercised by IS professionals has also become a primary concern for business leaders, the IS community and commentators (Lucas, 1984; Scarborough and Corbett, 1992); it is also a central feature of the present study. But we take a slightly different approach in noting that 'experts' have continually to re-create and legitimise their definitions and control of resources in order to sustain their expertise.

In his closing remarks on decision-making as political process, Pettigrew (1973) drew attention to variance in political intensity. This he attributed to the structure of a particular organisation, where complexity and heterogeneity were likely to lead to the generation of disparate demands. Later writers have also attributed this to the level of uncertainty faced by an organisation and the routine/non-routine character of particular decisional processes (Hickson et al, 1986). In conclusion, Pettigrew (1973) saw his primary analytical task as that of identifying the 'political structure' (the generation of demands and strategies that support them) through which organisational decision-making takes place.

Pluralist Theories

In the 1980s an important strand of IS research emerged in the USA. This was inspired by the publication of key texts (Pfeffer, 1981; Mintzberg,

1983) on organisational power that questioned rationalist views of organisational life. It was also prompted by the emergent discourse of 'user involvement' in systems development that began to gain significant ground in this period (e.g. Boland, 1979; Ives and Olson, 1984; Robey and Farrow, 1982; see also Friedman and Cornford, 1989, Chapter 8).

This new IS research began to explore the place of politics in both IS departments and systems development practices (Bariff and Galbraith, 1978; Franz and Robey, 1984; Kling, 1980; Klein and Hirschheim, 1987; Kling and Iacono, 1984; Lucas, 1984; Markus, 1984; Markus and Pfeffer, 1983; Markus and Bjorn-Andersen, 1987; see also UK contributions from Newman and Rosenberg, 1985; Willcocks and Mason, 1987). In this literature Pfeffer's notion of power as the control of resources (both ideological and structural, see Kling and Iacono, 1984) is largely taken for granted. Furthermore, politics is associated with *visible* conflict between organised coalitions of organisational actors. As such, there is an assumption that an absence of observable conflict means an absence of politics (see Kling, 1980; Kling and Iacono, 1984).

There is a general view in this literature that politics is pursued for purposes of securing control over often undefined or ill-defined 'private' or personal interests. These are in some way connected with maintaining control over resources and deflecting such things as blame and scapegoating (Franz and Robey, 1984).

In its time this development in the IS literature was both bold and pathbreaking in challenging the orthodoxy of rational systems development—an orthodoxy which was a condition and consequence of a technological culture and hegemonic organisation theory that appeared unassailable in their inherent common sense. However, its modest aim appeared to be that of adding a political dimension to this rationalist and realist model of IS practices rather than overturning the model altogether.

In terms of its prescriptive force, this literature advocated a general IS awareness of power and politics (e.g. Markus and Bjorn-Andersen, 1987). Often this takes the form of trying to bring power issues to the awareness of systems analysis (Markus, 1984; Klein and Hirschheim, 1987; Willcocks and Mason, 1987). This is done for a variety of reasons which include: (a) making analysts more astute political operators (Markus and Pfeffer, 1983); and (b) creating a quasi-therapeutic role for the IS professional as a dispassionate observer and facilitator in the power battles of competing system user groups (Klein and Hirschheim, 1987).

In so far as an increased awareness of organisational politics is generated, the aims of this literature may appear laudable. However, the limit of the approach is that it fails to analyse the systematic inequalities of resource distribution sanctioned by bureau-corporate organisations and the society in which they operate. While acknowledging power and a diversity or plurality of interests, it leaves the inequalities underlying these interests unexamined. As such, there is no account of how certain major social inequalities may be responsible for much resistance and mistrust in organisations.

A major weakness of this strand of IS research is its location in and identification with the IS community. This appears to have prevented it developing a more detailed analytical view towards the role of IS specialists. It also forestalled an in-depth questioning of the identity and beliefs of IS specialists, despite the recognition that there is an important relationship between a culture of technologically inspired rationality and IS practices (see, for example, Franz and Robey, 1984; Markus and Bjorn-Anderson, 1987). In short, while exposing the politics of organisation this literature seems oblivious to its own politics. We turn now to a literature whose politics blinds it to much else.

Marxism

Not surprisingly, Marxist approaches to organisational technology use are going through lean times at present. However, they have had considerable impact in the past through their concern with the labour process of capitalist production and the place of technology within this (Braverman, 1974; Zimbalist, 1979).

Marxist theory has tended to regard the deployment of IT as a conscious managerial plan to gain control of workers by deskilling work tasks and intensifying the monitoring of manual labour processes (Braverman, 1974). Most often it is assumed that this 'control imperative' is management's sole aim in introducing IT rather than being one of a number of conflicting objectives (Child, 1985; Hyman, 1987). It also attributes an omniscience and homogeneity to management that is rarely evident from research in the field (Elger, 1978; Scase and Goffee, 1989; Knights and Willmott, 1990).

The distinctive contribution of Marxist approaches, however, is their focus on power and conflict within the context of a historical and contemporary theory of organisational change in relation to the contradictory dynamics of capitalism. Applied in the field of IT developments, it has given rise to a number of interesting trade-union led interventions in the development of workplace technologies in Scandinavia (Ehn, 1989). Marxist approaches have also been important in informing the 'social shaping of technology' perspective discussed below. The Marxist perspective has also contributed to the development of studies of IS specialists themselves and the organisation and accomplishment of systems development. In the late 1970s Kraft (1979) explored and sustained Braverman's (1974) thesis regarding the deskilling of computer programmers. While sympathetic to Kraft's approach, a number of researcher's have challenged his conclusions (see Borum, 1987; Friedman, 1987a,b).

Following Braverman's thesis the fullest and most meticulous application of labour process analysis to the area of systems development has occurred in the recent work of Friedman and Cornford (1989). This research comprises an extended historical analysis of the management and organisation of systems development and systems development staff. Its particular focus concerns managerial strategies to control IS specialists and the way in which these strategies have changed as technologies and the relationships between IS specialists and other organisational functions have developed. We will return to this work in Chapter 4. Here we merely note the importance of this work in qualifying and challenging a straightforward deskilling thesis by insisting on the importance of contexts such as labour markets, the area of IT application and the availability and cost of hardware and innovations and organisational changes in the development of software.

The presumption that technology is principally a means of sustaining management control and deskilling labour was always questionable as the literature (Burawoy, 1979; Littler, 1982) stimulated by Braverman's (1974) thesis made clear. While we would not deny that it often has these effects, the intricacies of managerial politics can only be understood if research is comparatively 'open' to alternative readings and writings. But what from our point is valuable about Marxist analyses is their insistence that, at least within a capitalist order, political struggle is inescapable and cannot therefore be excluded in accounting for the development of new technology and IS.

Following Foucault (1980, 1982), we would go even further and argue that power and political struggle or resistance are intrinsic to social relations under any regime assuming human behaviour to remain under-determined or 'free'.

Gender Research

Traditionally, technology studies, like much else, has been seen as somehow gender neutral and this is a sure guarantee that it embraces all sorts of taken-for-granted gendered assumptions. To begin with, so-called high technology work is not only associated with men but frequently dominated by them. Furthermore, men resist quite vehemently any encroachment by women on their monopoly of technological jobs (Cockburn, 1983, 1985). But the relationship of gender to technology clearly begins in the home and is reinforced by educational and workplace environments. Perhaps as a result of socio-sexual development, a number of men are attracted to the certainty, 'hardness' and unambiguity of technological artefacts, inert matter and their manipulation (Murray, 1993). It readily fits the desire of masculinity for order, integration, linear rationality and control (Kerfoot and Knights, 1993) that is precarious or absent within social relations except where they are formally regulated as in bureaucratic hierarchies or total institutions.

As Hacker (1990 p.109) has argued, it is not so much the technology itself that generates a gendered response as the ways in which technology jobs such as engineering involve a 'testing and training in mathematics... [that is]... embedded in a very masculine-shaped professional organisation of knowledge and evaluation'. According to Hacker, women apparently have no major problem with mathematics as an intellectual activity (on the contrary, evidence suggests that women, on average, are better at maths than men), it is the testing that puts them off. It is not easy to ascertain the reasons for this. One interpretation would be to suggest that it relates to a weaker concern with achievement and 'success'—a characteristic of the 'passivity' in which femininity becomes constituted and reinforced in masculine cultures; another would be to see it as a refusal/resistance to the indignity or humiliation of continuous and unmitigated hierarchical judgements that are prevalent within masculine dominated institutions.

Apart from the obvious sense in which an examination of technology through a gendered perspective may help to adjust explicit and implicit sex discriminations within employment in this field, another value is that it provides a vivid illumination of the way that technology is inescapably a social and political phenomenon. In our case studies, there were few women working in the technology area and especially in the higher positions in the hierarchy. Partly as a consequence, it may be argued that technology in the company was managed in a highly masculinist manner such that, for example, there was a high degree of job segregation based on gender between the IS (systems developers) and customer services (users) divisions. However, the absence of one sex cannot be seen as wholly responsible for a particular set of gendered practices since masculine and feminine modes of thought and behaviour do not necessarily coincide directly with the sex of the person as respectively male or female (Kerfoot and Knights, 1993).

It is clear that in many spheres IT has been designed and developed with the view that primarily women will use it in their function as clerical, secretarial and administrative processing workers. So, for example, Cockburn's (1983) discussion of the history of typesetting shows that computerisation resulted in the abandonment of the original linotype layout to be replaced by the QWERTY layout of traditional typewriting. This, as Wajcman (1991, p.50) points out, was 'designed with an eye to using the relatively cheap and abundant labour of female typists'. Webster (1989, p.52) has shown that the design of early word processors was also 'aimed at the main users, women office workers who had formerly worked with typewriters. Yet the design and development of the systems that support such work is predominantly a male activity. However, this is not, as Wajcman (1991, p.38) makes clear, because technology is inherently masculine but more a matter of technological competence having been associated with masculine identity over several generations. Nonetheless it is certain kinds of technological competence—those that are seen to bestow power, prestige and status—with which the masculine identity is associated. Kitchen or domestic cleaning technologies though equally as complex as personal computers or home entertainment equipment, for example, are not treated with the same degree of significance largely because of the gendered divisions of labour within the household. Similarly, while not historically constant, the relationship to specific technologies is often gendered—men taking on an active relationship wherein they seek to maintain as well as use the technologies and women often depending on males (husbands or engineers) to repair breakdowns in domestic equipment.

So perhaps we ought to conclude, along with Wajcman (1991, p.162) and others sympathetic to a social shaping approach (e.g. Cockburn, 1983; Webster, 1989), that 'the production and use of technology are shaped by male power and interests'. However, apart from the difficulties that such unreconstructed or unproblematised conceptions of power and interests present, there is also a danger that their analysis simply replaces one set of determinants of change (i.e. technology) with another (i.e. interests or patriarchal power). (There is a vast range of literature (e.g. Butler, 1991; Hekman, 1990; Game, 1990) that questions the university of identity constructions which lie behind conceptions of patriarchal or class interests.) As is indicated in our critical examination of the social shaping approach more generally below, it is not just a matter of defining interests broadly and plurally to encompass all the major social inequalities (e.g. class, gender, race, disability). Our misgivings about social shaping theory are not an objection to interests *per se* but the way in which the shape of technology is almost unquestioningly seen to be determined by them such that what we perceive to be the political and social constitution of technology is left virtually unexamined.

When such explanatory weight is given to the role of gender interests, it is difficult to see how feminists can avoid the charge of political or patriarchal conspiracy. This is not to deny that technological developments frequently appear to coincide with what may be constructed as the interests of men. But our concern is to examine how this occurs in distinct localised instances largely through a diverse range of conditions and accidents. In short, we have to examine critically the conditions that make it possible for certain constructions of knowledge/technology to become plausible and thereby have power effects. In our case study, the systems project was defined as a success since any other option would have threatened the identity of the male senior management responsible for its development. An unintended consequence of the demand for success and, more importantly, the need to meet a target deadline was that clerical process workers (mainly women) using the system met with all sorts of difficulties. Moreover, at the point of their manifestation, these difficulties may well be seen by management as being related to the gender of those experiencing them. But it is important to avoid assuming that it is simply the gender or the interests of individuals filling particular occupational places that are entirely or exclusively responsible for the outcome. The functioning of power and identity also operate partly independently of those individuals who are their agents and benefi-ciaries or victims.

Also it is important to recognise that interests may themselves be constituted through the process of using particular technologies, as Wajcman (1991, p.105) herself noted when reporting on how women have often subverted the intended use of a particular technology such as the telephone which they used for social and emotional, rather than purely instrumental, forms of communication. This is just another example of how in a way parallel to the functioning of language (Quin-ton, 1966 p.11), the meaning of technology is contextually tied to the social occasions of its use.

The Social Shaping and Social Construction of Technology

We have already been introduced to the social shaping approach which will be examined in greater detail shortly but there are two other new perspectives that have emerged recently in technology studies. These are the 'social constructivist' (Bijker et al, 1987) and actor-network (Callon et al, 1986; Callon 1991, Latour, 1987) schools of thought. The common link between all three of these approaches is their desire to look inside the hitherto largely unopened 'black box' of technology. For until this point, the great majority of work in the area of technology research had been concerned with the development of technological trajectories (e.g. Barras and Swann, 1983; Dosi, 1982; Nelson and Winter, 1977) and the 'implications' or 'impacts' of IT on labour processes, employment pat-terns and gender relations (e.g. Braverman, 1974; Barker and Downing, 1980; Noble, 1984; Cockburn, 1985; Webster, 1989).

Advocates of social shaping and social constructivist or actor-network approaches are united in their hostility to such implied technological determinism. Rather, they are concerned to understand the genesis and crystallisation of new technologies in organisations and the marketplace. That is, both these perspectives refuse to take for granted the emergence of particular technologies—whether it is the bicycle, the washing machine or computer systems. Instead, they seek to understand why particular technologies emerge and are adapted at particular times.

In attempting to do this, both perspectives reject the splitting off of a 'technical' from a 'social' phase of innovation arguing that nothing is 'purely' technical. Although this is a view they share in common, actor-network theorists are more radical in their epistemological break with both humanistic and Marxist traditions in social theory. We begin by examining their work before returning to the social shaping approach which was partially criticised in the previous section.

The Social Construction of Technology

Actor-network analysts (e.g. Callon, 1986; Latour, 1987) perform a radical application of the social construction paradigm to the field of science and technology, thus challenging numerous taken-for-granted assumptions regarding the relation and boundary between the 'technical' and the 'social'. Broadly these theorists are concerned to document how specific knowledge and technologies are the outcome of a complex set of social processes or moments of translation involving the definition of problems (problematisation), the arousal of social interests (interessement), the enrolment of a variety of agencies and actors and, finally, the mobilisation of network members (i.e. those previously enrolled) when social investment reaches a point where withdrawal would be unlikely. If we subscribe to a consensus rather than correspondence theory of truth (Habermas, 1973), it is clear that technologies are incapable of transcending the social construction of their conception, design, development and use. Only when agreement about the nature of a problem to which some potential technology could serve as a solution has been reached will the interests of a group be sufficient to enrol and eventually mobilise support for the invention, innovation, construction and ultimately conversion to practical use of particular knowledge and technical artefacts.

But even this description of the sociology of translation may be seen as too mechanical and dualistic. Using less humanistic categories, Callon (1991) argues that it is through bringing into circulation intermediaries such as literary inscriptions (e.g. texts) technical artefacts (e.g. computers), skills (e.g. human knowledge), and money that actors define one another and their relationships. The resulting social networks are both a condition and a consequence of technological developments but the success of the latter will depend considerably on the degree of *convergence* of the network and the extent to which it become *irreversible*.[1]

A highly *convergent* network is one in which mutual definitions (translations) of actors and intermediaries are so compatible and integrated that any actor 'can at any time identify and mobilise all the network's skills without having to get involved in costly adaptations, translations or decoding' (Callon, 1991, p.27). In these circumstances members of the network can work together in pursuit of common objectives and do not feel their identities and activities under constant threat from one another or in continuous need of justification.

Irreversibility occurs when alternative translations (i.e. definitional relations between actors and intermediaries) to those currently in existence are blocked or are improbable because, for example, of the complexity and heterogeneity of the interrelationships comprising the network. A network that is highly convergent is also likely, though not guaranteed, to be characterised by irreversibility.

Apart from providing us with a rationale for researching technology without resort to either deterministic accounts or overly voluntaristic analyses of specialists, Callon's approach also facilitates the development of a more interdisciplinary approach—at least in this instance between economics and sociology. As he puts it:

> Economists teach us that interaction involves the circulation of intermediaries, sociologists that actors are only definable in terms of the relationships they enter into with each other. By joining their viewpoints, we have two pieces in the puzzle: actors recognise themselves in interaction, in inter-definition and this latter is materialised in the intermediaries that they put into circulation. (Callon, 1991, p.5).

When networks are characterised by strong levels of convergence and display irreversibility, they may be said to be highly stable and begin to resemble the 'black box' whose behaviour is readily represented, quantified and 'predicted independently of its content' (ibid. p.37) by theorists. Economists represent their subject matter in this way whereas sociologists have tended to assume that the black box is inherently precarious but that only becomes evident once it is opened up and examined. The former, of course, have enormous problems in explaining away the inaccuracy or reversibility of their economic predictions while sociologists are inclined to frame their accounts of shifting and precarious

---

[1]   The following few paragraphs are drawn partly from Knights et al (1993).

social constructions within some overarching universal or grand narrative such as the social structure, culture or class system that is their condition and consequence.

There is more stability than the sociologists are prepared to admit and less than the economists would like if their models are to correspond to the empirical world. Callon's perspective allows us to integrate the two perspectives but always from the point of view of empirical analysis. Convergence and irreversibility can only be decided by empirical observation, not through analytical fiat. Is it the case that when knowledge *works*, it is more likely to result in convergent networks characterised by irreversible translations or is the latter a condition that makes it possible for knowledge to work in the first place? Of course, it does not have to be either/or for there is clearly an interdependence between effective knowledge and the coherence of networks.

Callon has provided us with a useful framework to describe the phases or moments of a network's formation, and a way of avoiding a voluntaristic approach to understanding technological development. Elsewhere (Knights et al, 1993), we have argued that in this text Callon (1991) fails to analyse power preferring it to be seen like interests, as an outcome of practices rather than their explanation. But in drawing on Machiavelli (Callon et al, 1986; Latour, 1987), the 'sociology of translation' can be seen as 'a new approach to the study of power' (Bloomfield and Best, 1992, p.540). For power is exercised at each moment of a translation as, for example, when spokespersons struggle 'to speak for problems, to represent and define them and thus to win acceptance for particular solutions' (ibid. p.542). In this sense power is embedded in processes of systems development since the latter are frequently the outcome of a construction or redefinition (translation) of problems 'in terms of existing solutions' (ibid. p.536) that are available through prevailing technical–social configurations or their modification.

While the actor-network approach is predominantly oriented towards local empirically available instances of the reconfiguration of the boundaries and relationships between technical and social intermediaries (e.g. artefacts, texts, skills, actors, money, etc.), it identifies power as an irremediable aspect of actor-network formation or transformation. In contrast, the social shaping approach, to which we now turn, focuses almost exclusively on power, and the interests that are its medium and outcome, as the most important conditions in shaping particular technologies.

The Social Shaping of Technology

Whether as a result of a crude Marxian influence concerning the forces of production (technology) determining the relations of production (economy) or the Weberian view of the increasing domination of science and rationality on historical development, the idea that technology determines the character of social and economic life has frequently been given intellectual credibility. This despite a long line of continuous and diverse challenges to technological determinism. The social shaping approach is one of the most recent of these challenges but, like many that came before, appears only to substitute one determinism (interests) for another (technology). Basically its argument is that far from shaping society, technology is itself shaped by the interests of powerful groups, be it political élites, the wealthy classes, scientists or the patriarchal domination of men in society.

The social shaping perspective draws on Marxian and feminist concerns with class and gender. As such, it argues that capitalism and patriarchy are primary contexts that influence the development and use of technologies. That is, the emergence of new technologies in some way responds to the expression of class and gender interests—whether through the industrial military (see, for example, Noble, 1977), the domination of scientific and technological spheres of activity by men (e.g. Cockburn, 1985; Harding, 1986) or through the activities of particular organisations in the economy.

The social shaping approach is more broad-ranging than processual theory in encompassing major cultural and socio-political conditions beyond the micro-context of the immediate organisation or technology (MacKenzie and Wajcman, 1989; Wajcman, 1991). However, its predominant focus on social interests as the key determinant leaves it ill-suited to explore the accidental, unintended and often contradictory nature of the global context within which particular organisational and technological changes take place. This global context is very important in terms of constraining and opening areas for managerial choice and action in organisations. In the case study we present in later chapters, we will show just how important this context is and the way in which definitions of it can be manipulated to mobilise support for particular decisions and strategies.

We shall argue that individual and collective actors operate in specific conditions of possibility that concern both micro-contexts, within a specific organisation, and macro-contexts that encompass broader cultural and socio-economic practices in society. One of the major challenges of sociological writing remains that of showing how the connections and reciprocal relations operate between these contexts through the empirically observable interpretations, actions and network mobilisations of various subjects and their socio-political consequences.

In addition to the way that a restricted focus on social interests deflects attention from the broader contextual issues, it is important to question the undue explanatory emphasis given to interests in the social shaping approach. This blinds us to the way in which interests and the subjects to whom they are attributed are often already an outcome of the exercise of power (Foucault, 1982). It also obscures how the reproduction and transformation of social and technological relations occur often not as the direct outcome of the interests of individuals or groups, however constituted, but as their unintended consequence.

Recent writing from social shapers has gone some way towards recognising these difficulties. For example, Fleck et al (1989) insist on the complexity of forces acting on the development and implementation of technologies and the importance of their contextual specificities. Thus, in the case of computer aided production management, research (ibid.) uncovered a complex web of interests at play in particular organisational settings. These encompass both relations between systems suppliers and users and shifting alliances within user organisations that include managerial, trade union and shopfloor actors.

Another criticism levelled at the social shaping perspective is that, despite its insistence to the contrary, it does not take the task of looking inside the black box of technology seriously enough (Button, 1993). Rather, it looks at the forces shaping the contours of the black box while neglecting its contents.

However, the validity of this criticism depends on how the 'contents of technology' are defined. For Button (1993) the exploration of these contents appears to involve detailed and minute ethnomethodological examination of the work processes of, and interactions between, technologists and users. Advocates of social shaping would argue that a detailed examination of the design and use of technologies is important but that this cannot be isolated from the broader context which is both a condition and consequence of those micro processes. (These disagreements are underlain by a longer standing sociological debate between opposed traditions, paradigms and epistemologies which though we have discussed them elsewhere (Knights, 1992, 1993; Knights and Vurdubakis, 1994) are not the direct focus of this text.)

CONCLUSION

In this chapter we have presented a model that differentiates approaches to technological change by two criteria: their level of analytical focus (global v. local) and their view of organisational politics (abnormal v. normal). We then examined six different approaches to technological change, their location in this two-dimensional model, and the ways in which they attempt to explain relations between technological, organisational and societal change and the role that power and politics play in this process. In the next chapter we will explain more fully our understanding of organisational politics and change and the position of technological change in this process. In this brief conclusion we want to highlight where our theoretical sympathies lie.

As may already be suspected, we are highly critical of functionalist accounts of technological change which tend to see technological innovation as a progressive, independent and sometimes determining variable in societal development. In this perspective technology is a neutral factor of production with its origins in an asocial and ahistorical science. As such it presents itself to society as a given and taken-for-granted embodiment of a singular rationality that supposedly determines a one-best-way of organising production.

More refined localised accounts in the functionalist tradition of technological change have modified these stark assumptions under the force of detailed empirical research but there is still a marked tendency to explain away the existence of conflict and politics to unrepeatable contingencies and abnormal uncertainties. Despite these criticisms, processual and pluralist approaches have drawn attention to the importance of localised organisational contexts, practices and structures that were for a long time ignored by the other grand theories in our model.

On the other side of the model we examined the contributions that place political process and conflict over meaning and outcome at the heart of their approach. With regard to Marxism and feminism we argued that their identification of fundamental structures of inequality and hostile interests were vital for an understanding of the context of technological change. However, we questioned their tendency, particularly at the global level, to make a tight correlation between the achievement of capitalist and patriarchal interests and the direction, speed and impact of technological and organisational change. At their most extreme these two approaches are over-deterministic and conspiratorial in that they suggest all technological change is guided by an omnipotent and unseen hand that serves capitalist and/or patriarchal interests.

As we approach these perspectives with a localised focus that treat politics as inevitable this predeliction for over-determination is modified or cancelled out altogether. Here we find that technology is increasingly treated as neither a 'given' nor mere 'putty' in the hands of those dominant sectors who are deemed to have an all-pervasive control over society. Rather in this area of the model, social constructivism and actor-network theory radically question the independence of technology and argue that the genesis of technological innovations is profoundly social and political, obeying neither laws of technical nor structural determinism. Indeed, these approaches stress how it is active intervention on the part of networks of actors mobilising significant support that enables technological innovations to be brought to the market. Not surprisingly, then, power, politics, accident and unintended consequences are emphasised as inescapable elements in these processes. Recognising the huge advance that these studies make in 'breaking down' the boundaries between the 'technical' and the 'social' so prevalent in much of the literature in this field, nonetheless, we are uneasy about the way that the actor-network approach has so far given little or no attention to the broader powers and inequalities that are both the condition and consequence of network formations.

We now proceed to Chapter 2 where we present our own model of technological change. This draws selectively and critically on a number of the approaches outlined here but also begins a process of narrowing down the focus of the book first towards information technology, and, in subsequent chapters, to systems development itself.

2
The Social Construction of Technology as Political Process

INTRODUCTION

In reviewing the literature on organisational politics that focuses upon technology and systems development, we discovered two central weaknesses. The first, which is predominant within the liberal pluralist tradition, is one of identifying politics as a deviant, informal and irrational activity that disrupts the smooth running of organisations and the efficient achievement of their goals or strategies. Theorists subscribing to this view tend to focus on the localised or micro circumstances of a given organisation, neglecting the wider structure of social inequality within which such organisations and their divisions of labour and power relations are embedded. This wider context in which organisations function is a central focus of Marxist and feminist studies of technology who also overcome the weakness of treating politics as an aberration that must be expunged from the organisation. But they fall foul of a second weakness which is that of identifying politics as an uncomplicated reflection of class or gender interests arising from the capitalist and/or patriarchal politico-economic structures of society. For this reason they give little or no attention, as do the liberal pluralist theorists, to the way that politics emerges and displays itself in discrete and localised organisational contexts.

In this chapter we will argue that the process of organisational politics is central to the development and deployment of information technology. We do so by deploying an analytical framework that places organisational politics at its heart.

ORGANISATIONAL POLITICS

First we concentrate on general organizational activities returning to a focus upon technology systems once we have presented a thesis on organisational politics. A recent review (Drory and Romm, 1990) of writing on organisational politics (OP) suggests that two themes emerge from the broad and diverse literature in the field. These are:

(a) that OP in some sense is divergent from and antithetical to formal organisational goals. This suggests that there are formal organisation goals that are in danger of being subverted by OP;
(b) that OP tends to be associated with conflict in organisations.

In many approaches to OP there is an assumption that not only does OP tend to subvert formal organisation goals but also that OP is in opposition to the rational goals of organisations (Pfeffer, 1981; Pettigrew, 1973). As such OP is about the pursuit of self-interest or the pursuit of functional managerial interests in opposition to organisational goals.

As we have already outlined, it is our view that far from representing an exception to organisational process, OP is at the centre of events and practices in organisations. Indeed, it is through OP as an ongoing social process that organisations and their 'interests' and 'goals' are constructed. As such, we would argue that it is impossible and misleading to separate off the albeit problematic pursuit of self or sectional interests from those of the organisation itself. Rather, it is through the construction, negotiation and reappraisal of self, collective and organisational interests that the fragile reality of an organisation is sustained, reproduced and changed.

This is not to say that the construction of organisational reality takes place in a vacuum and can therefore be turned into any reality. Paraphrasing Marx, men and women make history but not under circumstances of their own choosing. Clearly, organisational realities are constructed, reproduced and changed within historically and spatially specific conditions of possibility (Bhaskar, 1989; Marsden, 1993). These both constrain and open up choices to organisations.

We argue, then, that OP is a process that stands at the centre of contemporary organisations. This process is highly structured and takes place within strongly delimited conditions of possibility. As such, it is not an anarchic 'free-for-all' but is instead played out within a complex set of conditions of possibility that include formal and informal rules and accepted customs.

The central motor of OP is the struggle of individuals and collectives to achieve and reproduce a sense of material and symbolic security in the world. Within management, in particular, this struggle centres around the individual pursuit of career and the symbolic and material achievements of success. The pursuit of career and success is a process that takes place in competitive conditions that vary in their intensity over time and place.

However, while placing the pursuit of career in the boiler room of OP we are not suggesting that such pursuits and 'organisational goals' are necessarily antithetical. As we have already indicated, career pursuits are not independent of the constitution and reproduction of organisational goals and, as such, can be productive as well as unproductive in relation to their achievement. In most circumstances, disruptive political behaviour is a consequence of previous exercises of power that have failed to secure the appropriate support from others. Here grievances may well result in individuals or groups denying consent to the official goals of the organisation. But while such behaviour may be seen as disruptive of the current goals, invariably and especially where the discontent is in any way shared by a significant minority, there will be attempts to build a nucleus of support for alternative ways of achieving current goals or a new set of goals. The point that needs to be noted is that organisational goals and the politics of their achievement and/or transformation is the site of career practices in pursuit of material and symbolic security.

Nevertheless, even though there is not necessarily a tension between the pursuit of career goals and formally defined organisational goals, it seems that the rules of the OP game prohibit too-explicit a display of these career goals. Instead, they remain concealed behind, though expressed through, the more legitimate pursuit of formally acknowledged organisational goals. Clearly, then, career development is sublimated, and often even lost from view, in the pursuit of ever-changing formal organisational goals and strategies.

It is largely for this reason, we would argue, that theorists like Pettigrew treat the politics within organisations as somehow aberrant, deviant and perhaps even subversive. What is happening is that the researcher identifies with those at the top of the official hierarchy whose interests often are to eradicate or annihilate the political ambitions of their subordinates partly as a way of protecting their own position and privilege. For while revolution may be a rarity, many examples of rebellion occur in organisations where those rising to the top actually displace the current regime. But even when political ambition is no more than a contest between equals for elevation in the career hierarchy, the basis of that competition has always to be couched in the language and collective values of the organisation as a whole. While everyone knows that individual career ambitions lie behind these various organisational practices, for the 'good' of the organisation and the standing and legitimacy of management in general, there has to be a pretence that it is not so.

Consequently, career competition is extremely complicated and takes place in small and hidden ways more often than in large and public disputes and battles. For example, successful managers develop an acute sense for creating an image of themselves as successful on a day-to-day basis. This includes treating superiors in a particular way, in putting on displays of competence for selected audiences, and massaging and manipulating the reality reaching superiors in such a way that it conveys a message of controlled competence, efficiency and innovation (Mills, 1956; Dalton, 1959; Burns and Stalker, 1961; Jackal; 1988).

It also involves complex alliances of managers within and between particular functions and departments. Thus, for example, managers from the same function may team up to convey a particular symbolic message of success to their senior executives, or they may seek allies in other functions to fight off challenges for their share of corporate resources.

The process of organisational politics, and the vast array of individual and collective strategies it involves, is necessarily riven through with a central paradox. For a great deal of managerial practice constructs a reality of its own activity that denies the *political* quality of that practice.

Neither managers nor many writers on management like to examine the fragile and precarious character of a conflictually negotiated order. Instead, a huge effort is made to give organisations the appearance that they really do run to clear formal procedures in pursuit of goals that are rationally derived from their 'objective' operating conditions. As such, we might say that *management is the political process of constructing a reality of management that denies its inherent politicality.*

Writing over 30 years ago, Burns and Stalker (1961, p.260) commented on this paradox as follows:

> The problem is no one regards himself as a politician, or as acting politically, except of course on occasions when he [*sic*] is led into accounts of successful intrigue and manoeuvring when he bolsters his self-esteem and reputation by projecting the whole affair into the safe social context of a game or joke.

Given their importance to the 'making' or 'breaking' of managerial careers, what might be termed metaphorically as the 'killing fields' (see Jackal, 1988) of politics are clearly disturbing and threatening to managerial identities. One way of coping with the anxiety and insecurity they engender is to discount their seriousness through joking or to deny the existence of organisational politics altogether.

There are a number of other reasons for denying or obfuscating the politics in organisational life. Apart from protecting the organisation and senior management against the fear that subordinate rebellion and even revolution are a distinct possibility, the very sense of what it is to be a manager is torn by a series of conflicting beliefs that an explicit acknowledgement of organisational politics only brings to the surface. On the one hand, fed by the meritocratic values of western democracies, managers will have some faith, however limited, in the merit-based nature of reward, and even when disillusioned, they will tend to act *as if* strategy is the expression of 'real' organisational interests and that their organisation is run by formal rules and procedures. On the other hand, they are aware that the whole process of management is a vast political game of intrigue, skulduggery, backroom deals, and career carve-ups. Only by elevating the formally rational and meritocratic aspects of organisations can the political and career competition be kept sufficiently 'under wraps' for the 'normal' business of management to proceed.

But a moment's thought reveals how a meritocratic system of rewards is an ideal that is unattainable if only because judgements of merit could never be so 'objective' as to be uncontestable. In so far as all judgements of merit are tied to interpretations of one or more superordinates, it is obvious that those with career ambitions will pursue various strategies to secure a favourable judgement even though success in such endeavours will often be related to their skill in obscuring what they are doing.

Despite much evidence to the contrary, meritocratic beliefs have the upper hand over views about political competition and intrigue. This is not surprising given the strength of rationalistic interpretations of management practice within academic discourses (see, Marsden, 1993) and the interest that managers have in promoting an image of themselves as rational and disinterested technocrats worthy of the power-infused privileges invested in them. But neither set of beliefs can be taken at face value since they are as much accounts of events as rationalisations of success and failure. If one is successful then it will always be rationalised as a result of merit whereas failure can be designated as due to the highly political nature of decisions or unfortunate external circumstances.

Perhaps another reason for obscuring the political character of organisational life is that its acknowledgement would only serve to intensify the existential and organisational insecurity prevalent in all organisations. By subscribing to a myth of orderly and rational decision-making, the inherent uncertainty of management and its potential to generate unintended and sometimes uncontrollable consequences is hidden. It is carefully laid to rest behind a durable façade of bureaucratic stability and fair play. In this way anxiety is controlled and managers do not have to confront the uncertainty of their lives; nor do they have to become conscious of the ways in which they may prostitute themselves and their sense of integrity in order to make the right political moves. Instead, this can be blamed on the dictates of 'the organisation' and removed from the realm of personal choice and responsibility. There is little doubt, however, that the devious and concealed character of the political conditions and consequences of organisational behaviour also generates anxiety and insecurity that cannot easily be released or shared without suffering career disadvantage.

As we have implied, all this political activity takes place within an apparently co-operative set of collective managerial practices that constitute the co-ordination and control of organisational activity. These practices are not only precarious because of pressures from outside but the co-operative veneer is continuously threatened by individualistic strivings to attain or retain a privileged access to comparatively scarce material and symbolic resources that grant security and status. This tension between co-operation and competition is reflected in, and reinforced by, the growing technical division of labour that separates employees into routine, specialist and managerial functions each of which gives differential access to organisational resources.

Overall the general intent of managerial action can be described as an individual and collective struggle characterised by co-operation, competition and conflict to secure a share of the material (e.g. income, control over expenditure) and symbolic (e.g. status, access to important projects or committees) resources organisationally available. This struggle for scarce material and symbolic resources reflects and reinforces stratifying practices that are anticipated to maintain or enhance individual security and socially valued identities, both internal and external to the organisation. The political process of organisational life, then, is fundamental to the striving of managers to create a sense of themselves that is coherent, manageable and convincing to significant others both inside and outside of the organisation.

The conditions under which managers labour to 'bring off' this deep sense of self are not generally of their own choosing, in that the individual manager confronts them as a given reality. That is, managers enter a national and local arena in which what it is to be a manager, what we here call the *subjectivity of management*, is already predefined. In other words, the idea of a particular sort of management, behaviour, attitudes and norms is established and treated as 'natural', such that deviation from certain routinised practices would be heavily sanctioned. The manager moving into this context has to come to terms with these normalised modes of behaviour (Foucault, 1977), and indeed will probably have displayed a capacity to do this prior to securing a managerial status. It may be possible to effect small local changes in management practice, but mere survival will involve the replication of existing practices to a greater or lesser extent.

POWER AND SUBJECTIVITY

Power is a central issue in organisational life and over the years various definitions of this concept have been developed. Within early functionalist interpretations (e.g. Parsons, 1963), power was defined as the active expression of consent which in circumstances of instability might take the form of force or coercion. In the long term, such manifestations of power would tend to be self-defeating for, in Parsons's view, in order to work power has to be legitimate or transformed into authority (Fox, 1971), where there is consent (or compliance) with respect to its exercise. This is essential if it is to facilitate the fulfilment of the four functional imperatives—goal attainment, adaptation, integration, and maintenance of activities, norms and motives—necessary to organisational survival (Parsons, 1951, 1959). Such crude versions of functionalism have been criticised (e.g. Giddens, 1971, 1979) for presuming rather than investigating value-consensus. They thereby treat the sectional interests of élite groups as universal, teleologically explain activities in terms of their consequences for organisational survival, and perceive conflict and resistance as aberrational and pathological.

This has not prevented the functionalist paradigm from influencing if not dominating much of the literature on technology and organisations. So, for example, socio-technical and systems theory were clearly functionalist in approach as was evidenced in the previous chapter. But, despite their claim to distance themselves from functionalism (Pettigrew, 1973), processual perspectives are also functionalist in so far as they take the survival of an organisation to be linked to its attaining the formal goals as identified by senior management and view 'informal' processes of politics often to be disruptive of organisational life. While not wishing to defend the paradigm, there is one sense in which the influence of the functionalist view of power might be seen as benign. For in contrast to the dominant decisional (Dahl, 1961) or what Lukes (1974) describes as the one-dimensional theory, functionalism identifies power as a *social* phenomenon not a matter of individual decision-making.

Early processual accounts, however, subscribe to this one-dimensional theory viewing power as the ability to secure one's interests against opposition from others. This is seen as being achieved through the possession of resources and their political mobilisation. Power, then, is dependent on the control of resources (Pfeffer, 1981; Pfeffer and

Salancik, 1978). In later articulations of processual theory, the two-dimensional theory (Lukes, 1974) is adopted where power is seen not merely as influencing the other's decisions but controlling which issues are available to make decisions upon. Here power operates so as to deny subordinates the opportunity to express their interests.

Emerging out of political science, both the one- and two-dimensional theories assume power to be exercised through decision-making. Advancing a more sociological approach, Lukes (1974, p.34) defines the three-dimensional or radical theory as recognising that power not only persuades others to support interests contrary to their own but also transforms people's views so as to make them think that what they want is on offer. In short, power works behind the scenes to manipulate social reality in ways that ensure conformity to the interests of the powerful. Through 'the control of information, through the mass media and through processes of socialisation' (ibid., p.23), human wants can be shaped or influenced in ways that are not in their 'real' interests. So, for example, B might willingly go along with A's wishes because B is unaware of the way in which these impinge on and curtail B's 'real', as opposed to apparent, interests.

This radical account of power of which the social shaping perspective is a recent variant, argues that the origins of power lie not in the personal control of organisational resources but rather in the division of society into antagonistic class and gender relations and the particular historical development and alignment of the state. Thus researchers in this field examined the organisation of a class's capacity for power (Miliband, 1973; Poulantzas, 1973) and the struggle for control between capital and labour played out within organisations (Braverman, 1974, Burawoy, 1985).

Recent 'realist' (Bhaskar, 1989) developments of this concept of power argue that an individual's capacity for power comes not from his or her behaviour as such, although political skill is an important facet of mobilising this capacity for power. Rather, an actor's capacity for power comes from the underlying relations of that actor and another's situation. Thus, for example, an individual manager, A, does not cause a clerk, B, to become a clerk. The manager may direct and monitor that clerk's activity but the positions of manager and clerk, and their radically different capacities for power, do not originate in manager A's behaviour. Instead manager A and clerk B fill positions created through the operation of deeper societal dynamics and relations than those immediately evidenced in their day-to-day interactions (Marsden, 1993). In this sense, power is not a personal possession but rather a *capacity for action* that resides in social relations.

Understood in this way, power can be seen as more than a repressive mechanism of control exercised by the powerful over their 'victims'.

Instead, power can both discipline as well as be enabling and productive. Thus, 'rather than A getting B to do something B would not otherwise do, social relations of power typically involve both A and B in doing what they *ordinarily* do' (Isaac, 1987 quoted in Marsden, 1993). That is, social relations of power enable the existence of the categories manager and clerk and provide the routines and relations that set the limits of their ordinary behaviour. As such, power may invoke our consent to everyday practices and can thereby transform the historical specificity of the manager and clerk into a taken-for-granted quasi-biological given.

This relational notion of power bears some resemblance to that developed by Foucault (1980, 1982) where power is seen to constitute particular subjectivities or categories of subject through its exercise and the knowledge it brings to bear on events and relations. The similarities reside in the tendency of both approaches to eschew theories which perceive power to be a property of the person and in their recognition that power can be positive as well as negative, productive of subjective well-being and not just destructive or repressive.

Where they diverge, however, is in their respective social ontologies for realists take their representations of social structure incorporating universal narratives and totalising categories of class, gender or race as real entities that are the determining force behind power relations. In contrast, Foucault (1984, p.249) recognises the dangers in becoming attached to or believing one's own representations since much violence and many atrocities (e.g. the Gulag, the Holocaust) have been perpetrated in the name of the class, the party, the race. For Foucault power does not have these or any other foundations and that is why it has to be examined in each and every occasion or local circumstance of its exercise. As he puts it (ibid., p.247), 'nothing is fundamental. That is what is interesting in the analysis of society ... There are only reciprocal relations, and the perpetual gaps between intentions in relation to one another.'

While power may invoke our consent, by virtue of the 'gaps in intentions' and unintended consequences there is always space for resistance. Only when it is understood as an essentialist and dualistic 'capacity for action' that some have, and not others, is power seen to be capable of exhausting a social relation in such a way as to preclude resistance to its effects (Knights and Vurdubakis, 1994). Why power often does generate consent is because it draws upon knowledge that is plausible or legitimate and this helps to transform individuals, whether exercising or being exercised by power, into subjects who secure meaning and identity through the practices it invokes.

Applied to the realm of organisational theory and OP the linked conceptions of power as social relations and power/knowledge suggest a number of things. Firstly, the realm of OP is a vital but limited one. The individual manager is not a free agent able to re-create the world in his or her own image. Indeed, the individual manager is a condition and consequence of a series of power relations, discourses and knowledge. Thus the individual manager is able to effect extremely limited change and only by the deployment of various social and political skills. That is, it is only by knowing the world around him or her that the manager can assess the room and scope for extra-ordinary actions.

Secondly, the prevailing order of power/knowledge relations and the existence of competitive mechanisms to fill the position of manager, places great normalising pressure on the manager. In order to retain his or her place in the hierarchy, the manager must create a convincing model of the normalised manager able to withstand the disciplinary gaze of superordinates and subordinates.

Thirdly, if the social relations of power often evoke consent to the routine and ordinariness of individuals' lives how are we to account for organisational and technological change? This we can only do by examining the dynamically situated conditions of possibility within which change takes place and where that change occurs in the gaps between intentions, between conflicting powers and as a result of the unintended consequences of diverse actions. Power relations are multiple, discontinuous and heterogeneous and they are often inconsistent and contradictory one with another. For these reasons they may stimulate as much resistance as consent, change as continuity and instability as order.

Lastly, we might say that power is least visible when things are most ordinary. In this situation the regulation of social and organisational life achieves its most routinised taken-for-granted status. As such the struggle to be secure almost loses its competitive, combative existentially 'open' character. Consequently, in this position of near stasis, OP is also a highly routinised and mundane affair. As a process it loses its raw, anxious feel.

This benign state of affairs is rarely evident within the dynamic social relations of capitalism in its search for ever new sources of profit. Accordingly, even at the moment of maximum security, subterranean changes are usually under way—whether these be political, social, cultural or technological—that combine to change, radically or subtly, the parameters of ordinary everyday existence.[1]

---

[1] See for example, the portrayal of the 1950s in the UK in Dennis Potter's T.V. drama *Lipstick on my Collar*. In this the emerging glow of post-bellum security and nascent never-had-it-so-good consumerism is undermined by the continued collapse of Empire, epitomised by shortcomings in the Whitehall bureaucracy, and the emergence of an antagonistic and autonomous youth culture.

From this perspective, power might be seen to infuse all organisational relationships such that rather than being an exception or aberration from the norm, political activity is *the* focal process through which organisations are sustained, reproduced or transformed. In this sense, politics is not just the backroom deals and intrigue of individual managers or their cabals and cliques (Dalton, 1959). It is also the more mundane, routine reproduction and control of organisational life. It is about the reproduction of normality and stability in conditions that constantly threaten, to a greater or lesser extent, to undermine or overthrow the established reality of organisations. Information technology and systems have then to be examined in the context of these political conditions and consequences of their development and use.

This view argues that there is no fixed, consensually agreed, authority that stands apart from a more naked and conflict-generating exercise of power. Nonetheless, part of what it means to exercise power is to render it legitimate in the eyes of subordinates (Gramsci, 1971). The reality of organisational life is seen to be precarious and open to constant challenge because it rests on nothing other than the time-bounded and context-related belief that this is the reality. Accordingly, one of the primary results of managerial action is the reproduction or change of this reality and the manager's position within it.

This realisation gives a certain poignancy and amplitude to the notion of the 'career politics' of managers. For chasing a career becomes an altogether more uncertain and difficult enterprise than that portrayed in the image of 'climbing the managerial ladder'. The process has been made more difficult in recent years by recession and the restructuring of organisations—the latter of which, in part, has been made possible by the increasing use of IT in management (Scase and Goffee, 1989; Zuboff, 1988).

THE ORGANISATIONAL POLITICS OF INFORMATION TECHNOLOGY

Having discussed our view of politics as the norm of organisational life, we now seek to elaborate this framework and to incorporate the specific issue of technology which is the focus of the remaining chapters of this book. We do this through a schematic representation (see Figure 2.1) of our understanding of the political process in organisations and an examination of the specific conditions through which it becomes possible and takes a particular form.

Figure 2.1 is a schematic representation of the politics of information technology. It forms the basis of our analytical framework. At the centre

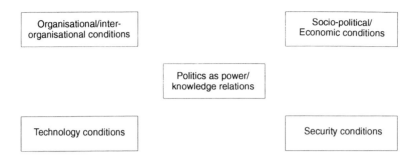

Figure 2.1 *A Political Processual Model of Organisational Change*

of this framework stands political process as power/knowledge relations which we have already argued is the motor of organisational life. It is through this process that organisational reality is sustained, resources claimed and allocated between competing groups and individuals, and careers made or lost.

This political process of power/knowledge relations is enacted in specific *conditions of possibility*, that is, conditions that make certain courses of action feasible while constraining or ruling out others. These concern both local and general conditions of possibility. Local conditions here are constituted by organisational structure and subjectivity, technological possibilities and context specificity. General conditions we here define as the global conditions of modern market economies. These refer to the broad divisions and market allocations of scarce resources within economically advanced societies and take in notions of class, gender and racial inequality.

To a certain extent the differentiation between local and general conditions is a false dichotomy. Take the example of technology, there are clearly general conditions of technological possibility such as the discovery of new technologies and the existence of a culture that equates technology with progress and cannot be readily separated out from the local conditions that are the stimulus to any specific technological development or application within an organisation. Equally it may be argued that the four distinct conditions of possibility are not so separate in the everyday reality of organisational life. Indeed in our empirical chapters we shall see this as, for example, when the personal security of senior managers leads them to define certain technological developments as 'successful' despite them falling down on a whole range of criteria. However, the distinctions are useful analytically for they allow us to unravel the complexity of the political process and show how these various conditions of possibility are interpreted, mobilised and interact to produce particular political outcomes and, of course, new conditions of possibility.

By combining these local and general conditions of possibility, we also seek to overcome shortcomings of the social shaping and social constructivist perspectives outlined in Chapter 1. The former perspective tends to concentrate on general (or macro) conditions of possibility while the latter concentrates on local (or micro) conditions. In addition, both neglect the crucial area of subjectivity and the preoccupation that individuals have in securing meaning and a socially respected identity.

While the following account continues to address the central significance of political process in our understanding of organisations, it does so through an examination of the conditions that make it possible for this process to occur. Given its central focus in this study, a disproportionate attention is given to the technological conditions and consequences of organisational politics.

The Conditions of Possibility of Political Process

Before proceeding to examine the four sets of conditions of possibility shown in Figure 2.1 we briefly state our understanding of the 'reality' of these conditions.

'Conditions of possibility' are not facts or objective realities, although they are often mistaken or portrayed as such. For example, a market exists only is so much as people believe it to exist and act accordingly. Similarly, a technological opportunity or constraint exists only in so much as people believe it to exist. Thus, not surprisingly we argue that conditions of possibility, just like organisations, are socially constructed. As such, conditions of possibility can be constructed in any manner of ways.

However, anarchy does not prevail because understandings of particular conditions of possibility crystallise through social discourse. So, for example, during the Thatcher years, considerable effort was made to convince public opinion that 'you can't buck the market'. Or, the assiduous efforts of technologists, governments, academics, and technology suppliers have generally convinced public opinion that IT 'is a good thing' and that, for a while at least, it offered organisations the chance of gaining competitive advantage over rivals.

At a more localised level, conditions of possibility are also open to multiple construction. However, in periods of stability they may become taken for granted. For example, in the 1960s the idea of an insurance company as an organisation in terms of its objectives, structures and appropriate culture and controls was largely taken for granted. In the 1980s and 1990s this was not the case and managers argued over the character of their organisations and the objectives they should be setting for them.

We might say, then, that conditions of possibility define a broad range of possible actions but that, particularly in conditions of rapid change, predominant constructions of these conditions can be challenged and overturned. So, for example, in the late 1980s the notion that IT was predominantly a labour saving device in production or administrative operations was increasingly challenged by proponents of a 'marketing led' use of IT. New and reconfigurations of existing knowledge are continually being produced that change the conditions within which particular exercises of power are possible.

The social construction of a particular organisation's conditions of possibility is therefore also part of the political process at the centre of organisational life. As such, managers will consciously or unconsciously attempt to construct their particular conditions of possibility in ways that are congruent with and legitimise their aims. So, for example, an IS executive may draw on market research or informal contacts in the market to argue for an increase in the IS budget because the company is not spending as much on IT as competitors.

What is interesting is the way that managers and staff interpret or construct reality within organisations and thereby mobilise specific conditions of possibility to justify particular actions or outcomes. In the course of our research we have also become aware of the way in which conditions of possibility can be seen quite differently by different members of an organisation (for example, with regard to our main case study company's existing IT infrastructure, see Chapter 9). Here the presence of organisational rules and the distribution of resources is an important factor in terms of which construction of particular conditions of possibility comes to be seen as the more legitimate and plausible within an organisation.

We now proceed to examine the four conditions of possibility—organisational, subjectivity and security, socio-political/economic, and technological—alluded to in Figure 2.1.

Organisational Conditions

Here we use organisational conditions as shorthand to incorporate a whole series of structures, practices and relations that make possible and are affected by the organisational politics we have been discussing. These include:

(a) an organisation's structure in terms of its divisional and hierarchical forms, the particular division of labour, and the distribution of resources and development of rules within this structure;

(b) an organisation's practices in terms of the way in which the organisation operates, and day-to-day tasks are carried out;

(c) an organisation's culture in terms of the particular norms and customs pertaining in the organisation.

The social construction and reproduction or change of these organisational conditions help to define what the organisation is and the rules of social interaction that constitute it. Often they will be taken on board at an implicit level by organisational members and take on a solidity and naturalness that defies challenge or change. At other times and circumstances they may seem arbitrary and fragile and ripe for rebuilding in new and different forms (see, for example, Child et al, 1990).

Subjectivity and Security Conditions

In Figure 2.1 we have separated organisational structure from subjectivity largely because we want to highlight the notion of subjectivity/identity and its relationship to managing individual insecurity as distinct from the organisational processes whereby particular hierarchical positions and inequalities are sustained or changed. We believe it is also important to focus on individual preoccupations with security and identity as these issues are conspicuous by their absence in most organisational studies of technology.

Subjectivity refers to the way we experience and make sense of ourselves and our world. By subjectivity we mean what it is to be a particular sort or category of person from the inside as well as in relation to others. Subjectivity concerns our sense of identity and belonging; it is the way in which we identify with a specific set of symbols and significations or meanings surrounding a function, specialism, or occupation, for example. While attachment to an identity may relieve some of the insecurity of living in an increasingly uncertain world, the difficulty of managing identity when it is dependent upon the uncontrollable perceptions and judgements of others is itself a source of insecurity. This is the ambiguity of identity; on the one hand, a respite from insecurity and, on the other, a source of threat and anxiety by virtue of being constituted in a world that is both precarious and unpredictable.

So, for example, the very idea of being a manager is an historically recent phenomenon associated with the development of large industrial bureaucracies and the separation of the ownership and control of industrial concerns through the form of the joint-stock company. This idea of being a manager carries with it a detailed code of behaviours, of ways of acting and thinking. By so doing, it structures the manager's existence closing down some avenues of action, thought and behaviour and opening up others.

This code of behaviour is constituted by particular forms of self-knowledge and knowledge of the world, often called discourses, which are immensely powerful. As such these discourses act upon and constitute the sense of what it is to be a manager. For example, a powerful contemporary managerial discourse is that of 'strategy'—strategic management and strategic behaviour. This is an historically specific discourse that has come into being in a particular set of conditions. But it has become naturalised, it appears as a natural condition of being a manager, and it prescribes new forms of managerial subjectivity.

The manager in the 1980s had to become strategic, display strategic ability, and act strategically. This idea of being strategic was not simply a new set of managerial clothes to wear. For these new forms of knowledge also constituted a way of looking at the world and oneself, conformity with which also generated a measure of order and security in conditions of instability and change. As such, managerial discourses do more than rearrange the façade of the manager's persona. Potentially, they act deeply and subtly on the very notion of what it is to be a manager (Knights and Morgan, 1991).

These discourses, whether of strategy, culture, chaos, total quality management (TQM) or whatever else happens to be the new guru-inspired managerial panacea, are powerful partly because they are not seen as forms of power. Rather they emerge and assume the mantle of common sense, as a new normality that obscures that which came before it. However, such discourses do not automatically 'colonise' managerial subjectivity. They are challenged and changed, resisted and rejected. Some win and others lose as managers play an active part in the formation, dispersion, birth and death of new and old forms of knowledge and understanding.

Organisational subjectivity, then, plays an important part in informing the political process of organisations which in turn plays back on that subjectivity. In the analysis we develop later in the book we are particularly interested in the different and competing strands of this organisational subjectivity with regard to the way in which managers think about and act on technology issues.

Socio-political and economic conditions

Here by socio-political and economic conditions we mean the particular general and local (sectoral) conditions within which an organisation operates (cf., Child and Smith, 1987). Within a market economy, these conditions largely concern labour, product and capital markets, their respective regulatory frameworks, and the social relations of class, gender and race. It is in this context that managers secure an understanding of their industry, developing and promoting specific competitive strategies appropriate to them.

Socio-economic Conditions

The general conditions of socio-political and economic possibility that pertained during the research conducted for this book were those of the British economy in the late 1980s. The defining features of this broader context were:

(a) the institutionalised inequality of resource distribution and life chances in a social structure characterised by class, gender and racial divisions;

(b) the legitimation of social and organisational hierarchies that create and sustain clear distinctions between owners, managers, workers and consumers;

(c) the pursuit of productive activity for profit rather than social utility;

(d) the promotion of an atomised and acquisitive individualism as the goal of personal endeavour and the means to achieving individual and familial security;

(e) the increasingly aggressive use of state and managerial power in the face of challenges from below (trade union reform, the emasculation of local government) which has become populist in its consequences if not in its genesis;

(f) the transformation of human labour into a commodity to be bought and sold in internal and external labour markets;

(g) a capital market system of corporate finance in which large financial institutions (e.g. insurance companies, pension funds) dominate equity ownership;

(h) an increasingly international, if not global, system of economic exchange constrained by large 'free-trade' blocs such as the EC.

Once again, we see that these conditions are constituted through political processes. In this sense, we argue that markets or any other of the representations listed above do not have an existence separate from the agents who constitute them. Rather, they are made and shaped by the constructions managers, analysts, economists and journalists project or impose on them. As such, markets become the subject of political process in that different managers may well constitute markets in different ways. Managers will make an appeal to 'the dictates of the market' as an objective reality that legitimises the view of strategy they put forward. This is not necessarily done as part of a disingenuous and self-consciously political manoeuvre. On the contrary, such is the power of the idea that 'the market' can be read in a singular and 'objective' fashion, many managers may genuinely believe that this is the way reality really is. When 'the market' assumes such a natural and commonsensical state, it becomes a powerful weapon for justifying and mobilising particular managerial demands and actions.

It may be suggested, then, that markets are unpredictable and precarious and cannot be treated as an external reality to which managers merely respond (see Auerbach, 1988). Rather, markets are actually constituted by the interpretations and actions of those who participate in them. Clearly, markets can be rendered more stable and predictable in the short-run through the combined regulatory efforts of their participants but in the longer-run they often operate in ways which undermine the managerial attempts at control they engender. Thus it is the case that the rational designs of managers can only be operationalised through the 'irrationality' of the market (Mandel, 1975).

If markets are not a uniform and external reality but are constituted through the perceptions and actions of their participants, there is no one single message that the market conveys. Perceptions of the market will depend upon one's position in the market and position in a particular organisation. But this is not all. Particular accounts and interpretations of the market are also strongly linked to the attempts by managers to advance or maintain their own material and symbolic security.

Gender Relations[2]

As already mentioned, gender relations are an important condition of socio-economic possibility. In contemporary societies those relations are characterised by large inequalities between men and women with regard to access to, and control over, material and symbolic resources. Thus, for example, in the area of the information systems (IS) specialism women are systematically excluded from managerial positions and are over-represented in the lowest grades of computing occupations (see Chapter 5).

The dominant position of men in commercial organisations and all their major functions has profound implications for organisational process. Not only are women marginalised or excluded from this process but the process itself is also profoundly 'masculinised'. That

---

2 The analysis of this brief sub-section on gender could equally be repeated with respect to race relations especially since one of our case study companies employed hardly any non-whites in its head office. But because of the minority status of non-whites in the UK, we believe the study of race relations and technology would require a broader range survey approach of a kind very different from that deployed in this study.

is, there are deep-seated and symbiotic relations between expressions and articulations of contemporary masculinities and organisational practices, structures and cultures. However, the very dominance of men in organisations, and management in particular, has tended to 'naturalise' and render invisible gender relations and their conditions and consequences.

We wish to challenge this situation and make visible the inter-linking and reinforcing of masculinity and organisational process. Thus, it is our contention that organisational politics, particularly where management is concerned, is inextricably linked to the achievement and articulation of contemporary masculinities.

Briefly, although research now recognises a plurality of masculinities (Brittan, 1989; Kerfoot and Knights, 1993; Collinson and Hearn, 1995), the bedrock of contemporary masculinity is its desire for, and identification with, an overriding rationality that renders social relations and an individual's position within them both predictable and controllable (Seidler, 1989). Here we do not have the space to go into the genesis of this socially constructed masculinity. Suffice it to say that it is closely linked with development of modernity and has sought to appropriate exclusive control of rationality in opposition to, and as an essential bulwark against, values attributed to femininity such as intuition, emotional openness and passivity.

Contemporary management practices are a major site of the achievement and reproduction of a masculinity that cherishes 'rationality', control, certainty, aggressive competition and instrumental action. As such it is an essential condition and consequence of organisational politics. Its dominance serves to maintain management as a privileged area of masculine practice which is highly resistant, in the main, to the incursion of feminine values and practices. As we shall see in later chapters (see particularly Chapter 6) this has important consequences for processes of organisational and technological change.

Technological Possibilities

In this analysis we have separated out technological possibilities from other conditions of organisational possibility. This is because we are particularly interested in technology and its social construction and management. But technology constitutes part of the other organisational and contextual fields we have already examined.

Before examining these technological possibilities we need a working definition of technology. We suggest that technology may be defined as a set of human and non-human artefacts, processes and practices ordinarily directed towards modifying or transforming natural and social phenomena in pursuit of human purposes. In the IT field it involves the following:

(a) technological artefacts, such as computers and software;
(b) technological knowledge, in particular systems development skills;
(c) technological workers and managers who are engaged in particular systems development and information systems (IS) specialists;
(d) the culture of technology, or the signs, symbols and values brought to bear in discussing, using and developing technology.

While in academic discourse and in the media, the term 'technology' is frequently deployed unproblematically, it has to be seen as a particular construct that might not have uses in everyday practice. And indeed, this is what we find in our research where people talked about 'systems', or 'the project', or 'the software', 'mainframe capacity', and the 'terminal screen' but rarely mentioned the word 'technology' as such.

Bearing this terminological qualification in mind, it may be argued that technological possibilities, in a more classical technical sense, refers to the range of technological solutions and innovations that can be developed from a given technology. Thus, for example, researchers have argued that information technology (IT) is particularly flexible in that it has a wide range of possible applications which can be developed in a variety of ways (Miles et al, 1988). However, when we begin to contextualise the use of technology this apparently inherent flexibility is confronted by increasingly restrictive local conditions that constrain both the use and development of particular technology applications.

Thus, major IT-using organisations like the ones we have studied are not free to deploy their technological means of production and distribution without constraint; indeed, there are both general and local conditions that restrain but also offer opportunities for the use and development of technology. At the general level, there are the upstream technological innovations being made that gradually emerge on to the market. These may then be developed for particular industrial applications.

The company, then, operates in a socially constructed technology market. Privileged actors within the company constitute this market within the organisation. They act as 'gatekeepers' (Pettigrew, 1973) able to develop particular views of new technologies and systems on offer. Here, in particular, IT research and development departments may be very influential.

These general conditions gradually merge into more sector-specific ones. Companies will watch their competitors' use of technology carefully. They may even identify 'winning recipes' of particular technology use (Child and Smith, 1987) which come to act as a major technological possibility on their strategic plans. Or they may play a more distant game of follow-my-leader technology use.

However, all the plans of technology and industry observers in a particular organisation have to confront the company's internal conditions of possibility. These are constituted by a number of different areas that we here make analytically distinct even though in practice they are often inseparably linked. These local conditions of technological possibility consist of what we have here called technology legacy, culture, structure and infrastructure, as listed below:

Local conditions of technological possibility

(a) *Technology legacy* where the prevailing, or competing, constructions of technology in an organisation are influenced by past experiences of technology use. Some organisations may be traumatised by particular failures, others buoyed up by successful innovations. This technology legacy is in turn informed by technology culture.

(b) *Technology cultures* are the general and particular attitudes and understandings of technology. These concern issues like the general role of technology: who sees it as what ? Is it seen as 'progressive', a 'necessary evil', a source of sustainable competitive advantage, a useful corporate image, building weapon, etc?

(c) *Technology structure* concerns the deployment, power and intra-organisational relations of technology specialists. Questions here relate to the material and symbolic resources controlled by IS professionals, their organisation in departments, their relations with senior and junior users and end users, and their position in the executive and senior managerial posts.

(d) *Technology infrastructure* which relates to the existing deployment of technology. What systems are running on what hardware? How easy is it to update and modify these systems? Who has a vested interest in seeing these systems stay in place or be scrapped?

From this examination we can see that the conditions of technological possibility are multi-layered and complex. And again we need to stress that these conditions do not exist as independent realities but are rather constituted through the political process that lies at the heart of organisational life.

CONCLUSION: ORGANISATIONAL POLITICS AS PINBALL

The picture we are here developing of the organisation may, with the usual caveats attached to all analogies, be likened to a pinball machine. Political process stands in the middle of the machine and is bombarded by the steel balls that are energised in different parts of the organisation. These bounce against the motor of political process and are shot back to bounce against other conditions of the organisation, such as those of subjectivity, structure, socio-political and economic context and technology possibilities. This constant process of steel balls bouncing around changes the shape and location of different parts of the organisation. Propelled by the motor of political process, the balls 'career around' fashioning new forms of understanding and subjectivity in the organisation and its contextual environment. At the centre of this process there is a knot of individuals scrambling to achieve a degree of emotional, symbolic and material security. The heavy metal balls of the organisation crash and wallop into them, reconstructing their sense of themselves and the reality around them thus, transforming subjectivities, identities and power relations as they go.

The pinball metaphor is, as we have already indicated, limited in its capacity to grasp the complexity of these phenomena since in social interactions, organisational members do not merely crash and collide with one another. They may anticipate, plan, manoeuvre, re-interpret and displace actions and events in ways that not only change the constitution of the balls but also the game itself.

This is not to argue that the political process is wholly random and accidental; it does display such moments but it is largely bounded and directed by well-understood rules, backed up by institutionalised and unequal power relations in, and outside, the organisation. For this process does not take place in splendid isolation as if the organisation were a desert island cut off from civilisation. Rather the political process in organisations is both a condition and a consequence of the more global sets of relations of the socio-economic world in which it operates.

In this chapter we have presented a new 'political' approach to organisation studies in general and IT development and use in particular. Its novelty lies in the central position it gives to political process and the efforts of organisational actors to achieve positions of symbolic and material security. In doing so, we have argued for an organisation theory that is both processual and firmly rooted in general and local contextual conditions of possibility.

In contradistinction to many other studies of organisational politics and IT, the approach presented here is based on a view of political processes in organisations that seeks to avoid empirical realist otologies and to advance beyond social constructionist and social shaping models of technological and organisational change. In rejecting the positivist notion that there is an external and measurable world, our analytical gaze falls on the process whereby the social world is constructed, reproduced and changed in and through exercises of power and identity-securing strategies. We argue that the contextually specific process of organisational politics stands at the centre of this constructional effort. Furthermore, we argue that the development, deployment and use of IT is in no way immune to this pervasive process of politics. Indeed, because it represents considerable novelty and uncertainty, and is associated with the rise of new and powerful trade, managerial and specialist groupings, IT has often been productive of particularly intense organisational politics. This is perhaps not surprising as the particular social reality and significance of IT has until recently been the source of much controversy in practitioner, organisational and sociological debates.

3
Responses to Complexity: Developments in IT Management and Use

INTRODUCTION

In Chapter 2 we argued that organisational politics is the motor of organisational life. The metaphor is apt for a number of reasons. First, OP provides the energy that enables IT systems to be transported to the destination of particular passengers but this is rarely a smooth trip; the traffic jams of systems development can be every bit as frustrating and time consuming as those of London or New York; often there is conflict in the vehicle as to where to go and what route to take, who should drive and sometimes the engine breaks down leaving the passengers completely stranded. Retrieval may take a long time and be very expensive. All of these probabilities were in evidence in our case study company, as we shall eventually discover. However, this political process varies in both its intensity and character over time. In this chapter we will examine a range of conditions that make such variations possible and argue that the intensity of IT-related politics has increased with the growing complexity of IT management and systems development issues.

In the first part of this chapter we introduce a discussion of the variability of political process in general and decision-making in particular. We then proceed to examine briefly the broad parameters of IT use in a particular sector of the economy, the UK life insurance industry, in order to explore empirically our thesis of a growing complexity and politicality of IT-related decision-making and practice.

In the third part of the chapter we describe some of the major changes that are contributing to the growing complexity of IT management issues. These include such factors as: (i) the growing range of technological possibilities available to organisations such as image processing, networked personal computers, electronic data interchange and electronic mail; (ii) the increasing range of IT applications in organisations and the related problems of (iii) systems renewal and (iv) systems integration. These technological developments do not, of course, take place in a vacuum, nor do they leave existing organisational relations unscathed. Thus, we also briefly consider: (v) changing intra-organisational relations between IS and other management specialisms; (vi) the growing range of actors demanding a share of IS resources and particular systems development projects, and lastly (viii) the rapid change in UK insurance markets in the 1980s and 1990s, in part made possible by earlier rounds of computerisation.

In the final part of the chapter we analyse one high level response to managerial difficulties in the IT area in the life insurance industry. This was the rapid spread and take-up of the discourse and practices of IT strategy. The application of IT strategy in insurance companies can be constructed in a number of ways. For example, a managerialist reading would argue that IT strategy take-up was a sign of managerial maturity and rationality in the face of growing complexity. In this perspective, strategy is seen to be a tool to rationalise resource use and inter-managerial competition in turbulent markets. Another, more cynical reading of the upsurge in IT strategy discourses might argue that this resulted from follow-my-leader practices that produced many written strategies but little application of strategy to the management of IT. Our political perspective suggests that the discourse of IT strategy followed an extension of a rapidly dilating corporate strategy discourse (see Knights and Morgan, 1991). As such, having an IT strategy became an important part of an IS division's competence and potentially bestowed considerable benefits on IS managers able to mobilise and articulate IT strategy techniques. From this perspective, IT strategy was grasped as a trendy technique that offered a possible 'technical fix' to the growing complexity of IT management.

Our interviews with insurance IS managers, suggest, however, that IT strategies tended to displace and placate growing tensions between IS developers and users rather than 'solving' them *per se*.

VARIATIONS IN POLITICAL PROCESS

Reviews of OP literature suggest that many writers (e.g. Batten and Swab, 1965) regard politics as an organisational exception (see Drory and Romm, 1990). In the IS politics literature some observers concur with this view. For example, Kling (1980) suggests that political analysis of IS development is appropriate when a multiplicity of actors are in open disagreement. Other academic studies suggest that different analytical perspectives can be used to illustrate different aspects of IS. So, for example, Franz and Robey (1984) analyse case material through a rational and political perspective.

In our approach we disavow this pluralist approach. For us, organisational life is about politics. That is, politics is not an exception or optional extra. It is a constant abiding presence at the heart of organisational life. Indeed, it is the motor or mechanism through which the reality or competing realities of organisational life are constructed. But while we insist on the centrality of politics in organisational life we also want to acknowledge that this political process is manifested in different forms and with different intensities. That is, the tenor and form of political process is not constant: it changes and is dependent on a number of different circumstances.

The variation of political process can be broken down into a number of different dimensions. Firstly, there is the *intensity* of politics. This stretches from the routinised banality of everyday organisational practice to open warfare. This intensity of politics is, secondly, associated with the *institutionalisation* of political process. That is, political process is not usually conducted through an anarchic free-for-all. Organisational processes are embedded within a system of formal and informal rules and norms (Crozier and Friedberg, 1980) where these are often established by a series of precedents that organisational actors understand (March, 1981). These rules and norms can and do change, as occurred within our case study Pensco. In this example, change was largely due to the arrival of a new General Manager, who used his powers of 'constrained domination' (Hickson et al, 1986) to overhaul Pensco's culture and management reporting procedures (see Chapter 6).

The intensity of political life is then associated with the degree of stability or change in an organisation. We would suggest that change is likely to be associated with intense political processes. However, change does not cause political intensity. Rather, they are intimately linked as change arises out of political process in the first place.

A third dimension of political life is the *self-consciousness* that actors have of the political character of their actions. Boland and Pondy (1983) have argued that rational and 'natural' (political) myths of management can co-exist in organisations. At least initially, we will suggest that deeply institutionalised political processes will tend to foreground rational, bureaucratic myths. In this situation organisational actors will be more likely to see the organisation as a set of rational processes. Some actors may be seen as particularly 'political animals' but they will be the exception rather than the rule.

In periods of change and instability the political character, or 'politicality' (Hickson et al, 1986) of organisational life may come rushing to the fore as actors realise that taken-for-granted rules are changing. As these change, actors can no longer rely on them and they may sense they need to assume a more active and calculating approach to organisational life. These approaches can also derive, of course, from changed commitments that are a function of particular political outcomes such as, for example, the success or failure to achieve a favoured career position.

So far, we have argued that there are three important dimensions to the process of organisational politics. These are the intensity of political process, the degree of institutionalisation of that process, and actors' awareness of political process as a self-conscious activity. While not wanting to fix these dimensions in mechanistic relations, we have suggested that political intensity will tend to increase with the lessening of institutionalised rules and regulations associated with periods of rapid organisational change. As the accepted norms of political process are undermined this will also tend to increase actors, self-consciousness of the conditional character of organisational rationality and the role of individual and collective political strategies within this.

We now look briefly at the politics of decision-making, an area that has received considerable attention in organisation theory (e.g. Allison, 1971; Cyert and March, 1963; Pettigrew, 1973; Hage, 1980; March, 1981; Hickson et al, 1986). In so doing, we argue that the increasing complexity and uncertainty of IT management issues and systems development is tending to increase the intensity of political processes in the so-called 'user relations' phase of IS practice.

It has been suggested that 'organizations are best conceptualized as political bargaining systems' where political intensity is strongest around the decision-making process (Bacharach and Lawler, 1980, p.213). This is because decision-making and taking can often unsettle existing organisational relations and is often associated with high-profile and risky projects. Again, though, this political intensity will vary depending on the types of decisions being taken. For example, some decisions will be relatively routine, involve well-known procedures and have relatively predictable outcomes. Such decisions are likely to be associated with low intensity, unreflective political processes. In a sense, these decisions almost take themselves and appear to comply with a rationalistic view of organisations. Alternatively, decisions can be associated with a high degree of uncertainty and complexity. Additionally, they may lack a well-worn path of decisional procedures and practices.

Decision-making uncertainty will tend to be high when a major decision is being taken for the first time and when its results cannot easily be predicted (Hickson et al, 1986, p.43-4). This can be further heightened by the range of interests involved in the decision and the form of the participation of those interests in the decision-making process (Hickson et al, 1986; Cohen et al, 1972).

The maximum uncertainty and complexity in decisional processes will tend to prevail, therefore, when decisions are 'sporadic' and 'vortex'-like, that is, where decisions are 'informally spasmodic and protracted' (Hickson et al, 1986, p.237) and where they draw in a wide range of conflicting interests and objectives. This can create a whirlpool effect of political conflict. A primary example of sporadic and vortex-like decisions are those concerning the launch of new products on to the marketplace. This is because these tend to be non-routine decisions, involve a wide range of different organisational actors and create considerable uncertainty as to potential sales in conditions the organisation does not generally control. This will be seen to be the case with the Pensco case study presented in Chapter 6.

So far in this chapter we have argued that while at the centre of organisational life, the political process is not a constant, unchanging phenomenon. Rather, its intensity and character is affected by changes in internal and external markets and by the degree of institutionalisation and self-consciousness concerning political events. But, as we have seen, organisational politics is particularly important and often intense in the sphere of decision-making especially when there is uncertainty and complexity. In the remainder of this chapter we will argue by reference to our research in financial services that the IS decision-making arena is becoming increasingly complex and uncertain: a change which is tending to intensify the politics of IT-related decision-making and systems development.

DATA PROCESSING IN INSURANCE IN THE 1960s AND 1970s

Insurance is often called an 'information-intensive' industry. As one manager we interviewed commented, the life insurance industry sells no more than 'pieces of paper and promises'. However, sales, underwriting, renewal and claims procedures all require the collection, manipulation, storage, retrieval and updating of considerable amounts of data. Furthermore, this data has to stay on record for many years as life policies can have a duration of up to and over 50 years. In 1990, UK per annum income for individual life insurance policies was more than

£14bn. and there were over 110m. personal life and pensions policies in force (Association of British Insurers, 1991).

General insurers (i.e. those distributing fire, accident, motor policies, etc.) began investing in punched card machinery in the 1920s to accelerate the processing of the masses of standard information with which they dealt. From the mid-1960s they were involved in the arduous task of converting and storing their punch card data on mainframe computers and extending the range of computer support to the preparation of policies and renewals. In these early days of computing the range of technological possibilities open to management was limited and the sheer size of developing back-office systems forestalled other uses of expensive mainframe processing time. There was a rapid take-up of computing by the general offices as it promised significant cost savings in the most labour-intensive areas of their operations (Barras and Swann, 1983).

The introduction of computers and the design, programming and maintenance of software gave rise to a nascent data processing function within the industry. This was something of a novelty in a sector which had never had much contact with, or made large investments in, technology and technologists. Investing in computer technology on such a sudden and massive scale had some major implications for management in that not only were they confronted with unfamiliar equipment and methods of processing but also a 'strange' group of technology specialists whose occupational culture differed sharply from that prevalent within insurance.

Managers used early computing applications to cut staff costs and raise clerical productivity (Sturdy, 1992). The advent of batch processing was used to further rationalise clerical work. This involved the creation of a special data preparation function staffed almost entirely by women who did nothing but punch or key data into the mainframe computers. This gendered division of labour around the emergent technologies was not caused by the technology as such. Rather it was informed by, and in turn contributed to the reproduction of, a systematic division of labour and job segregation based on gender (see Collinson et al, 1990).

Two developments in data processing technology greatly extended the potential range of technological possibility open to insurance managers. Firstly, the creation of on-line computing meant that data held in computer files could be accessed and altered in seconds whereas before access and amendment were only possible during periodic batch processing runs. This also opened up the possibility of direct data input. Secondly, the development of relatively cheap mini-computers, which could be linked to mainframes, meant that it was now possible to create a distributed network of processing capabilities.

On-line processing had a number of applications in the insurance industry. It was used to accelerate the generation of policy quotations from head office or branch locations. It also allowed the process of policy production to be speeded-up through the direct entry of client data on to the mainframe from the branches. However, the take-up of this technological possibility has been limited due to a number of factors discussed below. This unevenness in the uptake and utilisation of distributed processing suggests, as we would suspect, that there is no direct correspondence between technological innovation and organisational change.

The general insurance industry, at least initially, used distributed processing more than the life sector. This in part resulted from the previous location of a considerable amount of administrative work in the branch network of the big general companies. However, there were significant differences in the way managers in these companies adopted distributed computing (Barras and Swann, 1983; Storey, 1987).

Of the three large general companies studied by Storey (1987) in the mid-1980s only one had developed a comprehensive system of distributed processing, one had no distributed processing, and the other had developed distributed processing for some products but not others. From these observations Storey concluded that while managerial intent in all three companies was informed by an 'underlying "logic" of beliefs about organisational rationality' (ibid. p.48), manifested in a common concern with cost-cutting and operational standardisation, the mobilisation of these beliefs was mediated through diverse organisational cultures and resulted in the variety of technology uses observed.

In life insurance, decentralised processing and data input at branch level are still not prevalent. In many companies branches are regarded as sales outlets and have until recently been largely unaffected by computerisation, save for the provision of on-line quotations and enquiry services.

The lack of administrative decentralisation in the life industry also results from the economies of scale that accrue by keeping a specialised head office administrative unit for the more complex processing procedures in the life industry. This is also related to political considerations within life insurance organisations. On the one hand, the Sales and Marketing Division consider branches to be exclusively sales-oriented. On the other, the Administrative Division may not want to lose control of any of its work. Thus, although it has been technologically possible to decentralise administrative work for some time, or in some cases send it overseas, there has been little pressure to move in this direction in the life insurance industry.

This was illustrated at one of the companies we visited. The IS AGM commented with regard to administrative decentralisation:

There is nobody apart from us that maybe thinks it is a good idea, because everybody else has got their interests in leaving things as they are unless there is a...you know, I think the push is going to have to come from another direction like a major push to reduce costs.

With regard to the locus of IT-related decision-making our own interview evidence suggests that this was largely the domain of technologists in nascent data processing departments. Somewhat isolated from the mainstream of insurance activity, these managers have considerable decision-making powers based on the technical skills over which they exercise a monopoly control. Their major organisational relationship is with the administrative divisions of insurance companies who were the main recipient of computing investments in this period.

As such, computing in the insurance industry in the 1960s and 1970s can be characterised as technology- or systems-led and predominantly geared to the automation of back office clerical routines. Technology was largely process-oriented although with the increasing importance of unit-linked products (see Chapter 5), there were already moves to make a more substantial use of computer systems in product development and delivery.

In the early days of computing, senior managerial decision-making largely concerned the question of whether or not to invest in this new technology. Once this decision had been made the application of computing to the business was restricted by the limited range of possibility of early computers and the specialised knowledge required to program these particular machines (see Pettigrew, 1973). Thus mainframe computing was initially used to deal with standard accounting and administrative procedures. The sheer size of this task in the financial services industry effectively excluded other potential uses of computing in the sector for some time. The predominant use of early computing also created important organisational relations between computing and administrative functions. Managers in these functions have often resisted attempts by other departments to encroach on this relationship. Furthermore, the particular uses made of early computing technology, the specialist mathematics-oriented knowledge required and the organisational position and professional culture of these technologists helped to constitute and reproduce occupational identities sharply at odds with that of the conservative paternalism of the insurance industry, which has been likened to a quasi-civil service culture (Murray, 1991).

THE INTENSIFICATION OF IT POLITICS

As mentioned, political process varies in intensity and character over time as its conditions of possibility change. In the next two sections of this chapter we examine these changing conditions of possibility with regard to increasing managerial complexity within the sphere of IT and systems development. In this section we spell out broad and general changes taking place in those areas. In the next we focus on our site of empirical investigation, the UK life insurance industry, to further explore these changes and the high level response to them of IT strategic management. We now proceed to examine some of the factors that have contributed to the growing complexity of IT-related decisional processes. These are listed in Table 3.1.

Table 3.1 *Factors contributing to the intensification of IT politics*

- Increased range of available technologies
- Increased range of technology applications
- Changing focus of IT applications—front office and market-sensitive systems
- Problems of system integration and renewal
- Growing number and range of actors within IT decisional processes
- Changing intra-organisational relations—the rise of sales and marketing specialisms
- Changing product markets

The Increasing Range of Technologies Available

During the 1980s an increasing range of technological possibility was opened up by developments in computer hardware, software and telecommunications. This increasing range of possibility has been made possible by a number of factors: the falling cost of computer processing power, the increasing sophistication and flexibility of software systems, the diffusion of network capabilities, and the emergence of a series of tools and techniques that may have a profound effect on the manner and speed with which software is developed and managed (see Bessant et al, 1985; Miles et al, 1988).

The price of computer processing power fell dramatically during the 1980s. At the same time computer processing speeds greatly increased. The 1980s were characterised by the emergence and diffusion of the personal computer as a new and powerful local computing device. This gave rise to an increased measure of user control over some areas of IT use. However, despite this development, the 1980s were a decade that saw the continued dominance of large, centralised systems running on mainframe computers. This was particularly the case in areas, such as financial services, where companies were dealing with vast quantities of client and transaction data.

With the benefit of hindsight, a number of commentators suggest that the 1980s were a decade of profligate IT spending, encouraged by favourable economic circumstances and a belief that IT could deliver the future if enough resources were pushed the IS Division's way (e.g. Cane, 1992). However, such is the pace of technological change that 'yesterday's strategic coup often becomes today's high-overhead, inefficient liability' (McFarlan and McKenney, 1983 p.4).

Towards the end of the 1980s a new range of information and communications technologies began to emerge on the market. These ranged from ever-more-powerful mini-computers, work stations, PCs and portable and palmtop computers, through image capture transmission and processing technologies such as image processing and document scanners, to a broad range of new communications links and technologies epitomised by current interest in computer networks electronic data interchange (Benjamin et al, 1990; Cash and Konsynski, 1985) and the possibilities of wireless computer and telecommunications networks (Taylor, 1992). Linked to these were also new forms of information storage, such as CD-ROMs, and explorations in multimedia systems enabling the combination text, graphics, video, still photographs and sound.

The emergence of these new technologies in the early 1990s in a climate of recession and increased managerial concern to implement new organisational forms have given rise to a series of concerns with regard to technology management that differ from those dominant in the 1980s. These include increased senior managerial scepticism with claims regarding IT's ability to deliver competitive advantage; growing interest in the idea of information, as opposed to technology, management, and a realisation that IT has largely been used to automate existing organisational structures and processes rather than fundamentally transforming them (Hammer, 1990). More specifically, in financial services management, attention began to focus on two key issues of IT management in the early 1990s. These were downsizing and outsourcing. Both these issues have major implications for the very organisation and control of IT in financial services.

Downsizing implies the demise of the large mainframe computing facilities which are the hub of financial services IT use. Advances in networking technologies and the price advantages of using powerful mini-computers and PCs now means that it is possible to create networks of smaller machines managed through client-serving systems of network management. Advocates of client-serving argue that costs may be 25 percent of those of equivalent mainframe capacities. Defenders of the mainframe argue that centralised processing of vast quantities of data is cheaper and more reliable than the use of networks where software and data management systems are still relatively unproven (Cane, 1992).

Outsourcing or facilities management consists of the contracting out of an organisation's computer centre to a third party. As such, the third party may buy the organisation's computer facilities and manage these to an agreed level of service. The driving idea behind this controversial development, which threatens the continued existence of a strong organisational data processing presence, is that computer centres in themselves do not constitute a core business activity. Additionally, there is a belief that dedicated facilities management companies will be able to achieve levels of efficiency unattainable from in-house DP departments.

Increasingly cheap and fast processing is extremely important for information-intensive retail organisations. If the mass of client and market information held on databases is to be used to good business effect, it is necessary to be able to manipulate this information rapidly in as wide a variety of configurations as possible. In areas such as financial services, until recently the great majority of client information was stored by policy numbers in databases. Consequently it has proved difficult to build up client profiles from this data. The creation of relational databases and very rapid processing machines has opened up the possibility of using client information for strategic advantage. However, the conversion of large databases to this new architecture is a colossal task.

While hardware prices have fallen, software development costs have remained stubbornly stable. Some analysts (e.g. Dearden, 1987) suggest that the high costs of in-house software development will be circumvented by increasing resource to package software. However, off-the-shelf systems often require considerable customisation and there is a danger that they will eliminate the specific features of a company's products. That is, as systems become more product-oriented they increasingly embody the specificity of a company's service or products. In financial services a company's computer system may be tantamount to its product. In this context, the 'system is the product' and many companies will continue to allocate massive resources to the in-house development and customisation of their systems in the search for competitive advantage through product diversification and innovation.

If managers decide to build rather than buy new systems, there is now a rapidly growing range of system development project support tools which claim to raise software specialist productivity. Similarly, there are many system development methodologies sold on the basis that their use will improve the design and effectiveness of large systems. For example, in the face of continued IT staff shortages at the end of the 1980s the Norwich Union insurance groups invested £4m. in a computer aided software engineering (CASE) facility. IT managers hoped this would reduce the burden of maintaining existing systems, which then absorbed

70 percent of the IS Division's resources, and eventually lead to a 50 percent increase in IT specialist productivity (Dudman, 1989). There is also considerable development work taking place in the area of automatic program generation and new programming languages. However, the cost and productivity of software staff remains a large problem within the management of IT. And the lead times required to develop large systems are often at odds with the rapid responses managers want to make in fast changing markets. For these and other reasons the strategic management of IT has come to be seen as increasingly important for the success and survival of organisations in the 1990s.

The rapidly expanding range of information and communications technologies is creating increasing complexity for the IT manager. Major developments have thrown into doubt past certainties and modes of organising technology. The complexities are further complicated by the persuasive application of IT in nearly all areas of organisational activity.

The Increasing Range of IT Applications

IT applications were initially applied in areas of routine data storage and manipulation. As technologies have become more sophisticated and flexible, IT use has colonised 'front office' areas such as contact with customers, and been used increasingly in the process of management itself. More recently, there is a marked tendency to apply IT in areas such as marketing and distribution where powerful database systems can produce highly focused analyses of clients and markets (Bertrand and Noyelle, 1988; Touche Ross, 1985).

This growing interest in the marketing application of IT is linked to a gradual shift from very inward-looking organisational uses of IT towards more outward-looking applications in intra- and inter-organisational networks. This is the case, for example, in the UK insurance industry where major initiatives were underway in the early 1990s to develop third-party networks to make possible the electronic trading of insurance (see Knights et al, 1993).

The Growing Number of Actors Involved in IT Decision Processes

The increasing range of ICT application has been matched by growth in the number and range of people involved in the areas of IT strategy and systems development. In the early days the IT arena was relatively limited and concerned small groups of people from one or two organisational functions. Now hundreds of users and developers are involved in different projects and at different levels of the organisation. These levels range from the setting of top level IT strategy and its integration into business strategy, through the whole range of IS senior, middle and junior managers to *ad hoc* forms of collaboration on particular projects. Furthermore, increased interest in inter-organisational systems has further expanded the IT arena as managers cross organisational boundaries to develop intra- organisational systems (Knights et al, 1993).

The important points to note here are that the sheer number of managers involved in IT decision and implementation tends to increase complexity, particularly as this is associated with the disruption of established intra-organisational relations. Thus, for example, in UK financial services companies the rise of a powerful marketing function has subverted previous established relations between IS and administrative functions as marketing managers have claimed a growing share of IS resources for their projects.

Systems Renewal

One of the prices that the service industries such as retail and financial services are now paying for being early large-scale computer users is the pressure to renew old and outworn systems. This partly results from increasing demands in the industry for a flexible use of IT in order to meet divergent market opportunities. These demands for flexibility include such areas as rapid product development, client-oriented databases, and faster product distribution. It is the common experience of many IS managers that it is difficult to meet these demands for flexibility from a systems base and architecture that may date from the late 1960s and early 1970s. An IS AGM (Assistant General Manager) in a medium-sized industrial insurance company said:

> One of the difficulties [with the new demand for flexibility] is that the current systems had been bent all over the place and changed out of recognition from when they started, and it was getting more and more difficult to maintain them, and thereby the response time to the marketing people when they wanted to launch a new product was getting unacceptably long.

Many companies have renewed part or, more rarely, all of their systems at some time in the 1970s or 1980s with the emergence of on-line technologies. It has, however, surprised us to find a number of large and medium-sized insurance companies still using a mixture of batch and on-line systems running on different mainframe and database technologies. Perhaps in recognition of this problem many companies have placed a complete renewal of systems on the agenda for the 1990s when they hope the necessary 'window of opportunity' will appear. Whether or not this renewal is achieved is altogether another matter; without a let-up in the demands for new products coming from marketing departments and a general calming of the turbulent competitive and regulatory waters of the insurance and financial services markets there simply may not be the time or resources to undertake the high risk and resource intensive process of systems renewal. Yet the rub is that without this systems renewal the long-term viability of many companies will be threatened by a kind of creeping arthritic condition in their existing systems infrastructure. Ironically, new entrants not saddled with a legacy of ageing systems may be in a better position to exploit the flexibility promised by IT than the older established companies.

At one large life company a gradual programme of system conversion appeared to get stuck. Initially the high cost–benefit and visible systems were converted but the low benefit and less visible systems were not converted. In this case incomplete conversion was estimated to be costing the company in the region of £2m. a year in the enhancement and maintenance of programmes, while it seriously limited the use of on-line systems due to length of overnight batch processing run times.

The consequences of failing to complete conversions may be considerable but it is often difficult to persuade business managers to commit the resources to their completion given management's market-oriented priorities. A senior IS manager at the above company argued that when renewal is undertaken the logical sequence of renewal would start by converting the core operating and records systems, only converting the product systems at the end of the sequence. However, in effect this would mean the business 'pumping millions into the IS division with no visible return for two to three years so you can't do it that way.' Such decisions are made all the more difficult when the future direction of technology trends is uncertain, as was the case in the early 1990s around issues such as downsizing and outsourcing. Yet, it appears that the often *ad hoc* proliferation of IT applications in the past will impose an increasingly costly burden on organisations wishing to employ more recent IT developments to transform current business processes. Systems renewal not only presents senior managers with a high risk and resource-intensive operation. It also is beginning to bring to light hidden costs of past system infrastructural developments. It is to this that we now turn.

Systems Integration

Our interviews suggest that systems growth in the 1970s developed in an *ad hoc* way in the sense that little attention was given to the shape of an emerging systems infrastructure. New systems were often simply bolted on to existing systems (see also Sturdy, 1989).

The consequence of the combination of the existing technology, and the methods of system development at the time led to a growing integration of systems. This often gave rise to the development of a complex suite of interacting systems, some of which had been enhanced over time, others of which had been added on to existing systems.

Systems integration, of course, has its advantages. In particular, different systems can be connected so that changes in the data in one system are fed through automatically into adjacent systems. However, a number of problems emerged through the integration process. Firstly, integration increased complexity in the sense that a minor change in one computer system could have ripple effects throughout the infrastructure of different systems. Furthermore, these ripple effects were often only being discovered by trial and error. This significantly raises the costs of maintenance and new systems. It also places a premium on the clear documentation of systems and their interfaces. If such documentation is not provided the knowledge of systems and interfaces may come to reside with particular IS staff. This knowledge can then become a significant resource for such individuals in resisting or accepting change and it may be lost when key IS staff members leave the organisation. We return to this issue later (Chapter 9) where we argue that particular software practices become embedded in IS and corporate cultures and structures. These may act as a considerable constraint on the emergence of different methods of systems development and user relations.

Systems integration has also been associated with a so-called 'processing-driven' approach to the application of information technology. The approach is characterised by the piecemeal application of IT to different administrative processes. In the insurance industry this has meant that separate but interacting systems have been created for pensions, life insurance and mortgage administration in the same company. As a result, there is a considerable duplication of data and marketing information is fragmented across a number of systems.

Recently IT users in the insurance industry have begun to consider the possibilities of moving towards a data-driven method of IT application. This involves redesigning systems around data rather than the different processes in which this is manipulated. It is claimed that this approach will remove much duplication of data capture and data held. Perhaps more importantly this approach will improve the speed and ease with which client data can be assembled and manipulated for the cross-selling of company products to existing clients (see Jones, 1985).

Integration has also tended to mean that systems cannot be renewed on a piecemeal basis. This is because the systems are constrained by each other; to renew one system without renewing the others may seriously compromise and add to the cost of the new system. Nevertheless, piecemeal renewal often happens in practice for a variety of reasons. In particular, the sheer size of renewing all systems is a daunting and massive investment. And while individual company divisions may want new product and processing systems, no individual manager or functional division may have much interest in seeing the renewal of core 'bread and butter' accounting and record-keeping systems. This is because such renewals may show little direct cost saving, service improvement or added sales. They may thus be difficult to cost-justify and managers may be unwilling to act as 'champions' for such unglamorous and risky projects. However, the renewal of such core systems may be key to creating the much talked about flexible systems and infrastructures of the future. Lastly, the proliferation of hardware and software platforms based on different operating systems and standards creates considerable problems in the area of system inter-connectivity (see McFarlan and McKenney, 1983, p.5).

Product Markets

During the 1980s then, we see a gradual expansion of IT within the insurance industry from the back office towards areas such as marketing, sales and distribution. This was accompanied by the increasing use of IT in the development and delivery of new products to the market. In sum, IT use was becoming much more sensitive to the market (Friedman and Cornford, 1989).

However, this was also a period in insurance where there was considerable market turbulence as a welter of new government legislation changed the competencies of different financial services sectors and introduced new regulatory procedures for the industry. The application of IT to the area of product development itself contributed to this turbulence and change by facilitating the development of increasingly complex products that could also be changed and re-launched with increased speed.

New product opportunities and regulatory systems served to increase uncertainty in the industry as our case study in Chapter 6 amply illustrates. Managers from different areas of insurance companies struggled to come to terms with changing market expectations and the fine detail of government legislation, often finding themselves in conflict with each other as they vied for systems development resources to meet their particular needs.

The 1980s therefore was a period of growing complexity with regard to the management of IT and systems development within the UK insurance industry. We would suggest that this increasing complexity was not limited to the insurance sector but was widespread in industries using IT in a wide range of applications and settings. Indeed, in the IT community itself there were increasing signs during this period of a sense of crisis with regard to the role of IS managers, systems analysts and programmers.

One response to the growing complexity of IT issues and increasing and conflicting pressures on the IS resource was the turn to strategic management and IT strategies. It is to this that we now turn.

THE RISE OF CORPORATE AND IT STRATEGY

The increasing complexity of IT issues facing organisations in the 1980s threatened to throw IT management into chaos. The old ways of managing based on technology and technologist-led decision-making and an often *ad hoc* approach to long-term planning were no longer sustainable.

Not surprisingly, therefore, the IT community began to generate, and borrow, new ideas to manage growing IT portfolios and problems. This process gave rise to a powerful and sustained discourse of strategic IT management which argued that, even in an often unsettled environment, long-term business and IT planning could and should be achieved. As a discourse and through the specific techniques promoted, it promised to give managers greater control over their own futures and those of their organisations (see Henderson and Sifonis, 1988; Sutherland and Morieux, 1988).

This idea of strategic management was not, as it were, 'invented' by the IT community. Rather, it was borrowed from a more general and dominant corporate strategy discourse (see Knights and Morgan, 1991). In the IT community the idea of strategy soon gained great currency as it promised to resolve growing problems around the management of IT. In particular, it appeared to offer a solution to the issue of rationalising the increasingly wide range of systems development demands being placed on IS departments (Lederer and Mendelow, 1988).

A primary issue that IT strategy promised to solve concerned that of the difficult relationship between IT and business issues, and in organisational terms, the relationship between IT users and in-house IT providers. In the discourse of management and consultancy the problematic character of this relationship was labelled as the problem of integrating or aligning corporate strategy with IT strategy (e.g. Watkins, 1989). In recent surveys of the issues facing IS managers, 'planning and developing information systems to support corporate strategy' was the prime concern (Parker and Udundun, 1988, p.34) and the integration of corporate and line management uses of IT was signalled as a vital issue (Dixon and John, 1989).

Here we want to challenge the limitations of much of the strategy literature which tends to have a narrow and prescriptive focus. This literature often tends to reduce the problem and complexity of managing IT to an issue of creating the appropriate hybrid IS manager or chief executive (e.g. Dixon and John, 1988), management development programmes (Peat Marwick McLintock/Bristol Business School, 1988) or prescribing improvements to IS developer and user communications as a panacea to more deeply seated problems (e.g. Guinan, 1988).

Furthermore, the 'solutions' provided by much of the strategic IT literature often smack of a mechanistic application of slogans and techniques. While of some use in concentrating managerial thinking around key issues, the underlying theoretical assumptions of these techniques may, as an unintended consequence, reproduce the very problems they seek to ameliorate (see Knights and Murray, 1990).

Let us illustrate through our own research in the financial services area where we found increasing concern to implement corporate and IT strategies towards the end of the 1980s (see also Watkins, 1989). Managers felt these were needed in part to deal with problems to do with the proliferation of insurance products and distribution channels, the decentralisation of organisations into business units, and a tendency to give these business units their own IT and systems budgets. There was also clearly considerable kudos to be gained by taking up the banner of strategic management in the 1980s: it was a big and rolling bandwagon and many managers felt compelled to jump on it.

In the strategy-saturated discourses of IT management of the 1990s it is sometimes difficult to remember that 'strategic management' is a comparatively recent development (see Hoskins 1990; Knights and Morgan, 1991). Indeed, prior to the 1980s many insurance companies had no written strategy as such. In the 1980s professional managerial practices became increasingly prominent. One of the main signs of this new display of professionalism is found in the advocacy of strategic management. The great majority of companies we interviewed had yearly corporate strategy documents and regular strategy and planning cycles.

But precisely as strategic management has become more prominent so have the conditions to forward plan with relative stability declined. Major market and regulatory changes have affected the range of products sold, the manner in which products are sold and the distribution channels through which they are sold. Some of these changes are quite revolutionary for the life insurance industry, for example, the acquisition of estate agencies and tied agents such as building societies, whereas others are more incremental.

The massive changes that have taken place in the insurance industry in the last five years were summed up by one IS manager. He said:

> Five years ago there was just life [insurance]. Now there is unit-trusts, estate agency and investment goods. This adds up to a substantially different culture. Now the keywords are decentralised, profit centre and customer oriented.

The pace of this change and its often multi-faceted character have created major problems for the strategic management of insurance companies and difficulties for the management of information technology. In general, these problems can be summed up by the tension encountered between long-term strategic coherence and control and the rush to exploit short- and medium-term market opportunities. This tension is graphically evident in our case study (see Chapter 6).

As we shall see in more detail later this has upset the prevailing internal structural and political relations in many companies. For the time being we note the difficulties as perceived by IS managers who have often felt themselves to be outpaced by the changes being made by senior management and in particular the growing influence of the marketing specialism in the life insurance industry.

These difficulties were perceived at one medium-sized company to have greatly exacerbated the long-standing problem of renewing the company's core computer systems. These were already deemed to be in a 'creaky' state. However, rather than being able to concentrate on their renewal the IS Divisional Manager has found himself adding to and amending the existing systems. In his words this practice has arisen:

> because we have always been pedalling faster than we could really afford to pedal to keep up with the marketing guys.

This was a common lament in the UK insurance industry in the late 1980s. It reflects the speed of change taking place in the industry at the time, the increased importance of the marketing specialism, and the apparent subservience of IS managers and staff to a rapidly escalating series of new product and systems demands. In this situation companies were making very rapid decisions that often had major organisational implications. However, IS managers were often only informed of these decisions after they had been taken and were unable to assess them and inform their business colleagues of their possible repercussions on future IT strategy.

It is generally agreed that in the last five years it has become increasingly difficult to plan in the life insurance industry. Previous to this the life insurance world was described by various interviewees as 'cosy' or a 'sleepy hollow'. Now the emphasis is on entrepreneurial and proactive strategy. As one respondent put it: 'You can second guess and have multiple strategies. You need to be proactive but you don't know which way the industry will go.'

This was the case at one of the largest life insurers. Here strategic deliberations led to the production of a five year plan. However, the pace of change was so rapid that this was seen to be a rough guide rather than a detailed plan. The IS manager here likened the company to:

> a great big tanker going down the [English] Channel whereas insurance is suddenly trying to add all sorts of things on to it which are nearly as big as itself. So it will end up a different shape but you're not sure which sort of appendage will grow and which will not go anywhere.

At this company the emphasis was on the creation of a strategy that enabled the company to react flexibly to future changes. This resulted in a tension between a 'Utopian' plan five to six years away and a 'completely non-strategic version [of the plan] where you respond to every little request and you end up with a chaotic group of systems that in no way can be related to each other.'

The turbulent character of financial service markets and the pace of organisational change in the insurance industry have created particular problems for the formulation of IT strategy. The shift towards more flexible and decentralised structures and the rise of a marketing-led outlook with a stress on sales maximisation and rapid product development and diversification have placed new and novel demands on IS divisions. In some companies these demands have even led to the dissolution of a centralised IS function.

This was the case at another of the UK's largest life insurers. Here the management of IT had shifted from an emphasis on a technology-led style towards a 'customer, marketing and management decision-making led' style of IT use. This involved the gradual decentralisation of the centralised IS division, which had a headcount of 850, into the newly defined business units comprising the financial services group. The then head of the IS division explained this as a movement towards the 'integration of the planning and control of IS into the business units'. In 1988 these units were using different types of hardware and had differing systems' legacies. The senior IS manager hoped that a corporate computer services function would 'draw these strands together over the next few years after letting the business managers find their own feet'. This was something of a problem because of the new autonomy granted the business units and the wide variety of hardware and software utilised by them. Nevertheless, the corporate IS manager was hopeful of achieving overall coherence in the systems' area because 'there's been a good conversation between [the business units] and specialist management'.

However the heads of the new business units had not been constrained 'because that would not have been an unpopular thing to do'. Instead, business unit managers were being given an almost free hand 'because of a belief in profit centres and incentives for groups of managers; it's your shop, you run it is the philosophy. Divisional managers believe they need control over computing, rightly or wrongly.'

The manager charged with bringing together the different strands of this strategy was sceptical about his chances of success. He said:

> I will seek to find areas of common interest in the future so one can say—there is a good reason for converging, isn't there ? If there isn't [a good reason for converging] one is forced back on common sense and a sufficient identity of professional interest to get people to say—Of course, we should be doing such and such.

In other words, convergence and coherence were to be sought through a lightweight central IS planning function attempting to massage gently a consensus out of the different business units.

This example, in a leading IT user in the insurance sector, highlights the difficulties of creating appropriate strategy development structures that have the authority to bring together business units where the Managing Director's major concern is the achievement of profit targets rather than corporate coherence. It is an open question as to whether the mobilisation of 'common sense' can create the appropriate balance between decentralised profit targets and a corporate IT strategy.

The achievement of this 'common sense' may indeed be possible. But it is unlikely to be achieved by formal strategic planning structures and better communication between IT users and developers alone. This is because there may be fundamental clashes of interest between the new business units, vested with considerable IS autonomy, and the corporate IS function. And to come back to the central theme of this book, the resolution of such tensions is highly political within organisational life.

Here we see that strategic coherence is not likely to be achieved by simply putting in the right structures and methods and having 'a jolly good chat with the chaps'. There are clearly major interest conflicts at play along with the more personal aspects of organisational politics. As such, managers are unlikely to give up or compromise their perceived interests for the sake of an abstract goal like 'the corporate good'. In this sense, we would argue that far from representing a higher rationality, corporate and IT strategies are part and parcel of continuous political conflict in organisations. To see them as 'innocent' or apolitical techniques raised above the 'mess' of organisational life is both naive and dangerous. Yet academics and consultants continue to pour out the articles and prescriptions that promulgate such misleading interpretations of organisations.

This clash of interests was graphically illustrated in another large life company we visited. This company had recently established a new distribution channel through a direct sales force. This channel comprised a new business unit and was given considerable managerial autonomy from corporate management. During the establishment of the unit its managers decided to develop three computer systems to handle the sales generated by its commission-based sales force. (These were expected to expand rapidly and indeed they have surpassed the company's initial expectations.) It fell to the centralised Information Services Life and Pensions Department to develop these systems.

The three systems comprised a commissions system, a client information system, and a management information system. Now while these systems have all been used in various guises over the years at this company, systems managers and staff were presented with a novelty that was to cause them serious problems. That is, the above systems had in the past been developed for a very different type of distribution channel and selling method. Systems staff had considerable experience of these operations but had little or no experience of the business requirements of direct selling. Nevertheless, systems staff went ahead as instructed and built the software they thought would be required for the new distribution channel. They were also keenly aware that the systems being constructed would need to be integrated with the major core life and pensions systems run by the company in order to administer the products once sold.

When the new company started selling life and pensions, products systems problems quickly emerged. In particular, the commissions system assumed an importance that had not been forecast. Sales managers soon complained that the commission system was both inflexible and too slow. In the words of the Life Systems Development Manager:

> The commission system proved adequate but it was very difficult to introduce changes due to its reliance on our core life systems for its feeds of information. ... Now what [the new company] has seen as the slowness of that system has attracted some criticism. And when they've wanted to make changes to that system it has also meant changing the core systems. So they have had to compete for priority to get that work done. ... All this has not given them the flexibility and freedom to introduce changes which they see as crucial as quickly as they desire.

These problems appear to have led to considerable tension and hostility between the new company and the Information Services Division. As a consequence, the Managing Director of the new company decided to have a set of relatively independent systems developed by external software houses. This was a source of considerable mirth and anxiety for the in-house Life Systems Departmental Manager: mirth because the company the MD had chosen was small, and considered to be a 'tin pot' software house which had run into considerable problems; and anxiety because the 'relatively independent systems' being developed still had to communicate with the core life and pensions systems. This was forcefully expressed by the Life Systems Department Manager:

> There will still, of course, be some dependence on our own systems. In the end, I mean, they are not selling their own products; they are selling life insurance, they are selling endowments, they are selling pensions, they're selling whatever, but they are all *our* products. That business has to come into *our* systems and the commission payable still has to be identified and dropped out of the bottom of *our* system. So there is still that dependence there. We might be able to simplify that process. We might be able to simplify those features. ... But there will still be some interdependence there however independent they think they are making themselves by having their own systems developed.

Clearly the establishment of the direct sales force company has caused considerable problems for the managers in the IS Division. At the time of our interview these had in part been resolved when the new company had required the assistance of the IS Division to help sort out the mess it was getting into with its external software house. Nevertheless, there was an outstanding issue that concerned the integration of the new company's systems into the core systems and a more general threat to the position of in-house life systems managers who appeared to feel they had lost control of a significant part of their work to the new company.

An additional feature of this example that merits comment concerns the fate of the client information system. This was developed in the belief that sales staff would want to record their client prospects and dealings on a computer system. This was an erroneous belief because sales staff baulked at the amount of work required to key in the necessary information. Accordingly to the Life Systems Manager they were also unwilling to share 'their clients', as they saw them, with the company:

> because at the end of the day, at least at the end of next week, they might want to go and join another company. They don't want to leave all that data with [the company]. They want it on their own personal system.

The volatility of sales staff and their desire to 'own' their clients has been disastrous for the client information system. The Life Systems Manager neatly summed up this situation:

Yeah, I mean we've got this system now that cost us ninety odd thousand pounds to develop which hasn't got a single item of data on it. It'll never be used. It's in the bin. And the management information system, also, at the end of the day, proved not to be what was needed.

This example nicely illustrates the problems created for the development of a long-term and coherent IT strategy at the end of the 1980s. Here the tension between the operational autonomy of new business units, using new techniques and practices, and a centralised Information Services Division providing systems development and computing facilities to the whole of the organisation, comes starkly to the fore. In this particular example the problems encountered were eventually dismissed by our informants as an 'aberration'. This may be so, but it is our impression that such 'aberrations' are commonplace in financial services and elsewhere. And while it is the sincere wish of many managers in IS and other divisions that the market will settle down and that a window of opportunity will allow them to put their houses in order, this is unlikely. Indeed, the external stimuli behind the organisational change witnessed by the financial services industry have had a profound effect on the internal structures, cultures and practices of companies and their managers. Thus even though the regulatory changes made in the middle 1980s are unlikely to be repeated, the industry has now developed an internal dynamic that may well ensure that 'aberrations' continue to be commonplace and bring with them far-reaching impacts on the lives of organisations and their managers and staff.

CONCLUSION

In this chapter we have provided a broad overview of the management and use of IT in organisations from the 1960s to the 1990s. This shows a growing complexity of IT use and management issues and can be related to a number of factors: the expansion of computer applications available; the extended range of these applications in organisations and the concomitant expansion of the number of actors with an interest or involvement in the area of IT management and systems development; and the problems presented by the accretion of different layers and types of computer applications running in large and integrated suites of systems. The last part of the chapter noted that this growth in the complexity of IT management issues has in part been met by a strong interest in, and practice of, 'strategic management' techniques.

Here we argued that the complexity of IT management issues invoked a strategic response, in part because a strategic discourse was already part of the dominant managerial rhetoric in the 1980s. Many claims have been made for the efficacy and necessity of strategic management as a means of gaining a broad co-ordination of organisational activities in troubled times. In particular, strategic management seems to promise the attainment of a higher degree of rational management in large, multi-division organisations.

In this chapter we have questioned this adulation of strategic management in the area of IT and presented empirical material drawn from our research in the financial services industry which questions the efficacy of IT strategies. In so doing we want to warn against an innocent reading of strategy techniques, structures and prescriptions. Our research shows here that the simple introduction of strategic planning cannot be expected to achieve the new co-ordination and co-operation touted by IT consultants. For example, the co-ordination of centrifugal operating division uses of IT and a centralised corporate IT function will not be achieved by the implementation of strategic information planning systems or hybrid managers alone. This is not because organisations implement these methods with insufficient rigour, as claimed by some commentators (Lederer and Sethi, 1988), but because the implementation of these methodologies is in itself a political act. As such, these methods are as much about changing internal organisational power relations as about a new form of rationality where everyone wins. It is to an examination of some of these power relations in the area of IT management and use that we now turn. This we do through an examination of the constitution of the IS specialism and its organisation and culture, and the developing relations between IS specialists and their users in general and with specific reference to the financial services industry.

4
The IS Specialism: Organisation, Development and Culture

INTRODUCTION

Chapter 3 examined the growing complexity of IT and management issues in the area of IT. In this chapter we want to take a closer look at the specialist grouping which has developed alongside the prodigious growth and expansion of IT application and use. Thus, it focuses on the organisation, history and culture of the IS specialism. This in turn is related to our concern to explore the different conditions of possibility of technological and organisational change. Clearly, the organisation of IT-related knowledge within the IS specialism is of considerable importance here.

As already mentioned, IT has developed with remarkable, if uneven, rapidity since the appearance of the first microchips. Not surprisingly, the IS specialism has also developed rapidly in this short space of time and is subject to almost continuous change as new technology applications, techniques and practices are brought on to the market.

IS divisions have had an important change agent role in many organisations in the last 20 years. However, in performing that role IS divisions have also established their own particular cultures, practices and structures that now threaten to block the changes in IT management being demanded by senior user managers. In this sense, 'the change agent itself … must change to be relevant' (McFarlan and McKenney, 1983, p.199). This stricture has often been understood as a demand for structural change within organisations—the decentralisation of IS divisions and the integration and alignment of IT and business strategies. In addition, we understand it to have important implications for the collective and individual identity of IS specialists because the changes taking place in the management and use of IT present a challenge to individual IS specialists. In particular, the qualities and criteria by which IS specialists are judged and rewarded may have shifted rapidly in a short space of time. This happened, for example, at Pensco (see Chapter 7) when a new General Manager and IS chief attempted radically to change the control and management of IS specialists.

Given the unstable, although relatively comfortable, position of IS specialists in managerial and non-managerial labour processes, individuals in the specialism may feel an undefined pressure to change the manner in which they present themselves to their colleagues and the corporate world. This pressure may be particularly accentuated if they respond to career expectations to scale the corporate ladder.

In order to get a clearer and more detailed grasp of the politics of IT it becomes important to examine these changes and concomitant shifts in the organisation and identity of IS specialists. However, organisational change is fraught with difficulties and tensions that are resolved slowly due to the mutual embeddedness of organisational and political practices.

In the first section of the chapter we appraise the organisation of the IS specialism in the UK by examining its size, rates of pay, 'professional' organisation, location in the class structure, and forms of career mobility. We also pay particular attention to the managerial control of IS specialists and the degree of autonomy they continue to exercise in their working lives.

In the second section of the chapter we draw on the work of Friedman and Cornford (1989) to chart out the history of developing IS specialist and user relations, the forms of control that managers have attempted to exert over IS specialists, and the changing relationship between, and organisational position of, IS specialists.

Lastly, we look at the culture of science and technology in contemporary society. This we do in order to assess the position of IS specialists as technologists in a society where technology is generally seen as a positive and essentially neutral embodiment of rationality and progress. By doing this we are not attempting to assert that IS specialists believe that they are gods towering above ordinary mortals. However, the prevalence of the discourse of positive and rational technology that has accompanied the development of IT could be a powerful source of identification and legitimation for IS specialists practice.

Inasmuch as this is plausible we disagree with those accounts of the values of computer and IS specialists which claim that IS specialists basically share values similar to those of other specialists and managers (Holti, 1989; Mumford, 1972). Our disagreement here lies in part with the type of values that Holti and Mumford attempt to measure and in part with the empirical social psychological approach that they take in their studies. In contrast, we present a more speculative approach of a kind of meta-discourse analysis in order to assert that this discourse is an important condition and consequence of IS specialist subjectivity in the text.

This last theme is taken up empirically in Chapter 5 where we present empirical material to explore further the mobilisation of a distinct IS culture in the defence and negotiation of roles and responsibilities in a user-led systems development project.

IS SPECIALISTS[1]

Members of the IS specialism are those employees, contract or self-employed personnel, whose main job description involves one or more of the following tasks or responsibilities with respect to development, maintenance, sale and management of computer hardware and software, the management of such staff, and the control and direction of IT-related investments. This definition is necessarily imprecise but is meant to suggest the general, if shifting, parameters of the IS specialism. IS specialists in the UK can be found in a number of organisations: in-house computer and systems divisions, hardware and software companies, IT consultancy firms, and software agencies. There are also a 'substantial' number of freelance IS specialists (Friedman, 1987a, p.353).

The specialism is relatively young and has developed out of disciplines such as physics, electronics, mathematics and, with regard to systems analysts, system theory and control engineering (MacKay and Lane, 1989). It is characterised by a rapid numerical expansion (in 1988 there were 300 000 people in data processing jobs, that is, over 1 percent of the UK workforce; *Computing* 10 November 1988 and the proliferation of sub-specialisms within the area as technologies and the means of using them change and develop.

Data on the gender composition of IS specialists in the UK suggest that the pattern of gendered job segregation bears a broad similarity with other specialist groups. That is, women tend to be concentrated in the lowest grades and have found it particularly difficult to break into middle and senior IS managerial grades (Beech, 1990). This was born out in both companies in which we carried out case study research. In both companies no women were employed above the grade of project leader

---

[1] This first section of the chapter draws considerably on Murray (1991).

despite their dominance in lower level clerical work and women constituting approximately 60 percent of all employees. Detailed surveys of US computer specialists show a slight improvement in this situation over the last 20 years. For example, in 1970 only 15 percent of computer scientists and systems analysts were women whereas 90 percent of data entry clerks were women. In 1990 respective percentages were 34 percent and 87 percent. This data suggests that more women have moved into the system analyst jobs although there are still two men for every woman in these occupations. In the area of computer hardware this situation is far worse: women only accounted for 9 percent of engineers and 15 percent of technicians in 1990. The IS specialism, then, is still a predominantly male occupational group. It is, furthermore, a predominantly white male group. Data for the USA, for example, shows that of computer scientists and systems analysts in selected computer-related occupations in 1990 57 percent were white men, 30 percent were white women, 4 percent where black men and 3 percent were black women (Henwood, 1993, p.33–5).

IS specialists can be considered a relatively privileged, if internally divided, group of technical workers and managers. Since the widespread adoption of computing facilities there have been acute shortages of IS specialist labour. There is not a monopoly of IS specialist buyers or sellers but generalised conditions of excess demand pushed wages up faster than the national average until the recession of 1991–3. For example, in 1988 there were acute shortages of programmers, analysts, network and database staff and systems development staff were much sought after (Income Data Services, 1988), while Buckroyd and Cornford (1988) estimated that there was a shortfall of some 19 700 systems development staff in 1987. Wages in 1986–87 rose by 16 percent for computer operators, 15 percent for programmers, 12.5 percent for systems analysts and 10.2 for project managers. That is, these rises were well above the going rate of pay settlements and inflation. In 1987 the average annual salary for operators was £ 11 100 and for project managers, £ 21 360 (Income Data Services, 1988) which was again higher than for equivalent work outside of computing.

Despite enjoying 'high salaries ... and a relatively high degree of autonomy [in their work]' (Friedman, 1987a, p.359), the IS specialism has not emerged as a fully fledged 'profession'. It does not, for example, organise entry to IT jobs through universally recognised professional training and qualifications and, therefore, cannot define the relationship between itself and the clients who use its services—a condition that Johnson (1987) describes as necessary to the development of professional power. Nonetheless there are a number of 'professional' IT organisations (Massey, 1988). Two of the larger are the British Computing Society (BCS) and the Institute for Data Processing Managers (IDPM). Both set entrance examinations for potential members and BCS accredits degree courses and is 'well represented' on government committees. The BCS has 30 000 members and 65 full-time staff and is perhaps the best organised of the associations. But it only represents 10 percent of the IS specialism. Only if it were to secure monopoly control of the right to practise as an IS specialist could the occupation be transformed into a profession. This is unlikely to occur in Britain where recent public policy has been designed to undermine the restrictive monopoly practices of the established professions by forcing them to accept the 'discipline' of market competition.

Within the academic literature there has been an extensive debate regarding the values, abilities and legitimate roles of IS specialists. This has tended to concentrate on the evident communication problem that exists between technologists and other organisational members and has variously prescribed solutions to this problem. On the one hand these consist of generic calls to re-educate IS specialists such that they take account of the social and political aspects of systems design (Mumford, 1972; Willcocks and Mason, 1987). On the other, some commentators have seen the emergence of the IS specialist as a potential saviour of UK industry from the parochial amateurism of British managers (e.g. Rose, 1969).

The study of IS specialists is a new but well-established field of social enquiry. Radical contributions to this field of enquiry have been particularly concerned to establish the class and labour process position of IS specialists as either a subset of technical workers in general or a profession. Within this focus considerable attention has been concentrated on the dynamics of developing IS specialist labour practices and processes and the extent to which IS specialists may have been deskilled (Kraft, 1977; Kraft and Dubnoff, 1986; Friedman, 1987a, 1987b; Orlikowski, 1988; Tierney and Wickham, 1989).

We now draw on this literature to sketch out the position of IS specialists in contemporary social and organisational contexts. However, in doing so we also attempt to go beyond this literature's structuralist limitations by exploring the constitution and development of IS specialist workplace identities. In particular, we are concerned to examine the discourses through which IS specialist practices and beliefs are in part constructed and which in turn serve to legitimise the practices, beliefs and self-understanding developed by IS specialists.

At a general level IS staff and managers can be said to be part of the 'middle levels' of the class structure of advanced capitalist economies. That is, they are technical workers performing largely non-manual labour, who secure access to economic and symbolic resources through the possession of specialist knowledge and techniques. Recently they have been seen as a particularly important example of the increasingly popular category of 'knowledge workers' (see *Journal of Management Studies*, 1993).

In terms of the labour process the IS specialism might be said to stretch from proletarianised data preparation staff to the 'capitalist agent' represented by IS divisional manager (cf. Smith's, 1987, work on technical workers). However, there is no easy characterisation of the IS specialism at a schematic level, particularly as IS specialists are located in a broad range of sectoral and organisational contexts and the specialism itself is subject to rapid change (Orlikowski, 1988).

Within the systems development area of UK financial services, IS specialists are clearly separated from their office floor counterparts. That is, IS staff are recruited from a distinct labour market, have more exclusive life styles and residential areas and labour process positions different from those of their clerical counterparts. The social, gender, community and workplace divisions between IS staff and clerical workers in financial services are at present wide. Indeed, IS staff and managers often appear socially and politically isolated in the UK financial services industry. This in part is explained by the youth of the specialism compared to the antiquity of the mainstream specialisms occupied by bankers, actuaries and accountants. It may also result from tensions between organisational and 'professional' identification experienced by IS staff (Hebden, 1975; Tierney and Wickham, 1989). That is, IS staff may consider themselves to be IS professionals first and insurance or banking specialists second. In addition, the rapid growth of the specialism in the UK, the shortfall of 30 000 IS staff in the national labour market, and the concentration of many of the largest employers of IS labour in South-East England has tended to favour individualistic IS career strategies where 'job hopping' between companies may be an equally if not more effective means to advancement than single organisation 'management training' careers (cf. Friedman, 1987a). Such job hopping tends to limit the integration of IS specialists into corporate cultures and practices while it may reinforce patterns of professional, rather than organisational, identification. Nevertheless, IS staff and managers are wage labourers and subject to the discipline of labour markets and labour processes. At present, though, they occupy a relatively favourable and mobile position in the former which has a considerable influence on developments in the latter.

There has been a long running debate in the literature as to the extent or existence of a trend towards deskilling in the IS specialism. A number of researchers (Borum, 1987; Friedman and Cornford, 1987; Kraft, 1977; Kraft and Dubnoff, 1986; Pettigrew, 1973) have examined this area and draw different conclusions with regard to the internal fragmentation of the IS specialism.

Kraft (1977) and Kraft and Dubnoff (1986) maintain that computer programming in the US has been subject to a deliberate and unilinear process of deskilling leading to a rigid fragmentation of software development work between conception, design and execution. Programmers are subjected to direct control—a kind of Taylorism of mental work—which leaves them with little or no autonomy and few career chances beyond the position of senior programmers. For Kraft and Dubnoff, 'the key to financial success in software is to not specialise and not get too technical' (1986, p.192).

Friedman and Cornford (1987) and Borum (1987) suggest that such Bravermanian deskilling strategies are exaggerated in the literature or at least less successful in Europe than is apparent from Kraft and Dubnoff's studies in the US. This is not to deny that management is attempting to assert its control over the labour process of software development. But this is taking place in an uneven and contested manner where control strategies can be characterised as ones of 'responsible autonomy' rather than 'direct control' (Friedman and Cornford, 1989). Indeed, they argue that there is a tendency in the UK for the least skilled jobs in IS divisions, such as data preparation and 'ordinary applications' programming, to decline while the reintegration of analyst and programmer skills in the figure of the analyst/programmer is being actively sought by IS managers. Likewise, drawing on Danish empirical studies Borum (1987, p.3) sees a shift towards 'job enlargement and [the] flexible partition of tasks' in project-based work groups rather than a trend towards mass production- type work organisation predicted by Kraft (1977). He concludes that management have indeed mobilised control strategies but that these have been only partially successful due to resistance to them, tight IS specialist labour markets, and the unionisation of IS specialists in Denmark. Of late the favourite control strategy appears to be financial in that Danish IT divisions are increasingly being turned into profit centres subject to strict financial control and monitoring.

Pettigrew (1973) comes at the problem of the internal division of IT labour from a different perspective altogether: that of the pluralist wing of organisation studies. His detailed study of the battle between early programmers and a developing and discrete discipline of systems analysis suggests that the internal fragmentation and hierarchisation of the IS specialism cannot simply be seen as the outcome of a grand managerial design to control labour. Rather, an appreciation of the development of computing technology itself and the sectional battles this sparked off within particular IT workforces needs to be placed alongside, and integrated with, an analysis of managerial attempts to gain control of the labour process.

So, while there is ample evidence of the internal fragmentation of IS specialist labour it is also clear that this is a fluid process and not a simple, homogeneous, and unidirectional shift towards deskilling. Further, research suggests that individuals within the specialism tend to move up through programming into systems analysis and design and project management (Friedman and Cornford, 1989).

However, as Orlikowski (1988) and Derber (1982) argue, the broader autonomy enjoyed by IS specialists and other technical workers is often limited. That is, although they may exercise considerable discretion over the practice of their technical skills IS specialists have less control over the objectives to which their labour power and skills are harnessed, once they are in the employ of a particular organisation. This is not to say that they have no influence on the specific objectives to which IT is directed. Indeed, in financial services, IS managers appear to have exercised considerable influence over the direction of IT investments. However, this influence has been a response to, and has served to reinforce, an overwhelming managerial logic. Thus, computing has by and large not been used to democratise work organisation or enrich clerical work in the insurance industry. Instead, the predominant use of the technology has been guided by a dominant managerial discourse of profitability and the reduction of costs and improvement of labour productivity.

At present even this limited form of decisional autonomy possessed by IS managers appears to be under threat. Nevertheless, due to their control of important rules and resources IS managers may still be able to mobilise considerable, not to say too much (e.g. Lucas, 1984), organisational power. Orlikowski (1988, p.120) nicely sums up this tension as,

> the contradiction between the service [IS specialists] as workers provide their clients and the power they wield over these clients through their specific knowledge, skills and technical autonomy.

The responsible autonomy enjoyed by IS specialists is in part the result of tight labour markets. It is also facilitated by the specialism's ability to control and mobilise organisational rules and resources. This control is in large part based on their until recent monopoly possession of specialist knowledge and technique. This has allowed IS specialists to exercise considerable influence over the development of particular systems, the conceptual techniques, such as system design methodologies, used to develop and define these systems, and the purchase of software and hardware (Markus and Bjorn-Andersen, 1987). However, the extent of this influence has often gone unrecognised by IT users (cf.Lucas, 1984) and a number of researchers have recently argued that IT users and systems designers and analysts need to recognise the importance of organisational politics in systems development, and in particular the sources of IS specialist organisational power (Markus and Bjorn-Andersen, 1987; Willcocks and Mason, 1987).

A clear managerial function within the IS specialism has developed as IS divisions have expanded and IS specialists have progressed further up the IT managerial hierarchy. This is by no means a uniform process but it generally means a 'break' with the 'hard' technical skills to which they owe their specialism. Instead, general management skills are required such as planning, financial control and budgeting, combined with a range of broader inter-personal and political competencies and a detailed knowledge of the business to which IT is to be 'harnessed'.

However, the growth of IS divisions has had contradictory effects for IS managers. On the one hand, the shift from a small installation providing relatively straightforward batch-processed, labour-saving applications to a large, highly visible department responding to increasingly powerful user demands increased IS managers' legitimate claim on organisational resources. On the other hand, according to Friedman and Cornford (1989, p.162):

> this situation also exposed them to the approbation attached to more visible, more spectacular failures. Late systems and budget overruns became public.

And, as the above authors found in their survey research in 1981, the story of IS manager departures and dismissals became a frequent theme.

Recent reports from the IT community stress the disappointing results derived from much IT investment and executive management concern with the failure of IT to 'live up to its promise' (Touche Ross, 1985). There is also concern that executive management does not have the expertise to wrest this 'promise' from IT. For example, it was recently reported in the *Financial Times* that:

> It is universally acknowledged ... that there is hardly a board [of directors] in existence which has the necessary skills and experience to make informed decisions about IT strategy and spending. (Cane, 1988)

In other words, there appears to be a skills gap on boards of directors and this has led to suggestions with regard to filling that gap. A number of commentators argue for the promotion of IT managers into executive management (Coopers and Lybrand, 1988). Others claim that there is a dearth of IT managers with the suitable skills to take on this role (Mill, 1989; Sharpe, 1989). Others within the IT community have established various initiatives to develop a new breed of 'hybrid' IT/business manager to fill the perceived gap in executive management circles.

In the second section of this chapter we briefly consider the changing historical relationship between IS specialists and their organisational counterparts. This we do by drawing on the work of Friedman and Cornford (1989).

A HISTORY OF IS SPECIALIST ORGANISATIONAL RELATIONS

In their recent book Friedman and Cornford (1989) propose a three stage history of systems development. The first stage of systems development is dominated by the problem of hardware constraints in terms of cost and flexibility. The second stage is characterised by a concern to raise the productivity of software developers. And the third stage focuses on the increasing importance of relations between systems developers and systems users.

In the first phase of this history, data processing managers were largely concerned with the selection and evaluation of computer hardware. In the second stage a 'software crisis' focused managerial attention on the management of software staff. In particular, managers were keen to raise software staff productivity and increasingly attempted to use strategies of direct labour control to achieve this objective. These strategies utilised a fragmented division of labour in systems development and a diffuse use of structured systems development techniques. However, managerial attempts at controlling and monitoring more tightly IS labour in phase two were tempered by continuing IS skill shortages which allowed staff 'to resist unpopular management strategies by simply changing jobs' (Friedman and Cornford, 1989, p.159)

In phase three user needs came to dominate systems development. In this phase, which develops from the beginning of the 1980s, there was an explosion in user demands on IT use and IS divisions. Additionally, the systems being developed in the 1980s were increasingly business sensitive. This in itself increased pressure for the prompt delivery of systems (because late delivery would have a direct impact on the firm's relationship with the market) where usability was the key criterion of success. That is, 'producing the right system, rather than producing the system right', became the new philosophy of the third phase of system development (Friedman and Cornford, 1989, p.175). This in turn implied a changing relationship between IS specialists and the businesses in which they were employed. Increasingly systems developers were expected to take greater responsibility for the effects of the systems they produced on both their users and the organisation in which they were implemented. Simultaneously, a search began to give users greater control of the specification and development of individual systems and systems priorities. This latter was particularly important as user demands proliferated and came into conflict with one another. According to Friedman and Cornford, responsibility for setting systems priorities slowly migrated from the data processing divisions to top management because IS specialists failed to fulfil their promises.

With increasing expenditure on IT, senior management in the UK began to introduce accounting procedures to make IS divisions into cost or profit centres—a move that placed great emphasis on the clear specification of present and future systems demands in order that the divisions concerned could stay within budget.

This development in turn appears to have encouraged IS managers to adopt more formal systems development procedures in order to monitor operations and stay within tight budget constraints. These formalised procedures were in part aimed at internal divisional operations, but they also encompassed the formalisation of the interface between IS divisions and user divisions in the hope of improving business requirements specification and involving users in a manner that gave the appearance of user control while ensuring that IS divisions remained dominant in the relationship.

In many cases 'charge out' systems based usually upon 'man (*sic*) hours' involvement were introduced whereby IS divisions charged their users for services rendered. This had the benefit of apparently formalising the costs and benefits of particular systems developments but it also tended to focus attention on the quantity of systems produced by the IS division rather than their quality. In particular, it seems that the inter-divisional financial relations introduced with charge out systems risked driving a wedge between the interests of the IS division and user divisions, thus making it more likely that different divisions would 'pursue subunit goals at the expense of overall organisational effectiveness' (Friedman and Cornford, 1989, p.273).

With regard to managerial strategies towards IS specialists, Friedman and Cornford believe that a shift towards responsible autonomy strategies is now taking place. That is, the tendency towards the fragmentation of IS work and the close monitoring of IS specialists noted in phase two is giving way to a reintegration of system development tasks—a tendency illustrated by the reintegration of many analyst and programmers' jobs into the figure of the analyst/programmer. This change is taking place in part because of the changing relationship between system developers and user needs. In particular, 'uncertain and complex user requirements meant that changes to specifications at late phases had to be accepted as part of the development process'. This encouraged the reintegration of analyst and programmers' jobs because 'if user communication during programming phases had to be carried out via analyst intermediaries, it was likely that messages would be corrupted as well as delayed' (Friedman and Cornford, 1989, p.299).

This emphasis on responsiveness to business needs may have encouraged the reintegration of tasks in the IS area. However, it perhaps underplays the increasing subservience of IS managers and staff to user-driven IT needs. We have also found that IS staff feel themselves to be under growing pressure from the proliferation and aggressive mobilisation of user demands for systems development resources.

Friedman and Cornford's work provides an extremely useful backdrop against which to develop more focused enquiries into the dynamics of an organisational politics of IT. At this stage in our research we would surmise that each of the phases delineated by Friedman and Cornford has corresponded to changes in internal IS cultures in particular organisations and broader sea changes in the IS community at large. Thus, in phase one we would expect to find an emphasis placed on the relationship between managers in charge of nascent DP divisions and senior managers. This relationship would have been characterised by debate and negotiation concerning the cost justification and acquisition of computer hardware. In the second phase, having established the legitimacy of organisational computing applications, the attention of IS managers turned to the problem of controlling and raising the productivity of IS staff. This appears to have resulted from the growing perception of a 'software crisis' as the relative cost of hardware declined. This phase was characterised by a more inward-looking IS culture. Here attempts were made to formalise the work of systems development and control it through a detailed division of software labour. If Friedman and Cornford are right, we would expect a premium to have been placed on labour management skills of IS managers and their ability to adopt and apply formal systems development methods in their IS divisions. In the third phase of their periodisation, user relations come to dominate the organisational use of IT. This would certainly appear to be the case in the insurance industry and, as we shall see in further chapters, this shift is associated with important changes in IS culture and the organisational politics of IT. In particular, it privileges those IS managers able effectively to manage and defend the IS/user interface and speak the language of the new strategy discourse and its emphasis on the integration of IT into corporate strategy. This is not to say that IS managers will actually do as they say, rather they must at least be able to give the appearance of subordinating their specialist interests and culture to the demands of the user and business. As we shall see in Chapter 5, there is considerable room for both ambiguity and manoeuvre in this area.

SCIENCE AND TECHNOLOGY DISCOURSES AND THE IS SPECIALISM

We now turn to an examination of the prevalence of a discourse of science and technology in contemporary society. This discourse is linked to the status attributed to IS specialists as privileged interlocutors with an area of powerful technological knowledge. Furthermore, this discourse of a progressive and rational technology, that is also ascribed with an 'almost magical quality' (see Bill Clinton's Inaugural Speech as US President, 20 January 1993), can be mobilised as a powerful source of identification and legitimation for IS specialists.

The supposed subsumption of science and technology to the drive to accumulate capital is often remarked upon (e.g. Noble, 1977). This subsumption is accompanied by a discourse of scientific progress and technological advance—technical rationality—that varies in force over time. This has been particularly strong in the period of the post-war boom (1945–74) in which many of today's older IS specialists spent their formative work years. This discourse of science and technology was associated with an apparent coming to dominance of a discourse of technical–rational social regulation which has privileged the position of the scientist and technician.

The German philosopher Jurgen Habermas has argued that this 'ideology' of technical rationality differs from class-specific ideologies in that, 'it does not have the opaque force of a delusion that only transfigures the implementation of [class] interests' (Habermass, 1973, p.111). That is, technical rationality as discourse serves to obscure the exercise of self-interested class power behind the notion of an ever-advancing technological progress which signals the end of ideology and social conflict itself.

In the early 1970s Habermas (ibid.) argued that the dominance of technical-rationality was gradually but inexorably reducing the space for political action to a ritualised participation in elections where electors were presented with barely distinguishable choices between technical-administrative paths to progress. A condition and consequence of this erosion of political autonomy was the rise of a professional and scientific intelligentsia that increasingly led politics 'from below' (see also Boguslaw, 1982). This process gradually eroded the position of the politician to 'at best something like a stopgap in a still imperfect rationalisation of power' where the state increasingly appeared 'to no longer be an apparatus for the forcible realisation of [class] interests that have no foundation in principle... [and] instead [became] the organ of a thoroughly rational administration' (Habermas, 1973, p.63–4).

The prestige, visibility and importance of IS specialists is closely linked to this technical–rational discourse that depoliticises the development and use of technology for it supposes technologists to be impartial 'philosopher-kings'. Endowed with divine right these new kings 'rule' through the impersonal power of modern technology. However, in practice this rule is closely associated with and used to maintain and reproduce 'entrenched existing power centres' (Boguslaw, 1982, p.211).

The central focus of our argument here is that in the most recent period of history, a discourse of technical rationality achieved a dominance over competing discourses, and accordingly had important power effects on organisations and individuals. In particular, IS specialists, while occupying ambivalent class and organisational positions, may believe themselves to be 'philosopher-kings' with legitimate claims to a monopoly of certain key truths. While not contending that IS specialists in general in the past or the present see themselves as philosopher-kings, there is considerable evidence to suggest that IS specialists often treat their users with scant regard while considering themselves to be impartial technicians far removed from the subjective squalor of organisational politics (cf. Mumford, 1972; Newman and Rosenberg, 1985; Orlikowski, 1988).

A tendency to identify with technical—rational beliefs may be strengthened by the training that systems analysts and programmers receive. This training and the techniques systems analysts use are largely drawn from systems theory and mathematics (Mackay and Lane, 1989; Orlikowski, 1988) and are strongly constrained by the sequential logic required to write computer programs. These techniques tend to emphasise the technical character of information systems development at the expense of their social and political aspects. That is, they are based on a technical–rational ideal that often fails to recognise the socially constructed character of reality, its essential contestability, and the inequality and organisational politics that are a condition and consequence of its reproduction.

A second factor which reinforces identification with technical–rational ideals lies in the way IS specialists have been able to preserve an image of themselves as disinterested technological rationalists which often does not coincide with the way they are seen by their organisational counterparts. This has been possible due to the relative autonomy they have been able to secure in many organisations through their ability to maintain a monopoly of 'technological truth' until comparatively recently.

To summarise, the discourse of technical rationality attributes the technical expert with a peculiar authority. While not adequately explaining and often being at odds with social practice this discourse has important power effects. In particular, it raises the prestige and standing of the technical expert, and in so doing, it may become an important medium through which IS specialist identities are constituted, legitimated and reproduced.

However, the discourse of technical rationality and the subjectivity it in part engenders is in tension with the reality it attempts to construct. In particular, while often obscuring the inequality of social relations from which the discourse surfaces, it has not succeeded in transforming them into its own image of uncontentious technical progress; inequality and the unprincipled exercise of power remain and serve to render the technical–rational ideal unattainable.

This mismatch between discourse and practice is clearly visible in contemporary organisations where there is a considerable tension between the ideal of the manager as a technical rationalist selflessly pursuing unified and uncontested corporate goals and his or her embroilment in intensely competitive rivalries to secure the control of material and symbolic resources (Dalton, 1959; Burns and Stalker, 1961; Pettigrew, 1973; Armstrong, 1985; Jackal, 1988). There is then a considerable disparity between the security and promise of a tightly controlled managerial scientism, where disinterested authority determines the bounds and rules of social action, and the vagaries of market forces and inter-managerial competition characterise the context and content of much contemporary managerial practice. Furthermore, this disparity may be particularly acute for IS managers who, while being strongly wedded to technical–rational ideals, are still on the margins of executive power, at least in the UK experience (see Murray and Knights, 1990), and subject to control by executive managers who are less interested in an abstract administrative or technological efficiency than the pursuit of their own careers and the corporate profitability by which they are judged.

CONCLUSION

This chapter has examined the emergence of an IS specialism as a distinct organisational function and occupational grouping. We also examined the changing relationship between IS specialists and their users. This appears to have led to a gradual erosion of IS divisional autonomy in UK organisations as IT usage has shifted from back office, low profile services to integrated and market-sensitive systems that are key to corporate survival in increasingly competitive conditions. Lastly, we looked at the continued strength of a discourse of technology that attributes considerable power and prestige to the technologist. In so doing, we argued that this discourse of a progressive and rational technology can be mobilised as a powerful source of identification and legitimation for IS specialists.

This study of the emergence of the IS specialism, its changing contours and internal organisation, and its relations with other specialist functions and layers of management is interesting in itself. However, we see its particular utility as shedding light on the manner in which we theorise technology use within organisations. For it is the case with most technologies, and IT in particular, that their organisational adoption and adaptation shape them in specific ways. That is, they are not simply applied to organisations. Rather, there is a complex process whereby the technological possibilities open to a specific organisation are constructed, mobilised and assessed. And further, the way in which this process of construction and assessment develops is critically influenced by existing organisational practices, structures and cultures. In other words, the use of any technology is the result of complex decision-making processes which do not simply flow from the given state of markets and technologies. Rather, those decision-making processes are crucially dependent on habituated practices and relations of power between diverse specialisms in organisations.

Until recently the IS specialism has held a monopoly of IT knowledge and thereby occupied a crucial position in processes that determine the organisational use of IT. This has been particularly so as the organisational role and scope of IT use have expanded. Perhaps less clearly, but of equal importance, the IS specialism also plays a critical role in reproducing and/or transforming discourses of technology and technical rationality within a broader community of organisations and institutions.

5
Looking into User Relations

INTRODUCTION

Drawing on the analysis of the IS specialism in Chapter 4, this chapter examines some of the fundamental ambiguities of the IS/user relation in organisations. Through the presentation of empirical material from the insurance subsidiary of a major bank and the insurance sector more generally, we explore IS managers' perceptions of their relationships with users. This prepares the ground for the presentation of our main case study in Chapter 6 and develops our argument that 'user relations' and 'user involvement' issues are essentially issues of power, control and politics. As such, the organisational arena in which IS specialists meet their users is an area of contested terrain (cf. Goodrich, 1975).

Managerial and non-managerial staff treading this terrain employ a range of strategies and practices to protect their organisational turf, their career prospects, and their sense of identity, or what it is to be an IS specialist. Some of these practices are self-consciously political. However, it would appear that many are not. In this situation, IS specialists mobilise discourses about their essential neutrality and their elevation above the dangerous 'killing fields' of organisational politics.

This self-conscious protection of identity and autonomy in the organisation is often both more effective and economical than self-consciously and overt political actions. Such practices are effective because they are less vulnerable to the accusation of 'politicking' and accord with certain 'commonsense beliefs' about technology's inherent neutrality and rationality (see Chapter 4) while at the same time throwing up a smokescreen of often impenetrable technique and jargon. And they are economical because they minimise the often stressful tensions between being employed by an organisation and working for oneself (in terms of career, advancement, status and security).

The first part of the chapter initially outlines some of the formal changes that have occurred in the battle over the direction and control of increasingly powerful IS departments (Lucas, 1984). These include the reorganisation of IS departments, the inclusion of user managers in the management of systems development projects, and the use of new tools and techniques in systems development. Our argument here is not to deny that many of these changes were also concerned with, and were a response to, the growing complexity of IT management issues outlined in Chapter 3. However, we would stress that these changes were not an innocent, objective and singularly rational response to this complexity. Rather, this complexity itself and the responses proposed to it were constructed in particular ways by organisational actors concerned to protect careers, identities and the control of resources. This development is illustrated through material drawn from our interviews with senior IS managers in the insurance industry and our more in-depth study of the banking subsidiary we call Effessco.

The second section of the chapter looks in more detail at the negotiation and practice of 'user involvement' at Effessco. Here we are primarily interested in three things. Firstly, we are interested in the potential difference between user involvement, or co-option, in systems development and user control of systems development (cf. Franz and Robey, 1984; Markus, 1984; Markus and Bjorn-Andersen, 1987). Secondly, we explore the way in which IS specialists can delimit user involvement. And thirdly, we look at the way particular discourses of technology, or technical rationality, are effectively mobilised to protect the IS manager from the accusation of 'politicking'.

These issues are explored through the presentation of material drawn from one of our interviews with the project managers and staff during a key system development at Effessco.

USER RELATIONS

Significant interest in 'user involvement' in IS development began to emerge in the late 1970s and early 1980s (e.g. Boland, 1979; Ives and Olson, 1984; Robey and Farrow, 1982, see also Friedman and Cornford, 1989, Chapter 8). The problem of user relations was examined from a wide range of perspectives. These ran from those concerned to democratise systems development with regard to class (Ehn and Sandberg, 1986; Jones, 1985; Williams and Steward, 1984; Williams, 1985) and gender (see for example, Murray, 1989a; Avner, 1993; Green et al, 1993), differences through the socio-technical literature on the alignment of organisational efficiency and job satisfaction (Mumford and Henshall, 1979) to the more straightforwardly 'technical' literature on improving the development of information systems by ensuring that user requirements were clearly articulated (e.g. Ives and Olson, 1984).

The combined output of these different approaches was huge and we do not intend to review the literature systematically (see Friedman and Cornford, 1989, Chapter 8). Rather, our concern is to examine some of the cultural and structural changes associated with organisational attempts to implement user involvement or user-led systems development strategies.

In this chapter, when we talk of 'users' and 'user relations' we do so largely to refer to relations between IS personnel and managerial users—this is not to deny the importance of other user relations, for example, those between systems designers and users, rather it is to concentrate on our particular focus on inter-managerial competition. This focus has significant gender implications in the area of user relations in that our analytical gaze falls upon relations dominated by largely organisationally powerful men where the masculinity they mobilise is a condition and consequence of the user relations in which they are involved.

The development of user relations is associated with an erosion of the autonomy of IS managers in UK organisations even as IT investments have absorbed a greater percentage of resources and as IT applications have assumed an increasing centrality in the operational and strategic areas of organisational activity (Friedman and Cornford, 1989). This has also occurred due to the increasing use of IT in product and market-related applications. Consequently the style and centre of IT-related decision-making have shifted considerably from the early days of computing, when IS divisional managers had considerable decision-making power with regard to the direction and size of IT investments.

Various instruments were advocated to bring about a degree of user involvement. These included the creation of high level IT committees to consider and take IT-related decisions and system development; steering committees comprised of senior management representatives from user departments; the establishment of project committees comprising middle IS and user managers to pursue and co-ordinate the substantive work of systems development; the formation of so-called Model Offices to bring together system users and developers on a continuous basis, and the use of systems techniques such as phototyping to develop a focused dialogue with user managers. The rapid expansion of IS divisions in sectors such as banking and insurance was also used as a means to legitimate the reorganisation of IS managers and staff. Generic IS departments were subdivided into business-related units that were subordinated to the direct needs of business unit managers.

It is possible to interpret these changes as the almost inevitable result of the growth and increasing complexity of IS activities in many organisations. As such, the user involvement techniques outlined above could be seen as a rational development of organisational divisions of labour and lines of co-ordination and control.

Our interpretation differs markedly from these kinds of accounts which dominate the IS literature. Once again, the development of user involvement practices cannot be separated from the ebb and flow of organisational politics. However, while 'user involvement' may have been a discourse through which to legitimate incursions into IS strongholds, the results of user involvement practices are marked by considerable ambiguity.

In the user relation phase of IS development IS managers have found themselves in a quandary. On the one hand, they have been involved in a struggle to maintain their professional boundaries, identities and decision-making powers. On the other, they have increasingly come to accept their reliance on user managers for access to the detailed business knowledge necessary to build market-sensitive systems. Thus, the terms and conditions of user involvement in the IT decision-making and implementing process have become an area of contested terrain between IS and user managers. This is a theme taken up in more detail in Chapter 6.

On the surface at least, IS managers we interviewed in UK life insurance companies felt that they were losing control in the 1980s. For example, in a comment typical of many of our interviews with senior IS personnel, one IS divisional manager said:

> A few years ago I and a few senior people were probably making lots of decisions because no one else really cared. We shouldn't have really been taking them but I felt it was better to make a decision than to hang around. At that time *I was unaware of the need to understand the business and I didn't have enough time to keep in touch with the business*. The position has turned full cycle in the last five years and DP probably doesn't influence IT priorities enough. I'm not saying we have no influence but it is very difficult having handed the reins over to then pull them back.

In this manager's opinion, IS have handed over 'the reins' to the users and to him it seems politically unrealistic to think of getting them back again. However, while bemoaning a loss of control, a common complaint from IS managers concerned their sense that, while being divested of authority, they were still being made to carry the overwhelming responsibility for the delivery of systems to date and budget deadlines. This is captured by the following comment from a computer services manager:

> There seems to be a shift from DP [Data Processing] making or suggesting
> what was needed and now the users are saying what's needed. But DP are
> still held responsible for anything that comes in late.

At this particular company this situation had led IS managers to place
increasing stress on the formalisation and professionalisation of user
relations. The manager quoted above continued by saying:

> We have got to become much more professional with users in negotiating
> with them about what they want and then planning in a business-like
> manner how we would deliver those products.

In this way IS managers may hope to 'tie down' their users and
thus limit the users' ability to shift the responsibility and blame for
late system deliveries and budget overruns on to the IS division. This
is another theme developed in Chapter 6. Given the greater scrutiny
to which IS managers' performance was subjected they have responded by 'professionalising' their relationship with users. In some
respects this meant sharpening up IS practices to limit a tendency to
take on ill-defined projects with a kind of youthful 'can-do' attitude.
This was done through instruments such as 'change management'
policies in systems development methods where user requirement
changes had to be costed and approved by the Steering Committee
before these were accepted. Closer attention was also paid to areas
such as 'estimating' and 'quality assurance' because it was clearly in
the interests of IS managers to only take on responsibility for projects
they thought they could deliver on time and to budget. Or so it would
seem. For, as we shall see in later chapters, IS departments are inclined
on occasion to take on impossible tasks in such a way as to suggest
that there are deeper underlying politics than a mere struggle for
pre-eminence between IS and other departments.

One of the implications of user involvement has been an increased
emphasis on IS managers learning political skills. In the past, IS managers had a largely free hand with regard to IT decisions and systems
development practices. This feature, combined with the strong sense of
technical rationality mobilised by IS specialists, often created considerable IS intransigence. In our interviews, user managers often complained
of the tendency of IS managers to give their requests a terse brush-off.
One IS strategy manager we spoke to clearly recognised this tendency.
He said:

> We don't negotiate. We say: 'We know the answer'. That's it. We don't
> actually accept that someone outside IT could suggest something that
> might be worthwhile. We don't get into a negotiating stance. It's either all
> or nothing.

IS specialists are clearly not defenceless when it comes to the issue of user involvement. Their, until recent, monopoly of IS skills has often made it extremely difficult for users to 'get behind' the presentations of systems options given to them by IS specialists. There is also often a point in the systems development cycle where the users are obliged to hand the control of the project over to IS. This usually occurs at the technical design and programming stage (see Franz and Robey, 1984). At this point it is extremely difficult for users to monitor the context and achievements of IT programmes. Given the often considerable time pressures on the programming tasks, that often come after project timetables have already slipped, quick fixes and bodges may replace the more elegant and easily maintained systems envisioned at earlier stages of the project. Indeed, a considerable amount of 'unloading' of system features may take place at this stage (see Chapter 10).

IS managers may themselves be keen to set up certain kinds of 'user involvement'. This may be a not so subtle way of gaining control of user resources and also building user sympathies for IS departments. For example, we found evidence that user managers often show considerable resistance to involving themselves or releasing their subordinates for inclusion in the substantive work of systems development. This in part arises from their perception of pressure on internal resources and their wish to control these rather than second them to others. It may also be due to their feeling that systems development is not their job, not a competence they possess, and an area associated with high risks and spectacular and potentially career damaging failures.

In one company the support and help of senior business managers was finally enlisted by putting them in charge of the system development projects. As the Systems Development Manager put it:

> So we were faced with this problem whereby there was a growing need for fairly sophisticated systems. But we just couldn't get the commitment from the managers in terms of their time ... They wouldn't give the effort or time that was needed *so one way around that was to put them in charge of it.*

At Effessco, the company we will look at shortly in some detail, a 'Model Office' was established to bring together senior clerical users and systems analysts in one office. The initial purpose of this initiative was to give users a greater involvement in the development of systems through rapid phototyping and the training of senior user staff in systems analysis skills. In the event the model office was located in the IS Department, achieved the successful secondment of skilled users into the IS Department as glorified systems testers, and created considerable 'empathy' for IS staff in the user department (see Murray and Willmott, 1991). The Project Manager commented:

> We've picked up another benefit ... because of the users who were involved in a development with people from our department. They have now gone back to their own departments and are involved in servicing the product and they understand the [system's] problems which is a tremendous help.

The preceding examples suggest a fundamental ambiguity in the notion of 'user relations' and 'user involvement'. Often these concepts, with their implication of co-operation, seem to mean attempts at user manager control. At other times, they mean user supervision without user commitment. And at others they simply look like another area of political conflict where managers fight over the apportionment of responsibility, blame and achievement and the exercise of control and commitment of resources.

In the last part of this chapter we look in more detail at the character of this 'user relations' phase of system development. We do this by presenting empirical material from an interview we conducted with a systems development project in one of our case study companies. This material illustrates the ambiguity of IS/user relations as the Project Manager explained how he set about getting the users to take important decisions on the project.

IT TRAUMA AT EFFESSCO[1]

Effessco is part of a large financial services group operating in the UK. In the late 1980s, under increasing pressure to improve its financial performance and stock market rating, the company's executive managers were required to increase their profit contribution to the group by 50 percent. The combined results of past rapid growth and these ambitious future profit targets prompted a major company reorganisation at the end of 1988. The announcement of the results of this reorganisation was impending at the time the interview material reported here was recorded. Middle and junior managers already knew that the company was to be divided into separate units operating as profit centres; they also suspected that the highly centralised Information Services Division would be split up between the various profit centres. The distribution of

---

[1] Much of the material in this part of the chapter was first published as an article by F. Murray (1991).

new managerial posts and the fate of individual managers in the IS Division was then the subject of considerable, if muted, speculation at the time of the interviews.

The history of computer-based system development at Effessco is short and not particularly sweet. The first attempt to computerise administrative procedures, which had been brought in-house from a third-party bureau service in the late 1970s, was an expensive and embarrassing fiasco. This was nearly repeated two years later with another major in-house system development project.

These early systems development traumas had a lasting, if uneven, impact on the reputation of the IS Division and IT in general at Effessco. In the words of the Deputy Chief Executive they left 'quite deep scars on the organisation for years afterwards'. Indeed, eight years after the first system development failure it was not possible for the Deputy CE to discuss this with IS staff, 'without lots of shuffling in their seats and looking over their shoulders'.

Recalling the first major system foul-up the Deputy CE said:

> At the time all hell broke loose. Basically the company couldn't run a piss-up in a brewery. It was *only* a computer project that hadn't worked not the end of the world. But it was very difficult to see that at the time. Especially since the whole point of the project was to bring some order to the chaos in terms of administration... And the costs of it, even then... were big.
>
> In terms of the ethos of the place it was very hard, very hard at the time because the parents [the parent company] said—'I told you so. You don't know what you're bloody doing. You'll cause us problems by not being good solid bankers and doing all these nasty things and then failing.'

Thus, not only did IT and the IS specialists fail to deliver, thereby exacerbating the administrative crisis at the company; the system failure also caused serious embarrassment for executive managers at a time when they were attempting to establish their legitimacy and competence in the eyes of sceptical 'parents'.

Since these early IT experiences the company has tended to buy and customise software packages rather than attempt the development of large systems in-house. For executive managers, the early failures were a clear warning of the need to cost-justify and prioritise competing IT investments and place a series of controls on systems staff and managers. This was attempted by placing senior user managers at the head of systems projects, and the institution of an IT Committee made up of senior and executive managers to consider major IT investments and strategic decisions. However, this Committee was largely ineffective and folded after two years. In the late 1980s the direction of IT strategy and the prioritisation of IT investments remained a contested terrain between competing divisional priorities and systems developers.

It is, then, within this context that the interview material now presented is located. This concentrates on relations between systems developers and user managers and the negotiation of priorities and resource allocation within a large and strategic system development project. It draws on an interview with one of the subjects of our research, a Project Manager we here call Mike. At that time Mike was in his middle 40s and had been an IS specialist for 23 years. Like many IS managers of his age he had worked his way up through the IS grades in a number of financial services companies, progressing from computer operations through programming, analysis and project leadership.

In the course of interviews with Mike and a number of his colleagues a theme emerged concerning the relationship between IS specialists and user managers at Effessco. IS managers expressed ambiguity with regard to their sense of responsibility to their user managers and the 'business' in general For example, Mike said with regard to his section of the IS Division:

> I liken us to coal workers. We dig coal. We deliver things that are tangible to our users. We have a lot of ancillary workers in IS who don't produce coal, who produce intangible things, things that users can't identify and get a handle on. We're very fortunate because we'll be virtually untouched by the [impending] reorganisation because we are lean, very lean. We've got no fat on us.

A male project manager in the same department used images for IS Division personnel strikingly similar to those used by Mike. He talked of 'brickies' (bricklayers) and likened himself to the 'man who comes to dig the garden'. One of Mike's female project leaders, a fixed-term contractor, spoke of her desire to 'keep her hands dirty', while Mike's immediate manager saw himself as 'a bread and butter man'.

These images hardly confirm the notion of the IS specialist as a philosopher-king. Instead, they suggest humble if dignified and largely masculine images of manual labour strangely incongruous with the abstract mental labour performed by these managers. Above all, they stress utility and the production of tangible output in the form of coal, walls and vegetables which again is at odds with the rather intangible character of the software.

These images are connected to the ambiguous feelings IS junior and middle managers experience with regard to their role and the role of IT in the organisation. In part, these may be linked to a pervasive sense among IS specialists at Effessco that they are outsiders regarded with a good deal of suspicion by 'the business'. In addition, these feelings are related to changing user/system developer relations and in particular increasing emphasis on 'user-led' systems development. This may in part explain why Mike stated emphatically in the same interview that IT should be 'hooked to business needs', 'strapped' and 'totally tied to the business'. The project manager quoted above expressed similar opinions. While noting that he had to take decisions that should be taken by senior management or 'fall out' of a corporate strategy, he went so far as to say:

> I think we should be total slaves to the business. They [should] tell us exactly what to do. They[should] decide. And we'll do exactly what they tell us.

This desire to be firmly directed, if not controlled, from the top is echoed by Mike's line manager. He welcomed the forthcoming corporate reorganisation because:

> We're gonna have one guy who's not too far up the chain [of command] who's gonna say: You're gonna do that or [you are] not. And I think that's a tremendous boon. That could work quite well.

As will be seen in the material that is now presented, this apparent desire to be made 'slaves to the business' and subject to a labour process akin to that of a miner or construction worker is countered by a desire for autonomy articulated and legitimised through the mobilisation of a set of technical rational beliefs. It is also interesting to consider the expression of gender relations and masculinity within systems development at Effessco. For here Mike and his colleagues express a tremendous desire for certainty, for an organisation that will tell them 'you're gonna do that' and that will define their relationship with it, as slaves and miners tied to the business, without ambiguity.

This in part echoes and reinforces an overriding desire within much contemporary masculinity for certainty and well-defined and unambiguous roles within organisations. It also reflects the resurgence of 'the managerial prerogative' and, implicitly, ' a man's right to manage as a real man' that took place in the 1980s as successive conservative governments mobilised and often co-ordinated sustained attacks on trade union rights, professions, the poor and 'wimps', 'moaning minnies' and 'wets' of any persuasion. The managerial style engendered by aggressive free market rhetoric fell back on and adulated images of masculinity that emphasised the hard, the lean, the dry and the aggressive. In particular, it demonised and attacked 'feminine' ideas of negotiation, compromise, compassion and consensus in a quest for absolute authority and control.

At Effessco, these winds of change were clearly visible and infused much managerial discourse. Local conditions also heightened the desire for certainty within IS. Past systems developments had been disastrous and increased uncertainty connected to financial markets and the management of technology presented a considerable challenge to the achievement and sustained articulation of masculine certainties and control.

At the time of the interview Mike's project had 'slipped by three months' which was due to events Mike believed to be outside his and Effessco's control, namely the quality of the base software package acquired and skills shortages in the systems development labour market. These problems, and changes in the financial services marketplace, caused the initial scope of the project to be pared down considerably.

Senior user manager control of the project was established through two steering committees: a tactical committee responsible for the general direction of the project consisting of senior managers from the Marketing, Customer Services and the IS Divisions and an operational committee responsible for the day-to-day direction of the project.

According to Mike, relations with his user managers had been good. Managers from Marketing were initially 'very forthcoming... they were actually *part of us*'. However as the project go-live date approached 'they ... stepped back into their ivory towers [and came] up with new [systems] requirements almost as a whim'. In contrast, relations with the Customer Services Division (CSD) were 'very good, very healthy ... because of the way we communicate and operate here we don't hide, *we're very open about everything we do*'.

This latter view regarding openness was not one shared by CSD managers. For example, the main management representative from Customer Services on the project Steering Committee accused Mike of wanting 'to look after all the project from the product specification [onwards]'. He further characterised Mike as an 'I-want-to-control-it-all-person' and commented:

> Systems development teams aren't always as open as they should be about their problems. *They will only talk things through with us as a last ditch solution ... because they don't want the user to know too much.* [They are] subconsciously arrogant. They have a mystique. They don't say: How can I help people to do a job? They say: I will help you do what I think you need to do.

At the time of the interview Mike was preparing for a meeting of the tactical Steering Committee where important and pressing decisions were to be made. At the previous Steering Committee meeting Mike had alerted his user managers to a problem concerning a shortfall of ISD resources. This news was not well received. One of the project leaders commented when recalling the committee's reaction:

> I don't think people [in the Steering Committee] are really prepared to pick up the issues and resolve them. They don't want to know about them. Sort of: 'Don't tell me bad news', almost.

However, she continued by explaining that once the committee reached a decision and set a date for the release of that system 'people get *absolutely locked into that date*'. And it is upon the successful achievement of this date that IS project leaders and managers believe themselves to be judged. Given the increasing pressure these junior managers felt themselves to be under, Mike was at this time attempting to remove estimated end-dates from his Steering Committee reports and replace them with an approximation 'er, sort of, end of February, maybe [laughs]'.

Mike explained his role at the meeting as the following:

> My role will be to lay out all the various scenarios for the next 18 months on what we can do given our resources. I've got a number of scenarios which I'll be presenting. At the end of the day they [the Steering Committee] will pick one, and I'll run with it. *But they'll make the choice. I won't.* I've just got to do all the hard work and present all the scenarios. It's then incumbent on them to select one and say: 'Right, we'll go for that.' In which case I'll say: 'OK, we'll go for that but remember [laughs] I want no more increasing in scope.'

The presentation of an objective basis for managerial choice is not as simple as Mike's proposal to 'present scenarios' to the Steering Committee suggests. Computer systems are complex to analyse, design, program, test, correct and implement. Each of these phases of the development can hit unexpected problems and will vary depending on the system being built, the people building it and the involvement of the potential system users.

Nevertheless, Mike believed that user managers needed to be seen to take the major decisions with regard to the direction of the project and that this could be simply achieved by presenting them with the various scenarios. As the following quote illustrates, though, he entertained doubts regarding the extent to which user managers could really be in control of a project:

> Whether we are actually more user-led or not [after reorganisation] I don't think will actually make any difference, uh, because at the end of the day (pause) again we come back to the communication thing. We don't hide,

uh, we may force issues through to get resolved like what's going to happen with Release 3, you know [I say]. 'Come on, let's have a decision, a clear sense of direction'. That is the sort of thing that we'll be asking our users to decide. *Whether or not the users themselves will be deciding, uh, I don't think they can do so.* Unless they know more about [computer] systems and about this system they cannot produce for themselves the various scenarios I was talking about. They have to have the scenarios produced for them so they can take the decision [emphasis added].

Here, despite his stated view that user managers and 'the business' should be taking the decisions, Mike seriously doubts their ability to take them. His way out of this ambiguity, given that he professes a need to see IT 'strapped to the business', is to attempt to spoon-feed the user managers with what he sees as apolitical and value-free scenarios which will allow them to make informed choices.

The interview continued thus:

Fergus Murray (FM): Do the user managers have a way of getting behind the figures used in quantifying the scenarios?
Mike: They can't challenge the figures. The expertise is with muh [me?], is with my good self and my good people. They don't have the expertise to challenge the figures which, um, does seem a little, [pause] I mean, [pause] speaking the words does actually seem to me to be a little, [pause] yeah, OK, fine but at the end of the day its a matter of trust.'

In this revealing passage Mike starts to surface a perhaps reluctant realisation that user managers have no way of challenging the 'figures' he presents to them. Having realised this he is unwilling to voice the possible implications of this state of affairs. He tries twice but he cannot bring himself to say how it does 'seem' to him.

Mike was then asked how the 'figures' presented to the Steering Committee were calculated. He answered:

The figures are [long pause], the figures are reasonably accurate in so far as they are based on estimates. For instance, if I'm asked to produce a bit of functionality we'll typically have a brainstorming session on it, find out about it, talk about it, how complex [it is], what different processes it is to put in place and this, that and the other and out of that will fall an estimate of effort. So it is done, I mean, I don't just sit here in splendid isolation and come up with estimates. I do it, I do it with my senior people. We literally brainstorm a given topic, we talk about it, and out of that discussion will fall an estimate about the degree of difficulty.

Fergus then asked Mike if records were kept of the accuracy of past estimates of system development budgets and timescales. Mike answered that they had not kept records up until that time. With the first phase of the project:

We were just so end-date driven that we just said: 'There's November, lets get there' ... We always knew where we were within the project. [But] we didn't have at any point in time a very clear view of how much time we'd spent getting there.

With the present phase of the project Mike has kept more detailed records of time spent on the various parts of the development. From these he hoped to:

Be able to identify where there has been an overspend. [And these records], will give you some pretty clear indications for the future. It's a learning thing. You gradually refine it and refine it and refine it and you know where on the next [project] you need to put the emphasis.

I then asked Mike whether he thought these figures might be weighted by his colleagues or himself, to favour certain decisional outcomes. He bluntly replied, 'We don't do that.'

FM: Not consciously?
Mike: Not even unconsciously. There is not weighting of figures to suit our own ends. No. At the end of the day we are a service industry. We're here to deliver coal. To cut coal. Either for our admin. people, or marketeers, or both.

Picking up the mining analogy I suggested that miners might try to cut coal from easier seams if they had a choice, particularly if they were on piece rates. I wondered out loud if this analogy could be transferred to systems development.

Mike: It could be but it isn't. It could be but it isn't [sic]. I can see what you're saying. Yeah. If I wanted to I could sit back and say 'I want a nice comfortable release next month. I'll just pick, on this piece of work because it's nice and comfortable, its nice and controllable. I can see it very clearly, I can see all the traps very clearly. I think I'll go for this. I'll give myself a nice 6 or 9 comfortable months.' No, we don't do that.
FM: Do you think manipulating the figures ever goes on?
Mike: It must do. I should imagine there are people out there who are immoral, for want of a better word, who do things like that. I'd kill them. *I'd kill anybody if I ever caught them doing that.*
[At this point we both laughed thus breaking the tension that had developed during this exchange.]
FM: That's interesting.
Mike: Because it is immoral.
FM: Is DP a very moral profession?
Mike: I like to think that if we are not we certainly should be. At the end of the day we're here to provide a service. We're not here to sit in our wonderful ivory towers and dictate to our users. Our users should be dictating to us what they want. And we [should] turn round and say: 'This

is what you can get in the timescale.' And if it isn't good enough we go round the houses again. But there should be no hiding. [Just] the truth. *Users should be giving us clear direction. I don't think they can control us. I mean, they don't have the skills to actually control a system [development].*

DISCUSSION

The interview material presented here can be read as a series of consider-ations on the degree and type of control which user managers and 'the business' should exercise over IS staff and managers at Effessco. In the course of this Mike articulates a number of apparently contradictory opinions. At the end of the material presented he says that, on the one hand, IS specialists provide a service and their users should dictate to them, thus reiterating his belief that IT should be 'strapped' and 'tied' to the business. On the other hand, an apparent belief in the legitimacy of dictatorial user demands is tempered by Mike's opinion that user man-agers do not have the skills to control the systems development process, and by implication, systems development staff. Thus, he seems to end up saying that user managers should dictate but that in effect this can only be realised by a rather circumscribed user-direction of the systems development process which leaves IS staff and managers considerable professional and technical autonomy.

This conclusion accords with that reached by Friedman (1987a) and Borum (1987) in that they argue that 'direct control' strategies to 'strap' IS specialists to business imperatives have by and large failed. However, whereas Friedman and Borum, as academic researchers, largely explain this failure in terms of the organisational and labour market position of IS specialists, Mike explains it in terms of the technical and intellectual abilities ('skills') that IS specialists possess. That is, for Friedman and Borum the relationship between IT users and IS specialists is mediated by relations of power and characterised by a continuous struggle to encroach upon and define autonomy. For Mike, who appears to dismiss the idea of organisational politics out of hand, this relationship can be understood in the idealised terms of rational, functionalist management practice where trust, openness and the mutual recognition and respect for discrete areas of knowledge and expertise are the watchwords of organisational life. This denial of power, politics and uncertainty raises a serious problem in that it is by no means obvious that this mutual respect exists whereas the precarious trust relations Mike alludes to are open to chronic abuse, and the mobilisation of self- and specialists'-interests.

Mike attempts to establish the legitimacy of his control of major organisational resources by defending his trustworthiness and that of his colleagues. This he does in a variety of ways. He professes that relations with users have been very good because 'of the way we operate here, we don't hide, we're very open about everything we do'; he insists that although project Steering Committee members may not have the skills to take decisions, he nevertheless makes them take those decisions; perhaps given his ambiguity with regard to this latter point, he repeats, almost as a refrain, his desire to be dictated to by his users; and lastly, if all else fails Mike claims that the IS specialist should be 'moral' and implies that he will police and enforce that morality where it is found lacking.

However, these claims to trustworthiness are problematic. In the first instance, Mike's belief in the openness of social relations at Effessco is not shared by his user managers. In fact, one leading user saw Mike and his IS colleagues as closed, secretive and 'subconsciously arrogant' members of the organisation.

Secondly, the means by which Mike presents his user managers with choices cannot be abstracted from the power relations through which the reality of organisational life is constructed. Indeed, the cynical observer might conclude that the presentation of the various numerically calibrated 'scenarios' to the Steering Committee was a deliberate attempt to sustain and legitimise the relative autonomy of IS personnel as this came under increasing threat from the demands of other functions (cf. Markus and Pfeffer, 1983). The situation seems, however, to be of a greater complexity.

Despite recognising that the figures are estimates deriving from brainstorming discussions, Mike seemed really to believe in the possibility of capturing 'the truth' in numerical data. However, even within the limits of this technical rational discourse, the problems for the IS specialist are considerable. The development of software, even if this be 'only' the customisation of a large software package, is not like making cars or washing machines. That is, the product being produced is unique, and its success will often depend on the ease with which it can be integrated with other systems already operating. Furthermore, the production of software is often associated with the capture of complex and contradictory organisational relations subject to internally and externally generated change. It has proved, therefore, extremely difficult to develop a 'scientific' method for measuring the productivity of IS specialists or estimating the resources needed to produce a particular system. Nevertheless, Mike and many practitioners at the software engineering end of the IS specialism still believe that it is possible to produce a method for achieving these ends.

Mike's process of arriving at the figures for his scenarios was very approximate. This involved the interrogation of collective tacit skills and experience. This in itself may have much to recommend it, although in Mike's case it appears that he only agreed to the interrogation of collective skills, as opposed to his own, after his colleagues had persuaded him to include them in the brainstorming process.

The striking thing about this interview is not so much the looseness of Mike's methods but his apparently sincere belief in them and himself as an unbiased conduit of technical information. This belief seems to be a cornerstone of Mike's sense of identity and masculinity and he experiences considerable difficulty when it is challenged. Indeed, he goes so far as to say that he will kill anyone who contributes to the erosion of this belief.

This belief appears to be so important to Mike because it reinforces and gives credence to his 'objective' masculine identity and because he has doubts about the scientific status of the methods he uses. That is, while using these methods to legitimise his claims to autonomy they are not enough to do the job convincingly. Rather, it seems that it is his deep conviction in himself as a technical rationalist, as an unbiased conduit of 'the truth', that provides the guarantee that the looseness and enduring mystique of his methods will not lead him to abuse his position of power and trust.

Yet clearly Mike is not a disinterested party in the organisational changes taking place at Effessco. And it is evident from his actions that while applauding these changes, he also resists them particularly the encroachment of external user manager controls into the IS Division. For example, his attempts to remove precise project completion end-dates can be read as an attempt to blunt one of the more potent control mechanism's possessed by user managers for locking IS specialists into a particular project development time-frame.

Developments at Effessco suggest, then, that IS specialists are no longer the philosopher-kings they might once have been, and seen themselves to be. The collective memory of the specialism at Effessco is tainted by past failure and trauma; the basis of its organisational autonomy is under threat from company reorganisation and the erosion of its monopoly of technical knowledge. At Effessco, some philosopher-kings feel their wings have been clipped and now claim affinity with manual trades—the miner, the bricklayer and the gardener all doing 'bread and butter' jobs that provide a service to their employers. Perhaps this is not surprising given the pressure they felt themselves to be under to prove their utility and worth to their employer. Indeed, the metaphors they use may be a convenient way to distance themselves from their colleagues engaged in the 'ancillary' areas of the IS Division which were not producing tangible, measurable and laudable outputs, that is, 'coal'.

However, at least in Mike's case, behind the apparent approval of user-led systems development and its concomitant—'strapping IT to the business'—there remains a strong commitment to technical–rational ideals. These ideals appear to give Mike a strong sense of personal integrity and masculine identity and they serve to legitimise his continued claims to autonomy in the workplace. But, whereas in the past Mike's user managers may have been inclined to respect a discourse of technical rationality that legitimised the autonomy and 'clean' power of IS specialists, they are now more sceptical of these claims to a monopoly of technological truths. After all, users now have considerable experience of IT and in many cases they have seen that IT has not lived up to the promises made of it by IS specialists.

This is a fact of organisational life of which many IS specialists are increasingly aware and has stimulated concern regarding the legitimate role of the IS specialist in the future (e.g. Winkler, 1986). For IS managers like Mike who have lived through the golden age of the IS-specialist-as-philosopher-king these changes pose a considerable threat to their sense of security and integrity. However, for Mike at least this threat seems to make him cling all the more tightly to the technical–rational ideal rather than letting go of it and replacing it with something else. We think that this is so because these ideals are an essential part of Mike's sense of himself; through them he has been able to secure the symbolic and material resources to sustain a particular sense of identity for over 20 years. In the process he has become so 'strapped' to this sense of himself that he cannot simply drop his role as a technical rationalist and pick up that of the IS specialist as political operator or communications facilitator (Klein and Hirschheim, 1987).

CONCLUSION

In this chapter we have argued that the user relations phase of systems development was marked by the growth of techniques and structures to involve users in systems development. However, as we stressed at the beginning of the chapter these structures and techniques, while indicative of the increasing complexity of IT management issues, were not innocent of organisational politics. Rather, they were both a condition and a consequence of this complexity and became a battleground for tussles between IS and user managers and personnel concerning the control, direction and apportionment of responsibilities over, and the work of, systems development.

In the second part of the chapter we examined in more depth the way in which IS specialists have attempted to delimit user incursions into systems development while at the same time mobilising the politically correct rhetoric of IS subordination to business needs. In particular, we suggested that when 'innocently' deployed, a discourse of technical rationality that claims to raise the IS specialist above the 'hurly burly' of organisational politics has often operated as a potent weapon of political advantage.

This chapter has illustrated the considerable ambiguity and unresolved tension that continues to hamper IS and user relations despite, or indeed perhaps because of, the numerous organisational innovations made in this area in the last decade. For example, some IS managers feel that having ceded considerable control to users it is now difficult to pull the reins back into their control. But in the interview with Mike that we analysed we also showed how IS specialists can exercise considerable control through their ability to monopolise often tacit and approximate knowledge and present this to users as apparently cut-and-dried objective 'facts'.

It is perhaps tempting to speculate on these continued tensions and their underlying causes. So for example, perhaps there is a fundamental incompatibility between 'technical' and 'business' cultures and identities where highly mobile IS specialists identify with professional careers in IS rather than insurance *per se*. This may be exacerbated in a rather hidebound industry such as insurance, which lacks a certain sex appeal in the league table of occupations, and the rapidly growing ranks of the IS specialism which sees itself at the very cutting edge of industrial and, indeed, societal innovation.

Such factors as these certainly have a bearing on the politics of IS and user relations, as do past successes and failures in particular organisations, and the cultural and managerial specificities of particular industries and companies. Indeed, the very newness of IT and the IS specialism and the rapidity of technological change, in the last 20 years both as an accumulation of experience and continuous innovation, has forestalled a rapid institutionalisation of user/IS relations. It seems, in fact, that no sooner is a 'solution' found to these problems than new technological possibilities are used to undercut and reproduce them elsewhere.

It is this pace of change, continued managerial suspicions about the ability of IT to deliver on its own 'hype', and the increasing centrality of IT systems in contemporary organisations, that focuses so much attention on IS and user relations. Of course, IS staff and managers can be high handed, narrow minded in a technical sense and arrogant. Similarly, users can be obstructive, bloody minded and unwilling to part with hard won knowledge and experience. But we would suggest that the tensions that lie at the heart of the IS/user relationship are perhaps greater than many other interfunctional relationships in contemporary organisations, precisely because of the importance of IT and the huge uncertainties generated by the pace of technological innovation and the challenges of harnessing that innovation to often unclear, internally divided, not to say contradictory, strategic and tactical business requirements.

It is to a fuller examination of these tensions and the intermanagerial competition around the IT resource that we will shortly turn. But first in Chapter 6 we want to return to the issue of masculinity and gender in user relations raised earlier in this chapter.

6
Business Application Software: Masculinity and the Making of Software[1]

INTRODUCTION

In Chapter 5 we examined the ambiguities of user relations in software development in the increasingly uncertain and competitive conditions of the late 1980s and early 1990s in the UK financial services industry. In so doing we began to take note of connections between the social construction of technology, or the way in which technology is infused with social significance and contemporary masculinity. In this chapter we want to develop these connections by exploring the symbiotic relationship between certain masculinities and technology and the manner in which these can be manifested in the development of business application software.

We do this for two reasons: first, as was argued in Chapters 1 and 2, the constitution and reproduction of gender relations are a vital condition of possibility of organisational and technological change and are too often ignored by studies in this field; and, second, as we shall argue, contemporary systems development and managerial practices are suffused and constituted through the dominant position of men and the masculinity they embody and articulate. Indeed, we will go on to argue that the character of contemporary organisational politics and masculinities owe a great deal to each other.

As mentioned in Chapters 1 and 2, much research on gender and technology has examined the manner in which women are systematically excluded from jobs and professions that are defined as technological, largely through a process of job segregation and the cultural

---

[1] This chapter draws heavily on Murray (1993)

definition of technology as an almost exclusively masculine domain (see Cockburn, 1991. 1985; Collinson et al, 1990; Henwood, 1993; Wajcman, 1991). In examining gender relations our concern here is to examine this process of exclusion. From this perspective of the dominance and mobilisation of particular masculinities within the realm of technogical practice and discourse, we seek to provide a gender analysis of job segregation and, more specifically, the exclusion of women from the IS arena.

In this chapter, therefore, the relationship between masculinity and technology is examined in the context of our primary focus on systems development. Although we do not have the space or expertise to explore alternative forms of systems development, there is little doubt that alternative possibilities exist and draw the reader's attention to gender and feminist perspectives in this area. This we do by questioning the apparent 'good sense' of the prevalent method of developing business application software by dedicated project teams. We shall suggest that this particular form of organising software work, and the vocabularies of motive employed in so doing, are tied to prevailing masculine conceptions of work and technology.

Before examining intersections between masculinities and systems development we briefly look at the concept of masculinity and the rapidly growing literature in this area of gender studies.

MASCULINITY, SCIENCE AND TECHNOLOGY

This section of this chapter looks at the concept of masculinity. What is it ? Where does it come from ? Is it fixed or mobile, unitary or plural, stuck, stubborn and wholly negative or open to the possibility of change?

In its broadest sense masculinity is the way men behave; it is the way men think and feel about themselves. Far from being a natural or biological category, masculinity is a socially constructed way of seeing and being. As such it can and does change over both time and space. For example, concepts of manhood in medieval and contemporary times have changed considerably as they also differ between cultures and ethnic groupings. Furthermore, masculinity displays itself in a variety of ways within the same society depending, for example, on class or race, geographical location, form of power and sexual orientation.

If masculinities are plural and socially constructed it follows that a masculinity identity is not unambiguously conferred upon men as a function of their biological sex. It does not simply come with a penis at birth. Rather, it is the product of complex and often contradictory social processes. Moreover, while there are elements of ascription, living up to the image of what it is to be 'a man' is a continuous struggle where individuals feel 'driven', for no discernible reason other than as a part of what it means, and how it feels, to subscribe to an ideal of competence, and where the display of vulnerability is to threaten the image of that competence (Kerfoot and Knights, 1993, p.672). Masculinity is something that men struggle to achieve and maintain in highly competitive circumstances. Seidler says, 'Gender is not something we [as men] can be relaxed and easy about. It is something we have to constantly prove and assert' (Seidler, 1989, p.151).

Masculinity is a relational concept. It only makes sense, indeed it can only be defined, in relation to femininity. Masculinity and femininity are locked in a dance where their respective positioning constrains the space within which the other can define itself. However, the dance involves more than an uneasy partnership of a single masculine and feminine identity. It is more like a crowded club where different masculinities and femininities jostle and fight among and between themselves. The mutual stereotypings and 'put downs' cannot be separated from the fear that each represents for the 'other' but it is masculinity that is perhaps the most vociferous in its intolerance of that which (e.g. homosexuality, femininity) threatens its precarious solidarity.

In this chapter we argue that masculinity tries to claim as a core domain exclusive to itself the practice and culture of science and technology. This is closely associated with masculinity's claims to rationality (Seidler, 1989). It is also linked to masculinity's alienation from the body and emotion (Corneau, 1991). In making this claim, of course, masculinity also has a profound influence on the social construction of technology. That is, the very definition of technology, and the predominant discourses and cultures used to explain and mobilise the concept and boundaries of technology are hugely influenced by their identification with masculine practices. Indeed, it might be argued that in much contemporary discourse science and technology and the masculine define each other. In particular, technology strongly associated with women is seen by men as not really 'technology'. Thus, for example, few men in particular would identify people in highly feminised human/machine interactions, such as sewing or word processing, as technical workers whereas men using machines in metal working or printing are easily identified as engineers and technical workers (Cockburn, 1985).

In arguing that technology is a core domain of a socially constructed masculinity we suggest that it plays an important role as a boundary marker: what is perceived to be technological is frequently perceived to be masculine.

In the early 1980s Easlea (1983) argued that the historical development of scientific discourse was mediated by the deployment of an aggressively masculine imagery of invasion and subjugation. This involved the occupation and dissection of a passive and mysterious female 'nature'. Here science developed as a distinctively masculine activity where the 'deeper the mental penetration into female nature the greater the mental virility the man of science is able to claim' (ibid., p.171). This gave rise to a hierarchy of potency and status within the sciences where the most penetrative and dissecting activities such as particle physics stand above the 'softer' systemic approaches such as biology and ecology. Seen from this perspective science was articulated as a cold, dry, hard, aggressive activity that gloried in its own penetrative abilities in the pursuit of a complete 'mastery' over nature.

Science and particular masculinities developed together in the modern era. This involved not only the dissection of a socially constructed female nature but also the self-mutilation of the potentiality of a different kind of masculinity. For men's subjugation of a feminine nature proceeded apace with a need to 'subjugate and conquer the feminine within themselves' where this included the need to relate, to enter into dialogue, receptivity (listening/empathy), and the validation of and involvement in 'simple domestic concerns' (Easlea, 1983, pp. 146 and 37).

More historically grounded accounts of the development of science and technology (for a critique of Easlea's ahistorical method see Jordanova, 1987) have pointed to the incursion of women into this privileged masculine realm. However, Rossiter (1982) concludes that in the period 1880–1910 women's position within science was constrained in two ways: they were either limited to holding subservient positions as assistants and educators or confined to practise science in 'women's' fields such as home economics or cosmetic chemistry.

Harding (1986) also examines the subordination of women in the sciences in this and the post-war period. She argues that the cultural stereotype of science as tough, rigorous, rational, impersonal, competitive and unemotional has continued to be 'inextricably intertwined with issues of men's gender identities' in a mutually reinforcing manner (Harding, 1986, p.63). Science and technology not only seem to vest masculinity with a particular potency in, and claim on, the world: they also render masculinity and science particularly vulnerable to feminine 'dilution'.

> We should expect that in science more than any other occupation (except, perhaps, making war) it will take the presence of only a very few women to raise in men's minds the threat of feminization and thus of challenges to their own gender identity. (Harding, 1986, p.63)

While there are a multiplicity of masculinities that are fluid and shifting historically (Brittan, 1989), what remains comparatively constant is the dominant position of men *vis-à-vis* women (Kerfoot and Knights, 1993, p.663). Technology appears to be one sphere in which men and masculinity are locked into one another in ways that, whether by intention or not, exclude women and femininity.

MEN MAKING TECHNOLOGY, TECHNOLOGY MAKING MEN

This section of the chapter raises two questions: why do men become engineers and IT specialists; and what do they get out of their profession at a subjective level? In particular, we are interested in the connection between what we might call the psychic security that derives from these specialisms and the way in which it links with prevailing modes of masculinity. Hacker (1990) has explicitly addressed this concern in her work on engineering students. Kidder (1981) has not but the account he provides of the development of a 32-bit mini-computer provides some interesting, if inconclusive, pointers in this area.

Hacker set out to investigate the social formation of engineers through a comparative study of engineering students at the Massachusetts Institute of Technology (MIT). In this she explored the relationship between the childhood experiences of the engineering students and their decision to enter the profession. She found that the engineering students, 'painfully recalled children's bodies that would not do what they should' (Hacker, 1990, p.115). In addition, they experienced difficulty remembering the sensual pleasures of childhood in contradistinction to the humanities students she interviewed. From these and other findings she concluded:

> The men who chose engineering had early life experiences that emphasised aloneness, that allowed them greater distance from intimacy or the pleasures and dangers of 'mixing it up' with other people. Many became fascinated by things, and how they worked. These experiences heightened the value placed on abstractions and the control of nature. (Hacker, 1990, p.124)

Hacker here puts forward a very interesting thesis: that there may be early childhood experiences that take place within particular familial and societal contexts that predispose some individuals to become engineers. Further, these individuals grow up and seek psychic security in the world of things almost as a compensation for early disappointment or trauma.

Kidder's ethnography of an almost exclusively male computer development team touches anecdotally on this area: there is a link in the early life experiences of some of his subjects and their drift into computing. In particular, a number of the development team appear to have experienced themselves as failures either in terms of their sporting or academic achievements. Others found a reassuring solidity in the world of things. For example, one of the senior team members was a small, pale, weak child who felt himself to be at the 'bottom of the pile'. When he worked out how to take apart a telephone at an early age he says:

> This was a fantastic high, something I could get absorbed in and forget that I had these other social problems. (Kidder, 1981, p.87–8)

The project manager, branded an 'underachiever' at college, found a kind of security in the world of things. He said:

> There's some notion of control, ..., that you can derive in a world full of confusion if you at least understand how things get put together. (Kidder, 1981, p.158)

Kidder's ethnography only touches on these early experiences of the mini-computer engineers in question. It provides more material on the attraction of being a computer engineer. For despite the long, gruelling hours and poor working conditions, the computer engineers in Kidder's study are strongly attached to their work. As one says, they were breathing life into a new machine and by so doing making something bigger than themselves. They were also at the very 'cutting edge' of technological developments and in some senses were making history. This sense of going where no man has gone before provides considerable satisfaction to many engineers. One of the engineers Cynthia Cockburn interviewed says:

> You collectively are at the forefront of whatever it is you're doing. ... It doesn't have to be anything really [!] wonderful. The fact that you are at the limit of your company's experience: That's a marvellous feeling. And if it is the case, as it was with me, that you are involved in something which, without being mealy-mouthed about it, is doing humanity a bit of good. The scanner was such a tremendous breakthrough for the medical world. Everybody was so excited, swept up in it. It was terrific. (Cockburn, 1985, p.175)

However, such is the speed of technological change that this sense of being at the leading edge may be short-lived. This was the case for the project manager in Kidder's story of computer development. He stressed the tentative character of his 'marvellous feelings' when confronted with machines he had designed earlier in his career. These now appeared 'clumsy' and their makers 'dumb'. In a revealing quote he says:

> You spend all this time designing one machine and it's only a hot box for two years, and it has all the useful life of a washing machine. (Kidder, 1981, p.162)

The thrill of designing machines derives from the novelty, from the knowledge that no one has done this before, and that it will command the status of a 'hot box', the top kid on the block, for a couple of years. The project manager does not seem concerned with the utility of his creations. Instead, he is horrified by the way in which his cherished creations so quickly become ugly and lose their special and unique appeal, in which they become mundane and domesticated.

There are moments in Kidder's story where 'ordinary life' is almost completely excluded. The one woman engineer on the mini-computer project comments, 'You can end up staying all night. You can forget to go home and eat dinner' (Kidder, 1981, p.61); a microcoder on the project working on a small section of code notes: 'When you're concentrating on that little world you leave everything else out' (p.145); and the project manager likens the project to a computer game: 'It's like being in Adventure. Adventure's a completely bogus world, but when you're there, you're there' (p.95).

In *The Soul of the New Machine* the participants live in a world distant from 'ordinary life'. It is a world that asks little of its subjects other than that they be good computer engineers. It is a highly structured and seductive environment that may look bogus from the outside but that is forcefully real for its participants. One of its attractions seems to lie in its binary, black and white, character:

> The engineer's right environment is a highly structured one, in which only right and wrong answers exist. It's a binary world; the computer might be its paradigm. And many engineers seem to aspire to be binary people within it. No wonder. The prospect is alluring. It doesn't matter if you're ugly or graceless or even half crazy; if you produce right results in this world, your colleagues must accept you. (Kidder, 1981, p.134)

The project manager was aware of the fragility of the parallel, perhaps even virtual, world he had created in the basement. He worried over the future of the team of young men he had developed once the computer they carried in their collective womb was from them 'untimely ripped' by the demands of the marketing department:

The post-partum depression on this project is gonna be phenomenal. These guys [the team] don't realize how dependent they are on that thing [the machine] to create their identities. That's why we gotta get the new things in place. (Kidder, 1981, p.205)

Making the machine, breathing life into it, nurtures a particular form of identity and way of life only so long as the corporation continues to build new computers and values the particular contributions made by each team member. Once the machine is made and shipped out the basement door a potentially terrifying vacuum is left. At this point having given birth to a baby they no longer control—the marketing people even change the computer's name as soon as it is finished—the team is potentially at a loss. Thus, it becomes vital to 'get the new things in place' and repeat the exhausting cycle again. At this point re-entering the earth's atmosphere and the world of the ordinary and mundane can be a terrifying prospect. So rather than rest and relax there is a compulsion to do it all over again, and again, and again.

Of course this compulsive absorption in projects is not exclusive to men but it is, we argue, an aspect of masculinity where the involvement in linear and (phello) logocentric means–ends chains of events 'blot out' the precarious and uncertain 'reality' of everyday existence as well as the potential for that void of existential meaninglessness to 'raise its ugly head'. We suspect that this meaningless void, so well described by Durkheim (1951) as anomil but popularised by the philosophical and literary writings of the existentialists (e.g. Sartre, 1962, 1966; Camus, 1960; Gide, 1960), is gendered. It is so in the sense that the purposive–rational and linear logical pursuit of material objectives that can resemble mathematical certainty is a feature of contemporary masculinity. At the risk of reinforcing the stereotypical dualism, femininity appears more comfortable with the circular, amorphous, uncertain and unending 'reality' of organic as opposed to mechanical life. Since these gender stereotypes are conferred upon the biological sexes in a quite rigid fashion, it is not surprising that men attach themselves to these masculine conceptions of reality as do women to more feminine perceptions.

Although masculinity and femininity are conferred upon men and women respectively, they are by no means 'fined' or ascribed identities in contemporary society. The amount of physical and psychological energy that is invested in fashion, diet and personal appearance reflects how the achievement of gendered identities can be a perpetual struggle for both sexes. However, the desire to produce results, complete projects, generate exhaustive accounts and control material of realities (e.g. technology) that are seen to offer less resistance than social and symbolic life are characteristics specifically of masculinity, and perhaps why men have traditionally been attracted to technology. But the uncertainty and insecurity that does appear to reside more frenetically in masculinity also gives to technology the appearance of a refuge from the amorphous and irreducibly reflexive nature of social reality. Paradoxically, as we hope to show in our case study research in later chapters, this is a false refuge for technology turns out, despite protestations for its neutrality, to be every bit as political and uncontrollable as any other organisational activity.

We now move on to explore relationships between masculinities, organisational politics and systems development.

MASCULINITY AND SYSTEMS DEVELOPMENT

Most application software development is organised in discrete projects (Friedman and Cornford, 1989). There are considerable areas of software development that are not project based, such as software maintenance, but these tend to be seen as low status and unchallenging areas of IS work. High status work tends to be associated with high profile new software development. It is prized for the inherent challenge it offers and the promotion prospects that follow the successful completion of major projects. Despite much debate about software quality assurance, the success of new business applications software is still judged foremost by the ability of IS managers to meet system development time and cost constraints.

Project-based work has a particular culture and tempo that sets it out from much routinised work. A male project manager defined the 'project mentality' thus:

> It is a different mentality. The mentality in admin. is very much nine to five. Here, I mean my God, I come in at eight in the morning, I leave at seven in the evening, and there are still people here. It's a different mentality. If you ask people for a little bit of extra effort you get it.

We asked this manager if he could have developed computer systems, with (women) clerical users in their offices:

> No, because at the end of the day we're still a project, at the end of the day we've still got to have a project mentality, you've got to run it [laughs] like a project; there must be very clear milestones, deliverables, objectives ... which I think we would have lost sight of if we'd plopped the whole lot into the admin area.

So while project work is 'a lot of fun, hard work and a challenge' it also requires very clear parameters. These make it visible and controllable.

Put it in the administrative division and this visibility would have been diluted, dissipated, lost. Better that the technologists control it even if the rest of the company think they are 'weird fish'. Better to be 'weird fish' in your own pond than invisible in the admin. area.

So what is the 'project mentality' ? It is the ability to give a little bit of extra effort, to work odd and often long hours and the possession of demonstrable competence in the discourse and techniques of 'milestones, deliverables, and objectives'. Increasingly, it is about having the right 'methodology' and being a 'software engineer'. In business software development, project work means long hours. This is commonplace for project managers and team leaders. But programming and analyst staff are also expected to work long hours as projects near their release dates. IS staff, according to Holti (1989, p.470):

> strike a 'bargain' with organisational employment. They internalise an acceptance of the nature of project targets allocated to them in exchange for autonomy, lack of close surveillance and self-expression in the performance of their work.

Clearly working these hours can have benefits for individuals. If overtime is paid already, well-paid staff can make considerable amounts of money. And where overtime is unpaid there is an expectation that there will be a payback in terms of promotion or preferential treatment. But for anyone with even minimal childcare responsibilities there are major problems when working hours are extended. Given that, in our society, women assume or have imposed upon them such responsibilities, their participation in such projects is restricted.

Informal arrangements can be made for staff with young children up to a point. For example, one woman junior manager commented that she tried not to pressure people with families into working late or weekends 'unless it's absolutely necessary'. She said, 'We don't actually ask them [people with small babies] to come in if we can help it. [Pause] Well, I don't anyway. I don't think it's fair.' But often within the area of programming and analysis, particular individuals will have skills and knowledge that are not easily transferable; a situation exacerbated by the tendency to allocate particular parts of programming or analysis to individuals. And in this case either these staff do the work or the work may not get done. Staff with childcare responsibilities are not 'actually asked', at least if their managers 'can help it', to work long hours. But as a woman senior software developer and single parent who read an earlier draft of this chapter commented:

The fact that some people can live up to the expectation of long hours is nevertheless threatening to those who can't—a project I worked on got into difficulties and everyone was offered overtime incentives—although my manager accepted that I would not be taking advantage of them and quoted all the above stuff [regarding the company's respect for the individual] to reassure me that it was okay, I still felt almost guilty going home when the others stayed, particularly because almost everyone else was in a position to do so, which was stressful.

Even if work can be shared and some staff can work 'normal' hours this involves all sorts of hidden costs: the sense that you are not pulling your weight, that others are suffering for you, and that you are missing out on perhaps the most exciting and visible parts of the system development. And for those with aspirations to get into the managerial grades in IS, the inability or unwillingness to work long hours may be read as an insufficiency of organisational commitment. If bouts of superhuman effort work against those who have other commitments or simply do not want to allow work to dominate their lives to this extent, what do they do for those people who 'buy into' or feel compelled to work in this way? And, in particular, what can we glean from these practices about the relationship between the development of a particular work-based masculinity and making software? It is our impression that male IS staff and managers rather revel in the long hours they work. There is a tendency to glorify or accept as a technological inevitability the time they spend during the evening and at weekends at work. This separates out the IS man from the 'normal' business types; he might be a weird fish, and in the 1960s and 1970s he might have had long hair and strange clothes, but he could be relied upon to work long and unusual hours (see, for example, Pettigrew, 1973). The IS man, in his more unguarded moments, is apt to adopt a 'have a go' attitude, a 'we will deliver' mentality and a 'we'll-make-you-your-system-even-if-we-don't-have-the-resources' approach that is simultaneously self-defeating and self-aggrandising. This has a lot to do with the particular pressures IS men feel themselves to be under (see Knights and Murray, 1992). There is a kind of *Boy's Own* heroism about working these long hours. IS staff talk about preparing for the 'final push' and the 'muck and bullets' character of intense stages of project work. There is an ambiguous feel to the excitement that accompanies these phases of project work. An engineer in Kidder's (1981) study comments: 'It was a lot of fun, a lot of pressure' (p.54). The project manager says, 'I'm flat out by definition. I'm a mess. It's terrible [pause] It's a lot of fun' (p.109).

Project work appears to take on a life of its own; it is bigger than any of the individuals making it happen. You can either embrace it or take the difficult path of the conscientious objector. But in order to instil the project with glory and with a 'this thing is greater than us but we have to do it' dimension, frequent recourse is made to war imagery. Again, the woman software developer who commented on an earlier draft of this chapter recounted an incident which graphically illustrates this point:

> A project I worked on got into difficulties and the lab manager set up a special project room with a label on the door of 'War Office'. Quite a few of us found this slightly ridiculous but nonetheless I know others enjoyed this sort of thing and the phrase 'Blood all over the walls of the War Office' was a frequent one whenever a project manager got grilled over not meeting his dates. As a woman once active in the peace movement I found this attitude particularly alienating and there is no way I would have been able to 'buy into' it. The fact that a fair number of my male colleagues also found the whole thing puerile was an important factor in minimising the tension at work.

From one perspective the comparison of software development with warfare is preposterous. Sitting in front of a workstation in well-appointed office accommodation in the Home Counties in the 1990s is a world away from the 'muck and bullets' of trench warfare. But from another perspective these evocations of another theatre of masculine practice tell us something about the psychic reality of at least some men's experience of work. In this version, work is seen as war, as a matter of life and death struggle, of collective and individual heroism and sacrifice for an obscure and greater good.

War imagery can mobilise deep psychic energy in men. It also helps to make sense of the competitive social relations of capitalist work processes. This refers not only to the classical Marxist understanding of 'class warfare' but also to the warfare of inter-managerial and inter-specialist competition. (See, for example, Jackal's, 1988, account of US corporate alliance building and back-stabbing.) But making sense of work through warfare and mobilising energy through the evocation of war does something to the way work and masculinity are organised. Work becomes a dangerous and heroic struggle and the imagery and practice of a dominant masculinity mediates, shapes and personalises market forces. And, as in warfare, so in work there are many casualties.

In the practice of software development particular pressures fall on project managers, project leaders and team leaders. Anecdotal evidence of the results of this stress on the health of junior IS managers suggests that the pressures are not to be taken lightly. Yet it is often only by succeeding and being seen to succeed as a project manager or leader that the aspiring IS staffer can gain a foothold within the ranks of IS management. This clearly creates a dilemma for those who aspire to move into management. It also leads to the worst excesses of self-destructive macho behaviour.

One of the IS middle managers I interviewed talked surprisingly openly about his experience as a project leader on a highly visible project. His main recollection of the experience was being 'squeezed'. He said:

> Pressure definitely settles on the Project Leaders. The reason for that is you're not making the decisions...As a Project Leader I was receiving decisions and then you're squeezed; you've got close responsibility for the team under you who are also under pressure so you're bang in the middle where you're squeezed.

This manager has seen some of his peers move out of IS or into quiet backwaters of the department as a direct result of having had enough of this pressure. But despite believing that project leaders are made scape-goats and squeezed he wanted to have a go, to accumulate the right stuff in his climb up the ziggurat: 'You're trying to prove yourself, to get up to the next level.' Consequently this manager became a project leader and got his project in more or less on time. But as the project neared completion , as it was born, his body gave up on him. He said:

> I was probably keeping myself going during [the project] and then when I'd finished my body said, 'Forget it'. Management were very sympathetic. I dragged myself back into work for a week to do the budgets. I couldn't delegate it. The last two days I was told I was slurring my words.

When the tape recorder was off this manager recalled how he had been 'doubled up in pain' in the office during this period. Finally he went to see a doctor and was rushed to hospital. Nevertheless, he was back at work in a week to show, as he said, 'that I was OK'. After all, he said without a trace of irony, 'I'd never been ill'.

Having clawed his way back into the office to show he was OK this manager was then off work for over two months. In this period he had time to reflect and a number of consultants suggested to him that his worklife and his illness were probably connected. This led him to con-clude that his illness was 90 percent due to work stress. According to this manager his problems were created by the 'macho attitude in DP' based on the motto 'We will deliver'. Here though in order to fight his way up into management he ended up playing the very game he criticised and it was only when his body said 'Forget it' that he began to reflect on where he was going. Still, when we spoke he seemed determined to continue to play this game in order to progress beyond the destabilising position of project leader. Indeed, he felt the danger for someone like himself who had moved up the hierarchy pretty quickly was 'that if I stop at a certain level people will say I've reached my level of achievement'.

CONCLUSION

This chapter has argued that gender relations are an important condition and consequence of organisational and technological change. In particular, the dominant relationship between masculinities and technology practices and cultures has a profound impact, along with the operation of other conditions of possibility, on the way in which technology is developed, utilised and understood. Thus feminist researchers, for example, have argued that the supposed superiority of 'technological knowledge' and a predominant male appropriation or possession of this knowledge gives IS developers a dominant position in systems development particularly when the users they confront are women often concentrated in the lowest occupational grade (Green et al, 1993).

Thus, gender relations are clearly an important condition of systems development. They are also an important means through which gender relations are reproduced and/or modified. This concerns not only the continued domination of men in systems development but also of particular masculinities. For example, the realm of IS appears particularly amenable to a masculinity that values and elevates the linear–logical pursuit of project objectives that are deemed to provide a predictable, controllable and comparatively certain set of outcomes.

The material reported in this chapter on systems development also suggests that IS may be an organisational area that engenders and reproduces a particularly 'gung ho' form of 'macho' masculinity. This tentative conclusion is supported in subsequent chapters (see particularly Chapter 11).

This macho masculinity glories in its own public and 'heroic' approach which may be related to pressures that IS managers put themselves under in an almost celebratory fashion. However, underneath its heroic exploits there are more painful, private stories of illness and breakdown. And while bolstering a particular masculinity these practices clearly serve to exclude the vast majority of women, and some men as well, from senior and middle management positions. This exclusion, while not only being repugnant in terms of its implications for democracy and equality and impact on women, is also counterproductive in that it holds in abeyance characteristics constructed as 'feminine' that systems development clearly needs, particularly in times of uncertainty and competing user demands. These include such skills as listening, negotiating, coping with uncertainty, and forms of emotional sharing and openness. These latter, in particular, might lessen the tensions involved in systems development by encouraging a more open, less conflictual approach to resolving the competing demands made on, and by, systems personnel. But this will require a greater degree of reflection on how masculine powers and identities may be equally as self-defeating as productive.

In discussing not merely how masculinity reflects and reproduces the politics of organisation that an 'escape' into technology seeks to eradicate or deny, we hope to have made some minimal contribution to understanding these complex social processes.

7
Building Computer Systems at Pensco: The Pensions Project

INTRODUCTION

This chapter describes a large systems development project at Pensco, a medium-sized mutual life insurance company where intensive case study research was undertaken over a period of three years. The systems project was crucial for the company's future and was intended to place it favourably in the expanding though increasingly competitive market for group and personal pensions products. For Pensco, the project presented a number of novelties: it was the largest systems development project the company had ever undertaken; it aimed to develop product and process systems simultaneously (and thereby brought together actors from all the main divisions of the company); and although the second IT development since the appointment of a new General Manager (GM), it was the more important in that it updated and extended the range of products on which the company had built its growth and reputation. Furthermore, though smaller, the previous project had been seen as successful and therefore represented a model of 'progress' from which, it was anticipated, that slippage or deviation would be severely reprimanded by no less than the GM. Given these special circumstances and the importance of the project for Pensco's future, the systems development here described was a considerable test for Pensco managers and the Information Services Division in particular.

Our account follows the pensions project through from its inception to the launch of the systems developed. As will be seen shortly, this was a process fraught with tensions and difficulties. This was in part due to the regulatory changes in insurance and pensions markets and governmental interventions concerning the partial privatisation of pensions that were a condition of the project. But we believe other factors are more important in explaining the tensions and difficulties surrounding the project. Specifically, the intensity of inter-managerial competition and conflict over resources during a period of dramatic change in the company need to be emphasised.

In this chapter we are concerned to document the details and difficulties of the pensions project which we analyse in subsequent chapters. So, for example, in Chapter 8 we stress alternative interpretations of the project to the official ones described in this chapter. And in Chapter 9 we analyse inter-divisional tensions and conflicts during the project. Overall our concern is to examine what we call Pensco's 'technology context' and to stress the multi-faceted conditions of systems development and the manner in which the systems so produced are socially constructed and open to multiple interpretations. Therefore, the systems development process can be regarded as a process that inseparably constructs technological artefacts (in this case software) and meaning. And, as we have already indicated in Chapter 5, the constitution of meaning in organisations is a complex and highly problematical process through which organisational actors are crucially involved—morally, intellectually and politically. For example, in the case presented here the overall management sponsor of the project, the IS Divisional Manager, had a considerable interest in ensuring that the project was seen to be a success, as did his project manager and many others implicated in the project. This was because their assessed stature within Pensco and a broader IT-in-insurance community was tied to the outcome of this high profile and strategically vital project.

The account we present may take some readers into unfamiliar territory. For, in contrast to much of the literature dealing with IT, we refuse to treat IT development processes as a black box of little sociological interest. Here we focus not on the 'impacts' of IT on the labour process—a frequent preoccupation in the sociology of technology (Crompton and Jones, 1984; Shaiken, 1986; Attewell, 1987; Scarborough and Corbett, 1992, pp.31–48); rather, we concentrate on the construction of a vital part of IT, namely business application software. In opening up the black box of technology, of course, we also highlight the complexity of the social world in general and technology practices in particular. To an extent then we ask the reader for patience as we present the detailed story of the pensions project at Pensco for it is a complex and sometimes confusing phenomenon. It is also radically different from the sanitised and simplified accounts of systems development presented in normative and prescriptive texts.

Given the importance of software for contemporary business organisations, it is quite surprising that there are so few sociological studies of the systems development process for it is a crucial site of the social construction and development of technology and its particular form will have important, though not necessarily predictable, consequences for organisations and their members across a wide range of functions and specialities. There has been a literature examining the participation or non-participation of users in the design, development and implementation of information systems (Hedberg and Mumford, 1975; Bariff and Galbraith, 1978; Boland, 1979; Markus, 1984; Franz and Robey, 1984; Robey and Marcus, 1984) and a steady stream of research on the effects of technology upon organisational structure, process, labour and employment, and society at large (Braverman, 1974; Noble, 1977, 1984; Kling and Iacono, 1984; Strassman, 1985; Shaiken, 1986; Wield and Smith, 1987; Knights and Willmott, 1988; Zuboff, 1988; Kling, 1991). While drawing on many of the insights from this diverse range of research, we find it is limited in its depth of investigation of both the technological and socio-political processes of software business applications—this despite much of the literature focusing particularly upon politics within information systems design and development. The full details of our departure from the theoretical perspective informing these studies of information systems and politics will have to await a later chapter. Broadly, however, our view is that the resource dependency (Pfeffer, 1981; Hickson et al, 1971) conceptions of power that are adopted by these authors are too narrowly based upon the principle of reciprocity emanating from social exchange theory (Blau, 1964).

So, for example, resource dependency theories subscribe to the view that power is possessed by those who have access to or control, the resources upon which the organisation is seen to depend for its survival. While we would not wish to dismiss such a theory in its totality because clearly we can see how, for example, the wealthy exercised power especially prior to the development of the joint-stock company, those with actuarial skills have tended to control life insurance companies, and presently, those with accounting skills are dominant in most PLCs. The assumption underlying the theory is that the control over important organisational resources (e.g. capital, knowledge or skill) will secure the compliance of other organisational members. This is because in exchange for these resources, there is seen to be a reciprocal obligation on the part of the rest of the organisation to put them to productive use. Although the assumption of reciprocal exchange suggests a relational conception of power, this is limited by the implicitly *instrumental* nature of the relationships which exist exclusively on the basis of carefully calculated reciprocal benefits and obligations. No doubt many power relationships conform to this instrumental form but resource dependency theory assumes a universality that itself has the effect of reproducing precisely the organisational behaviour that it presumes. For in learning of the theory practitioners tend to adopt the behavioural characteristics that it describes. Often the relational conception of power is abandoned altogether by such theorists as the control of resources does appear to establish power as the property of certain individuals or groups and not others.

While we acknowledge that the effects of its exercise will vary depending upon the formal position of individuals within a hierarchy or their access to scarcely valued resources within a market economy, power is a social relation, the outcome of which can never be precisely predicted as following the strict lines of formal hierarchy or the particular intentions of individuals. It is this perspective on power, we argue, that helps to improve our understanding of the interrelatedness of markets, managers and technologies for it demands, at the very least, some analysis of contemporary systems development that identifies its complexity in the context of socio-political uncertainty and change.

Before presenting our account, a brief note on method is required. The account that follows is constructed from a longitudinal study of Pensco which took place in the mid- to late 1980s. However, well before we became interested in the pensions project, considerable on-site real-time research had been carried out in the company. This had consisted of semi-structured taped interviews with senior and middle managers, observation at different managerial meetings, and the consultation and analysis of Pensco archives, committee minutes and strategy papers. Research proper on the pensions project began towards the end of 1987 and continued until the middle of 1988, although limited contact with the company has continued since then. The period of research coincided with the most intense period of the pensions project as managers and staff struggled to meet the deadlines that were largely a function of governmental legislation and the budgets for the system. During this period we interviewed the main personnel involved in the project from the members of the Steering Committee down to the first clerical team leaders to use some of the systems developed. In all we conducted some 48 in-depth interviews with participants in the pensions project. We also attended a number of different Steering and Project Committee meetings and had full access to the minutes of all meetings and supporting papers concerning the pensions project. Thus we are in a position to be able to present an account from various perspectives and levels within the organisation. Initially, however, we have attempted to reconstruct an account of the project that favours no particular participant's perspective. This is not a claim to scientific 'objectivity' for we are not of the (positivist) school that believes it possible to eradicate values from research; clearly the values we invoke are those that inform our theoretical perspective discussed in Chapter 2. All that we are suggesting is an absence of direct side taking with respect to the participants themselves and a healthy scepticism regarding certain prevailing conventional wisdoms regarding technology and management. We now provide a brief introduction to Pensco and its context in preparation for the more detailed examination of the pensions project.

ORGANISATIONAL CHANGE AT PENSCO

Our examination of organisational change and the impact of information technology at Pensco now follows. In it we concentrate on: (i) the process of negotiated change between divisions and senior managers over the use of the company's IT resource; (ii) the relationship between this change and the firm's sectoral context; and (iii) the relationship between management intention and outcome.

Currently, transformations are occurring in the whole of financial services as a result of economic deregulation, political regulation and an intensification of both domestic and international competition. Insurance companies, in particular, can no longer ignore the pressure for change, and Pensco is no exception. Although having a history of paternal complacency against the background of steady growth, increasing turbulence in the market place in the mid-1980s had coincided with dramatic internal changes in the company as a result of the new General Manager (GM) and other senior management replacements (Knights and Willmott, 1987, 1993; Kerfoot and Knights, 1994). This resulted in the development of a corporate strategy that involved detailed business planning based on a rolling six month period through which the General Manager imposed and monitored key tasks on his senior managers. Corporate self-reflection of this kind resulted in a number of questions being asked as to whether the huge capital investments in information technology gave value for money and the extent to which IT strategy could be brought more closely into line with business strategy (Knights and Murray, 1990).

Gender relations at Pensco were dominated by gross inequalities between men and women: the vast majority of managerial positions were occupied by men (there were no women in senior management) while women, in the main, occupied senior and junior clerical positions. Within the IS Division there were no women in senior or middle managerial positions. The most senior women, of whom there were four, were in junior managerial positions, as project leaders, trainers or staff developers.

In general, Pensco was a company dominated by particular masculine managerial styles. However, the hegemonic masculinity within the company was undergoing profound changes during our research. Briefly stated, this involved a dramatic shift from a paternalistic style towards a 'professional' or competitive masculinity stressing aggressive assertion and individuation of responsibility, blame and success (see Chapter 11; also Kerfoot and Knights, 1993). As a form of management, paternalism engages a highly decorous and 'gentlemanly' [sic] set of behaviours which may appear to be the opposite of the 'cold', calculating and rational characteristics that we have been attributing to masculinity in this book. However, paternalism cultivated a form of masculinity in Pensco that generated perhaps even a stronger element of male domination than is currently the norm. This is because paternalistic masculinity seeks to 'protect' subordinates from the responsibility to make decisions and women, in particular, 'from the harsh world of business and politics' which is seen as potentially corruptive of their 'angelic, other-worldliness' (Kerfoot and Knights, 1993, p.671). The shift to a more aggressive and strategic style of management, although uneven in its development, is more compatible with modern competitive forms of masculinity where conquest is a defining characteristic and 'everything becomes an object of and for control' (ibid.). In contrast to paternalistic masculinity which was always self-assured in its 'right' and responsibility to protect women and subordinates, competitive masculinity suffers enormous self-doubt by virtue of the difficulty, if not impossibility, of meeting the escalating demands of its own ideal image of indomitable confidence and competence. A refusal to contemplate failure, competitive masculinity sacrifices everything, including emotional and physical well-being, at the altar of successful conquest. As we have intimated, systems projects display more than their fair share of the characteristics we attribute to competitive masculinity and this partly accounts for the events described in this chapter. But the preoccupation with success and competence reflects a reassertion of an aggressive masculinity within UK political and civil society at large. In Pensco, it was also linked to the rise of a discourse and practice of marketing and its assertion of a series of Darwinian, 'survival of the fittest', beliefs.

The Information Services Division

Up until the mid-1980s, Pensco had been moving quite rapidly towards providing customers with a better administrative service. This was partly achieved through the conversion from batch processing to on-line systems and, at this time, IS managers had a fairly free reign as long as they could cost-justify their IT expenditure. Once the new General

Manager (GM) was installed, he immediately began to thrust the organisation in the direction of a market-led, sales-maximising approach. In part, this was a response to the Company's falling market share which was occurring because of competition from the big corporations that had technology and marketing resources way beyond those of Pensco. But it was also a function of the GM's reputation (partly a reason for his appointment) in stimulating sales and marketing in a previous company. In addition to introducing a new pensions product, which, in placing major demands on IT, disrupted the on-line systems development plans, the GM restructured the Information Services (IS) Division, splitting it into three distinct business-related departments. This was very much in line with the growing discourse of user-led computing discussed in Chapters 4 and 5.

Later the GM brought in an old colleague from his previous company to act as the head of the Information Systems Division, while shifting the incumbent IS head sideways to become Customer Services AGM. In turn, the IS AGM brought in his former Technology and Planning (T&P) manager as his 'right hand man'. At their former employer he had developed control mechanisms to co-ordinate, standardise and closely monitor the social complexities of the systems development process. The IS AGM asked him to establish similar controls at Pensco. This was then attempted partly through introducing tight planning, reporting and monitoring procedures, backed-up by a striking degree of aggressive autocracy on the part of the AGM, with the intention that new computer systems were to be developed within budget and in accordance with a strict and closely monitored timetable of system development milestones . Moulding the IS culture around a market-driven approach meant that IT had to be directly responsive to external changes and internal executive demands for product ranges that were attractive in the marketplace. The IS Division had thus become less autonomous with respect to other parts of the business and the senior management team. As we have already seen in Chapter 5 this process is fraught with difficulty and ambiguity. To reduce IS autonomy is to risk ceding at least partial control of the politics of systems development to potentially hostile parties. Alternatively, to hold on publicly to that autonomy is to risk approbation from powerful user groups and IS managers who are keen to prove their ability to mobilise the rhetoric and uncertain practices of user involvement in the 'user relations' phase of systems development.

To summarise, it is against this socio-political and organisational background that the development of the new pensions products and their systems support was developed: that is, government legislation offering new opportunities in the market for personal and group pensions; a general push towards a market-sensitive and user-led development of IT; a half completed conversion from batch to on-line processing; and a new aggressive and autocratic IS AGM with little knowledge of the particular and peculiar nature of Pensco systems.

THE PENSION PROJECT AT PENSCO

In order to examine the development of information systems to support the new pensions project it is necessary briefly to trace the political developments leading to the partial privatisation of pensions. In the spring of 1985 the Chancellor of the Exchequer announced his intention to reform UK pensions legislation. In brief, this reform aimed to lessen the pensions burden on the state by encouraging citizens to arrange personal pension provision through the private sector in place of the State Earnings Related Pension Scheme (SERPS) that had been established by an earlier Labour Government. This move created considerable excitement in UK insurance companies because it was seen to provide the opportunity for considerable market expansion.

At Pensco these changes in state policy created considerable ground for speculation. In particular, the GM was anxious to maximise the opportunities he believed the proposed legislation presented to maintain and expand the company's market share in its key pensions markets.

Initial Response to the White Paper

In December 1985 the Minister for Social Security, Norman Fowler, issued a White Paper outlining the forthcoming Social Security Act. This provoked an immediate response at Pensco; the day after the Paper's release a bright young manager from the traditionally dominant actuarial specialism, on the fast track to a senior management position, circulated his initial analysis of the Fowler proposals and solicited comments from Pensco middle and senior managers.

Pensco managers had been considering possible responses to the forthcoming Fowler proposals since the middle of 1985 and had worked out a whole range of scenarios built on assumptions that involved informed speculation. While preliminary work had begun on revamping the product range to accommodate some of the expected changes, the publication of the White Paper provided the much needed knowledge and impetus for the project team working on the proposals to come up with an initial concrete set of products and their supporting systems to develop. Thus, in January 1986 there was a tentative agreement to develop a new group pension scheme to be launched on 1 May 1987 and a substantially revised and modernised personal pensions product to be launched on 1 January 1988.

Additionally, these initial plans foresaw the creation of an on-line system for the company's existing executive pension product and the development of a new 'Cash Driven' accounting system to replace Pensco's outmoded accounting systems developed in the early 1970s. And although these decisions were only tentative the project team began working on the development of these products.

The First Product Mix

Although it turned out to be something of a false start, this particular product mix and the process of its development was characteristic of the management of the project in general. In the subsequent two months of 1986 two young up-and-coming managers from the Marketing and Actuarial Divisions worked up what appeared to be a more considered response to the Fowler White Paper. This consisted of product definitions and discussion of the products and administrative systems that could be developed to secure Pensco's presence in the personal pensions market.

At this time a number of key themes emerged that were to be central to further developments in the project. Firstly, the idea of the 'core contract' rapidly gained a hold on the collective imagination of personnel working on the project. This was based on the notion that in the future pension clients would seek considerable flexibility within, and portability between, pensions contracts. The beauty of the core contract was supposed to lie in the possibility of using a master set of contract features to encompass a range of different products. At the time it was believed that this would cut out the duplication of laborious actuarial calculation for different contracts, make possible transferability between products, and maximise the possibility of customising or personalising individual policies. Further, given the commonality of the core contract it was also believed that the computer systems developed for both the preparation of quotes and processing the new products would constitute 'reusable system building blocks' easily adaptable for future product launches.

Having once agreed a mix of products and administrative systems the project proper got under way. Initially, it was decided to go for a 'middle of the road' development in keeping with the GM's predilection, as recorded in corporate strategy documents. This was an approach that emphasised continuity with limited change 'around the edges' with regard to the company's orientation to its main product markets. Thus, it was decided to concentrate the company's resources on the development of a new personal pensions and executive pension product while providing an on-line administrative system for this latter product. The group pensions product was at this stage dropped from the mix partly because of the complexities of revising a somewhat outdated existing product but also due to a prediction that it would not be a particularly extensive market. This view was later completely reversed and the reintroduction of a group scheme caused consternation and overload in the IS Division (see The Group Money Purchase Product on page 140). Initially, it was decided to launch these new products on 1 January 1988 while the executive pensions on-line systems was to be released on 1 October 1987 in order to gain significant productivity increases in clerical processing before the launch of the new products. It was also intended to launch the new cash driven system at this time (see Table 7.1).

Table 7.1   *Systems and products planned in early 1986*

Product/System	Planned launch
On-line system exec. pension	1.10.1987
Cash driven accounting system	1.10.1987
Executive pension product	1.1.1988
Personal pension product	1.1.1988

Project Management Structures

In the first quarter of 1986 considerable energies were expended in setting up the structures of the project. These consisted of a project Steering Committee (hereafter SC) and a Project Committee (hereafter PC). The former was made up of four of Pensco's five AGMs and the Project Manager while the latter was made up of the Project Manager and managerial representatives of each division of the company (bar the Investment Division) who were to be responsible for progressing project work in their divisions. Overall responsibility for the project was assigned to the Information Services AGM, who then delegated the work to his Pensions Systems Manager who became the Project Manager (hereafter PM).

Through the spring and the summer of 1986 work began on the first stage of the project which consisted in developing the features of the core contract and the specific profiles of the pension products to be launched in 1988. This largely involved the Sales and Marketing and the Actuarial Divisions establishing the key contract features of the products and then passing these business requirements to the Customer Services Division (CS hereafter) and IS Divisions in order for work to begin on the design of the product delivery and processing systems and policy documentation.

During this period the SC and the PC were still getting their control and reporting mechanisms in place. The PC committed itself to meeting on a weekly basis and its various members were given terms of reference outlining their responsibilities. Further, they were asked to produce quarterly schedules of project work in their divisions; they were also given personal responsibility for ensuring that the action points so generated were achieved within the dates assigned to them. Concern was expressed at this stage over the difficulty of getting the Finance Division to commit a member of staff to join the PC—an issue that was to drag on for over six months. The SC itself decided to meet on a monthly basis scheduled for one hour with the possibility of a half hour overrun.

Many a Slip Twixt Plan and Delivery

Already in mid-1986 problems were beginning to emerge with the progress of the project. In particular, the Sales and Marketing Division was slow to provide business requirements relating to their core contract demands. In part this seems to have been a result of the reorganisation the division was undergoing. It also, however, resulted from uncertainty in the marketplace and the great difficulty the division was experiencing in finding out what other companies were doing about the Fowler White Paper. Indeed, Sales and Marketing seemed somewhat ambivalent about the product mix to which the project had committed itself.

The SC expressed its concern with regard to slippage in the project and the PM informed the Committee in June 1986 that he would divide project tasks up into milestones and that he would be 'asking for copies of all action points with a view to chasing the individuals responsible for achieving them'.

This same meeting decided that it would seek approval from Pensco's Board of Directors for the expenditure on the project in the first quarter of 1987. At this time it was estimated the project would cost £3 m. to develop.

Interdivisional Hostilities

At about the same time the PM was expressing his frustration and concern with other divisions involved in the project. In an internal report to the IS managers working on the project he reported that 'if Actuaries/Marketing answer a question you get the feeling they're doing you a favour'. Furthermore, he put the backbiting that was beginning to emerge in the project down to the undue haste of the Marketing and Finance Divisions. He wrote, 'their objective is to tick off an action point ... even when they know they haven't given enough information'. The next month the PM received his own comeuppance when the Customer Services AGM admonished him for being over-concerned with quantitative progress at the expense of the quality of the work being done on the project. He further added at a later SC meeting that he believed the Sales and Marketing Division was simply rubber-stamping the work being done by Customer Services rather than working out what products they as a division wanted to sell. In conclusion, he demanded that Sales and Marketing must 'define what the market wants' and then Customer Services would do the detailed work on developing appropriate clerical systems and policy forms for the new products.

Product Uncertainty

Before discussing the problems emerging over the product mix to be included within the core contract, let us summarise briefly the situation so far. In response to the White Paper proposing that the Government encourage large sectors of the population to contract out of the State Earnings Related Pension Scheme (SERPS), through being offered a series of financial incentives, Pensco had set up a project and steering committee and decided on a product mix. This was to be supported by a core contract system that allowed for a range of alternatives and options encompassing not only diverse products but also flexibility within individual products. Of course, the core contract system had to be designed to incorporate a particular set of products and, at this point (August 1986), the two managers responsible for the original product/system mix in the project had begun to have second thoughts about the exclusion of a group pensions product from the project. However, the project management sponsor, the IS AGM, argued that if they wanted the group pensions issue reconsidered 'they must achieve it by submitting a paper to their AGMs outside the forum of the pensions project'. It was also reported that the company's sales force were very keen to have a group pensions product developed alongside the personal and executive pensions product.

Who decides? Who does?

At this time the core contract details had been more or less finalised and plans were well under way to present them to the GM. The Sales and

Marketing AGM was now reassured that the core contract was viable and decided against bringing in external consultants to examine it. However, he was increasingly concerned by the product mix the project was developing. As a consequence, the SC proposed an awayday to reconsider the product mix in order to assert the project's right to 'decide what is and is not present at the launch'.

It would appear then that here there was a degree of confusion over the roles of the SC and the PC. The SC, under the chair of the IS AGM, appears to have wanted the fairly minimal role of adjudicating over major policy disagreements and keeping a watchful eye over the progress of the project in line with the GM's professed desire to release his senior management for strategic tasks. Instead, at this stage the SC was relied upon to make all major decisions regarding the project. In other words, the PC was not mediating the demands made on the project before these reached the SC. This influx of unprioritised demands into the SC made its work far from easy and certainly heightened conflict within it. Speculating somewhat in the light of our interviews with the IS AGM and others who knew him, we would suggest that he was keen to suppress conflict and challenges to his authority in the SC. He attempted this by trying to ensure that his trusted, but ineffectual, PM resolved conflicts before they reached the SC, especially since the latter only met for one hour each month leaving little time to settle disputes.

IS Resource Shortfall Uncovered

Apart from increasing concern over the product/system mix, the need for the awayday arose because in August 1986 the PC Progress Report noted that there was a major problem in determining the scope of the development that could be delivered at launch. In particular, the estimate of IS resources required to meet the launch items had risen from 48.5 person years in February 1986 to 63.5 person years in August of the same year. In an attempt to reduce the demand on IS resourcing, the PC had established a working party that re-examined the core contract in an attempt to simplify its requirements with regard to systems development. This proved impossible. Indeed, the PM despairingly reported, 'There is even a danger of the estimates increasing as a result of the greater understanding [of the core contract] now being achieved.'

In the meantime, in his capacity as representative of the IS Division, the PM had calculated the maximum IS resource available before the proposed launch dates. This he estimated at 35 person years provided the major development effort got underway by 1 October 1986.

There was then a major problem in that a demand for 63.5 person years of IS resource greatly exceeded the possible supply of 35 person years. The PM proposed to resolve this problem, firstly, by finishing the detailed core contract proposals and re-evaluating the systems requirement for these and for product servicing. And, secondly, by ensuring that the PC produce 'a recommended package for launch which balances product and service demands within the overall constraint of the IS resource available', albeit based on the product launch priorities of the Actuaries and the Sales and Marketing staff. The PM added at this point, 'I do not expect this to be an easy task, I therefore propose the PC spend two days away at a hotel to tackle this task.'

This proposal appears to have found favour with the SC. However, it insisted on its attendance at the meeting and consequently asked that this take place over one, rather than two, days. Initially, the awayday was scheduled for September but this was deferred by continued disagreement within the PC.

The proposed agenda for the awayday was that the PC members of Sales and Marketing and Customer Service present their respective product and servicing requirements of the project. The PM was then to indicate IS resource availability and the extent of the imbalance between this and estimated resource requirements. Before opening up for a more general discussion the PM would then propose a package for the launch that eliminated the imbalance. With regard to this last item, the PM wrote in somewhat whimsical style:

> Whilst it may be hoped that this [proposal] has an air of realism to it, it is only meant to act as a basis from which discussion can ensue. It will be a product of [the project manager's] imagination and *may not have the backing of any of the Project Committee*. [Emphasis added]

The Group Money Purchase Product

At the very start of the pensions project it had been decided that a group pensions scheme should be made available for employees wishing to contract out of the State Earnings Related Pensions Scheme (SERPS) on a collective basis. Initially, this was to be achieved by modifying the company's existing group pensions product. However, this proposal was quickly dropped when the product/system mix was reconsidered by the PC's two up-and-coming Actuarial and Marketing Managers.

This was not a move favoured by all the personnel involved in the project. In particular, the company's sales staff began to argue that the Group Money Purchase market would be an important one. These sentiments were articulated by the PC member from Marketing Support who wrote to the PM at the end of June 1986:

The marketplace now seems to be moving towards the expectation of a significant amount of GMP business being effected. Therefore I am of the opinion that Pensco would be missing a great opportunity to increase its profile in the group pensions market if we did not react favourably to that situation, *particularly in view of the low level of resource required*. Any decision not to proceed will probably sound the death knell for Pensco in GMP contracts.' [Emphasis added]

Thus, the memo suggested that the existing group pension product be revamped to allow it to cater for clients contracting out of SERPS. It estimated that this would require between one and two person years of resource from the IS Division to do this. And it requested the PM to approach his IS AGM to seek approval for the commitment of IS resources to this end.

The IS AGM appears to have subsequently agreed to this proposal and allocated one person year of IS resource to it. However, towards the end of September Marketing Support sent the PM another memo in which it was argued that it would be a waste of resources to modify the outdated existing group pension product which would have a limited sales potential in the marketplace. Rather, Marketing Support now argued that that it seemed better to develop a completely new GMP scheme under the core contract particularly as this would involve a 'minimal' development cost.

This minimal development cost was, as we shall see later, one of the great fallacies of the entire project. However, in the memo this cost was believed to be minimal because after discussions between Sales and Marketing and Actuarial staff 'the view emerged that there [was] very little difference between a GMP contract and an executive pension contract'. This was a view that did not appear to be significantly challenged, at least in part due to the company's ignorance of the GMP marketplace, and was based on the idea that developing a GMP contract would simply be a question of rejigging the executive pension contract and the administrative systems that were to be developed for it. Subsequently IS staff produced an estimate for developing GMP of 5.5 person years. As it turned out this was an underestimate of monstrous proportions. In the event the nominal ISD resource expended on GMP was closer to 20 than 5 person years.

The Awayday

A number of papers were circulated prior to the awayday. These raised the issue of the allocation of resources between service and product requirements, the IS resources shortfall, and the desirability (referred to above) of including a GMP scheme in the project. With regard to the paper prepared on the allocation of resources between product and service requirements this appeared to show that the majority of resources in the project were committed to service, as opposed to product, development requirements. As the PM commented at the time, 'The emphasis of the project seems to have shifted from product to service.' In particular, the development of on-line processing for the executive pension and the new cash driven accounting system accounted for 21 person years of the 46.9 person years of IS resource required before 1 January 1988 whereas, from the figures presented, product development only appeared to have been allocated three person years of the requested IS resource. This left a total of 23 years of requested IS resource divided between requirements that were not clearly service or product oriented. That is, from the way these figures were presented it appeared that a small proportion of IS resources were to be devoted to product development and this provided the Sales and Marketing staff at the awayday with considerable ammunition to bargain for more of these resources.

In addition to the growing emphasis on a GMP scheme, Sales and Marketing had also begun to question the importance of having a new accounting system that was primarily designed to deal with an expected increase in variable premium payments. S&M now thought that Pensco was unlikely to receive much business of this nature. On the other hand, a paper presented to a special SC meeting held shortly after the awayday noted: 'As 1986 has progressed the SC have [sic] become convinced that we must have Cash Driven in place *before* the personal and executive pensions products are launched.' But it went on to say that even without the restriction placed on IS resources by the 1987 company budget, the launch of the cash driven system by October 1987 'was looking a very risky proposition'.

The PM thought he could see a way of resolving the excess demand for IS resources. By pushing 23 person years of systems development into a post-launch phase (after January 1988) and paring down the systems requirements for the cash driven and on-line systems he got close to balancing IS resources and systems requirements.

A Strange Kind of Compromise

The awayday attempted to reduce the tensions that had been building up in the project from the date of the first decision over the products and systems the project was to deliver. In the end a strange kind of compromise solution was to emerge that nearly resulted in the project's complete failure. The major decision taken at the meeting was to defer the launch of the new personal pension product by three months meaning that it would not be available until April 1988, while including the development of a GMP product to be launched alongside the PP

Table 7.2 *Planned product and systems launches in October 1986*

System/Product	Planned launch
Cash driven accounting system	October 1987
Personal pension	April 1988
GMP product	April 1988
Revamped self-employed pension	January 1988
On-line system executive pension	January 1988
New executive pension	January 1989

product in April 1988. In the meantime a stopgap revamped self-employed product, serving to fill the personal pension policy gap created by the legislation, would be launched in January 1988 to be in the new pensions market from day one. Further, the launch of a new executive pension would be deferred until 1 January 1989 (see Table 7.2).

This compromise was achieved by shifting 6.8 person years of IS development into post-launch work. However, considerable doubts were raised with regard to the achievement of the cash driven accounting system by its target date of 1 October 1987. Indeed, the PM more or less admitted that this was impossible when he wrote in a report to the senior management team that this target 'appears very difficult to achieve'. And without actually officially deferring the project, he announced that the Project Committee was 'looking at the possibility of adapting our existing accounting system for use as an interim measure from 1.1.88'.

The Steering Committee Objects

In their review of the awayday in October 1986 the SC raised a number of queries and criticisms. For example, the Sales and Marketing AGM noted that his division wanted to launch as many products as possible together thus achieving their 'big bang' publicity strategy. Meanwhile, the Customer Services AGM noted that the deferral of the redevelopment of the executive pension until 1989 would imply: (a) another year of operating an inefficient product at a time when he was 'being pressed very hard by the GM on minimising staff numbers', and (b) that as contracting out would be possible with executive pensions, some work would need to be done to make this possible with the existing executive pension. Subsequent estimates of the IS resource required to achieve this emerged at 3.75 person years. Given this pressure it was decided to develop on-line systems for the existing executive pension product given the 'urgent need to reduce the administration running costs of this product'.

However, the most pertinent point of the Customer Services AGM concerned the development of the GMP product. His line of argument attacked the idea that it would be easy to develop the GMP product. This idea had been based on the view that GMP would simply be a rejigged version of the new executive pension. He expressed concern because the GMP product was not to be developed before the new executive pension and he asked, 'If GMP is a scaled down version of the new executive pension how can you logically develop/launch the former before the latter?' No satisfactory answer appears to have been given to this question.

With regard to the cash driven system the SC resolved to put the PM's complicated proposals into action. These consisted of rapidly developing a basic systems outline of the project by seconding staff to the project on a full-time basis. A few weeks after this process was started, he then proposed developing a contingency solution by either reworking the old accounting system or launching a scaled-down version of the cash driven system. In order to achieve this the IS Division hired a systems design consultant with considerable expertise in developing life insurance accounting systems.

Confusion and Rescheduling

These changes in the pensions project created considerable confusion as all the work schedules had to be rearranged and new schedules for the GMP product and the systems to support it were produced. At the same time the PC was under considerable pressure to once more provide the necessary data to allow the SC to satisfy itself and the GM that the project was a viable and profitable proposition.

Despite the air of crisis at this time, however, the PM felt able to report, 'We are on the threshold of defining realistic goals and time scales which, whilst not being the ideal for every division, should enable the project to roll forward on the crest of a wave.' This was not a view shared by all divisions. Indeed, the Customer Services AGM expressed considerable alarm at the way the product/system mix had been rejigged and was particularly concerned at the prospect of the deferral of the cash driven accounting system until after the introduction of the GMP products and systems.

Profitability: Will the Project Continue?

Having appeared to reach an agreement on the systems and products to be launched from the beginning of 1988 onwards, the PC turned its attention to the pressing business of finalising the details of the core contract, which now of course had to take account of the GMP product, and tying down the constantly changing business requirements emanating from the Sales and Marketing and Customer Services Divisions. Meanwhile, the SC was increasingly concerned to prepare its presentation and justification of the entire pensions project to the GM and the Board of Directors.

With this end in mind the SC resolved to have four papers prepared in order that it might examine the staffing, profitability, project budget and sales implications of the new product and service mix the committee was in the process of agreeing. These papers were to be considered at a special SC meeting towards the end of November 1986.

Profitability and Staffing

Pensco is a mutual company, that is, it is legally owned by its policy-holders and, therefore, any profits made are redistributed as bonuses to policyholders. In 1986 the measure of an adequate return on capital investment had been set by senior management at 25 percent of the initial commission paid to sales intermediaries. To be cost justifiable, therefore, any large investment was expected to show a return of between 12 and 18 percent of the capital spent on that particular project.

In August 1986 the SC had been presented with the first report on the estimated profitability of the pensions project and the time needed to pay back its substantial development costs. At this time the minutes of the meeting noted, 'the great concern of all members of the committee' at the poor profitability figures and it was 'seriously questioned whether the project should be cancelled now'. Further, the project's management sponsor took it upon himself to inform the GM 'that the value of the project was being questioned'.

By November considerable additional work had been carried out with regard to potential sales arising from the new product releases and the profitability figures were looking considerably healthier. At this stage profits from extra sales generated by the project between 1988 and 1992 were estimated at £9.33m. This implied that the £5.6m. development cost of the project would be paid back within four years.

With regard to staffing the projections were less optimistic. Based on the assumption that administrative procedures would be improved (resulting in a staff saving of 15 percent) but remain largely unchanged particularly with regard to the division of labour between head office and branch staff, these estimated that the number of staff required would be considerably higher than that permitted by the company's 'allowable expenses' model. For example, by 1992 it was calculated that 256 staff would be required to process the projected business volume in the personal and executive pensions area whereas the allowed number of staff was 155, a difference of 101 full-time staff.

Given this finding the report on staff cost and profitability reported:

> The administration staff requirements are considerably in excess of those supported by the expense loadings in the policies. Based on the current method of administration it is not viable to proceed with the development.

In its recommendations the report argued that the profit assumptions and competitive position of the products in terms of their cost loadings could not be jeopardised. Therefore, it argued for a reduction in the number of administrative and support staff and a more efficient distribution of work between the branches and the company's head office. As a result, the SC commissioned a report into the possible means of raising administrative productivity.

While the SC meeting that considered these figures reported that 'the general view was that the payback period looked promising', the Finance AGM criticised the reports for not being 'sufficiently numerate particularly with regard to whether we could demonstrate how the Customer Services staff number would be brought within the bounds allowed by the profitability model'. Despite this warning the SC put its weight behind continuing the project although the report on staffing raised serious problems.

As it was, it was only in April 1987, four months after these initial discussions of the staffing problem, that the GM became aware that there was a serious problem relating to excess staff costs with the executive pensions product. And when this was announced one member of the SC simply suggested deferring the discussion of staff costs until the second phase of the project. The rest of committee did not agree and decided to give the 'true facts' to the GM as soon as possible. However, by this time the continued pursuit of the project had already been agreed by the Board of Directors.

In the next three months the project's main work consisted of developing the business requirements for the various products and systems being built, developing the systems overview, and the marketing and training plans while also preparing a paper seeking approval from Pensco's Board of Directors for the first phase of the project.

The First Board Paper: 12 March 1987

Since the middle of 1986 the SC had been preparing the necessary materials to present the pension project to Pensco's Board of Directors. When the project was presented in March 1987 it had already spent £861 000.

To an extent the Board paper is a *post hoc* rationalisation of the pensions project. For us it is interesting because it is the clearest portrayal and legitimation of the company's intentions under the new senior management team.

In summary, this paper set out to establish the legitimacy of the pensions project by cost justifying the project and demonstrating its strategic importance for the company. In its summary it argued that the Social Security Act created opportunities to sell personal and group pensions products. Pensco was responding to this opportunity by developing new products and administrative systems to take advantage of these opportunities.

The paper formalises a split in the project timetable and deals only with Phase 1, the key features of which were:

1. Provide a personal pension product based on the existing self-employed pension plan.
2. Provide a GMP product.
3. Enable the existing executive pension to be used for contracting out.
4. On-line data entry for the existing executive pension plan.
5. Commence design of cost-driven accounting system.
6. Provide reusable system building blocks for Phase 2 of the project and subsequent product development.

The estimated cost of developing these products and systems up until 1.4.88 was £3.81m.

The paper then stated that the personal pensions and GMP products were 'just about' profitable. However, it does not mention whether the executive pension will be profitable. Rather, it implies that it will not be profitable but failure to implement the project will result in £2.19m. lost profit on self-employed and executive pensions sales. The paper thus argues, 'Phase 1 is therefore seen as a very sound defensive measure which will give Pensco a realistic presence in all the major pensions markets.' Further, it states that all the products must be developed to maintain Pensco's claim to be 'a complete pensions office'.

In completing the summary the paper goes on to note that a second phase of the project will complete the work originally envisaged in February 1986. In other words, the pride and joy of the project, its core contract, was not to be developed until the second phase of the project. And the paper ominously noted, 'The implementation date for Phase 2 is yet to be decided and is dependent on the amount of resource allocated to it in 1988 and 1989.'

This paper was written by the GM and the IS AGM. Given the unfortunate profit figures that emerged from the cost-justification exercise they appear to have decided to sell the project by stressing its importance as a defensive measure aimed at protecting market share and ensuring that the company continued to be seen as a complete pensions office. The paper was accepted by the Board, although unfortunately we have no details of the discussion that took place.

For us a number of interesting points emerge from the paper. The first of these concerns the issue of profitability. In a company where the GM was known to have constantly chided his senior managers for their lack of quantitative precision, it comes as something of a shock to find phrases in the paper such as 'very nearly' and 'just about' profitable.

However, when all the caveats provided with these figures are taken into account it appears that there is no profit to be made. Nevertheless, no figure is presented for the estimated loss. Indeed, 'loss' is a word that is only used when referring to a failure to implement the project. But the paper tells us that the personal pensions plan 'is not profitable' and that the GMP product 'just about pays for itself over five years'. As for the executive pensions plan, failure to implement it will result in a loss of £2.19m. Further, no mention is made in the paper of the problems already alluded to with regard to bringing staff costs for administering the new products within the company's allowable expenses plans.

It appears that the shaping of the pensions project was largely accounted for at this stage by the GM's strategic decision to consolidate Pensco's position as a complete pensions office. An alternative could have been to specialise in the markets in which Pensco had considerable strength and forego the GMP development, as was initially envisaged. This path would have freed up IS resources to complete the on-line systems and concentrate on the development of new, rather than stop-gap, personal and executive pensions products. However, the force that the reorganised Sales and Marketing Division was able to exert on the project was growing all the time, and coupled with the CE's predilection for a marketing-led approach, was sufficient to change the definition of the project by mobilising a particular view of markets within the company. Once established, the commitment to GMP was a dangerous precedent for the IS and Customer Services Divisions, for as we shall see later, when the GMP market profile changed, Sales and Marketing were able to insist on major changes to the product and the development and launch of a Group Personal Pension product.

From this time on one might have imagined that with the definition of the project set and ratified by the company's highest authority, conflict over the service/product mix and the range of products to be delivered would have largely ceased. If so, one would have imagined wrongly.

The Administrative Review

The March 1987 Board paper appeared to show a clear swing back to a product-led project orientation: the presentation of the project costs suggested that nearly three-quarters of costs were accounted for by product, as opposed to service, developments. However, in the meantime the SC had been considerably shaken by the problem of squeezing the administrative costs of processing the new products into the allowable expenses permitted by the company's accounting norms. As mentioned, the SC chose not to worry the Board with regard to this matter and it appears that the GM himself was not aware of the problem until April 1987.

The administrative review issued to the SC in April 1987 which aimed to tackle this problem offered little comfort. Its main recommendation for increasing staff productivity was alarmingly simple; it consisted of issuing branch staff with a checklist of documentation required before a policy could be processed by head office staff. It argued that if all the documents were not sent to head office, the policy proposal should be returned to the branch until they were all sent together. It was hoped that this would significantly cut down on the average of nine memos per executive pension policy, exchanged by branch and head office, in order to assemble the required documentation at head office to permit the installation and processing of a policy proposal.

The administrative review was unable to place an accurate estimate on cost savings arising from this recommendation. This was due to an absence of past productivity data from which to extrapolate the potential productivity gain. It did hazard a guess, quaintly referred to as a 'ballpark figure', of a saving of 1–1.5 hours per policy (total policy installation time of 17 hours). However, it immediately added, 'This is only intended to indicate the scale of the saving and should not be taken out of context.' There was little cheer then in the administrative review for the SC.

Despite the slimness of the staff savings suggested by the administrative review it was recorded as a 'good report' in the SC minutes and its main author was charged with implementing its proposals. However, it appears to have come nowhere near achieving the scale of labour saving required by the allowable expenses model, which called for an increase in productivity of over 50 percent.

The Project Continues

At the end of March 1987 the Project Manager felt able to announce:

It is very pleasing to be able to report that the contract features and business requirements were agreed within the very tight deadline of March 31st.

Although much government legislation is still outstanding, we are in a strong position from which to move forward.

This view was not shared by the SC, and although progress was undoubtedly achieved in the following months the minutes from the SC, and the comments of the PM, register their increasing alarm at the slippage taking place within the project. There was also considerable concern with regard to the IS Division's ability to deliver the resources it had committed to the project. For example, the Sales and Marketing and Customer Services AGMs felt the division was being too ambitious.

In August 1987 the Government announced a further change in the details of the Social Security legislation. This now put back the date from which personal pensions could be sold from January 1988 to July 1988. This had considerable implications for the launch of this product at Pensco but it did not affect the bulk of IS work being done on the project.

At the same time there had been a major review of the project's progress and considerable work had been carried out to reschedule systems development as further slippage occurred. In particular, the On-Line Data Entry system for both the GMP and executive pensions products was suffering and a project budget increase was permitted to allow an additional extra four IS staff to be transferred to this part of the project.

By this time pressure in the work teams in the IS and CS divisions had become intense. Indeed, so intense that the project leader for the major part of the GMP system suffered a nervous breakdown. The dilemma of staff working in this area was not helped by the fact that despite the PM's assurance that business requirements had been finalised in March 1987, in reality these continued to change and be refined.

In October 1987 the IS Division was reporting to the senior management team that slippage on the project was running at unacceptably high levels. Authorisation was given to recruit a further four IS contract staff to work on the project.

Controlled Panic? October 1987 Board Paper

This paper was issued to the Board in order to formalise a number of decisions that had already been taken. Despite its even tone it represents the low point of the project. Substantively it announced a number of changes. Firstly, it noted the Chancellor's decision in March 1987 to bring forward the date from which personal pensions could be sold to 1 January 1988, and then his subsequent decision in August 1987 to defer this until 1 July 1988. This allowed Pensco managers to make a number of changes with regard to their product plans for the 'stopgap' personal pension.

Secondly, the paper announced the deferral for six months of the on-line systems for the executive pension product as it was felt to be unrealistic to have this system fully tested before June 1988.

Thirdly, the paper let it be known in the most sanguine tones that an experienced computer project manager had been taken on at great expense as a consultant to manage the IS Division's input into the project. This decision was taken because of 'the size of the project and the tight deadlines' and the need to allow the PM to concentrate on his overall, as opposed to divisional, responsibilities for the project.

Fourthly, the paper noted the administrative review and the implementation of its recommendations. And fifthly, it was announced that the cash driven system was now clearly seen as a Phase 2 development (i.e. it had been deferred) for the foreseeable future.

The estimated cost of the project had risen by 24 percent in this paper from £3.71m. to £4.61m. Over £300 000 of this increase was accounted for by improved IS estimates or further systems required from IS.

In the section on the repayment of the development costs the rise in the cost of the project was duly noted. There was, however, no comment on the profit situation. Instead, it would appear that the figures were left to 'speak for themselves'. That is, as in the March paper a nominal profit figure is presented alongside a cost figure. However, in the March paper when profits appeared to outstrip costs by £1m., the paper claimed that the project was 'just about profitable' and that it had to be seen as a defensive action. In the October paper the putative surplus has fallen to just £300 000. Other things being equal one would expect this to imply that the project was now less than 'just about' profitable. However, the paper is silent on this issue.

If this paper failed to make a full revelation about the changing cost and profit position of the project, it also rather skated over the redefinition of Phase 2 of the project. In the March 1987 Board paper Phase 2 consisted of the completion of the core contract and its 'underlying philosophy and bonus structure' derived from the executive pension. This also included the completion of the cash driven system. Once completed this was then to act as a springboard from which to launch a new self-employed, personal and executive contract. In the October paper this grand plan had been reduced to the launch of a new personal pension product, and as we shall see, even this modest proposal was eventually scrapped.

Growing Pressures

By the end of November 1987 the project was the centre of attention for all areas of the IS Division. Initial systems were released for system testing and appeared to be 'reasonably successful'. However, there was concern about the organisation of the testing of all the systems together and progress on the on-line data entry system, parts of which were deferred until the post-launch period. Even at this time new work was being discovered; a further 40 person weeks of IS time were estimated to be needed for one sub-section of the project.

The November SC noted its serious concern that the first system launch, the GMP quotation system, would not take place on time. This delay was immediately blamed by Customer Services, who were developing the system, on their colleagues in the Actuarial Development Department, who they claimed had not provided them with sufficient data to finalise the details in the system. The actuary at the meeting responded by saying that he would lighten the load on his junior colleague so that the latter might concentrate fully on providing the data needed. Further, the IS AGM put the actuary working on the data on a daily personal report to inform him of progress.

GMP Is Deferred

Despite these measures, in December 1987 the GMP quotation system launch was deferred for two weeks and the Sales and Marketing Division scrambled to rearrange their launch plans and publicity. The Sales and Marketing AGM stressed that it was absolutely vital that the GMP quote system be in place for launch on 18 January. Once again the junior actuaries on the project were heavily criticised and their commitment was questioned.

Despite all these recriminations and the intensification of monitoring, the GMP quote system had to be delayed for a further week. This was due to the 'somewhat fraught' process of getting the GM's approval for the Sales and Marketing product launch plans.

On 25 January the GMP quotation system was finally launched. The SC minutes noted that here there was 'a rather long list of [system] enhancements requested of GMP' still outstanding.

In the meantime, another conflict was breaking out between the sales and marketing and actuarial managers over the exact contract terms of the GMP product. A major competitor had recently launched its GMP product and the sales staff at Pensco felt their product to be uncompetitive. The actuarial staff were not keen to change the GMP contract terms because they felt the marginal profitability of the product would be adversely affected. In order to beat these objections, the sales and marketing managers on the SC argued that past projected sales and losses for the pensions products, largely constructed by marketing staff, were highly speculative and should not be allowed to overly restrict the setting of competitive terms. This made considerable space for the Sales and Marketing Division to get the terms it wanted.

Development Costs Written Off

In this it was greatly helped by the news that the GM and the Finance AGM were at this late stage, 'prepared to consider writing off the project development cost on the grounds that we have to spend it to stay in business'. That is, the profit terms were reduced from 25 percent of initial commission to 15 percent.

Meanwhile major problems were occurring around the GMP processing system. The December SC minutes noted that when IS had passed part of the system to Customer Services for testing, 'poor communication resulted in CS's reactions being significantly unfavourable'. That is, the minutes continued in slightly less verbose and diplomatic language, 'There were two [system] errors known to IS which would cause the system to crash.' Not surprisingly the system did crash repeatedly and as a result no satisfactory user testing could take place for four days.

In less fraught circumstances a four day delay might have not generated the 'significantly unfavourable impressions' of the system recorded by the CS AGM. However, at this stage in the project with only three months to go until the launch of the product processing system, there was no contingency left in any of the planning schedules. Consequently user testing and training, which always comes at the tail end of a project, was increasingly concertinaed. This constant pressure on testing and training contributed to a terrible 'foul-up' in the testing of the systems and minimum training for Head Office administrative staff, while training for branch staff was only made possible by hiring a helicopter and flying the training team around the country for three days just before the launch of the administrative systems.

The Cost of Success: GMP Administration Problems

As if this were not difficult enough, the launch of the GMP product (which could not be sold before April 1988, but for which prospective clients could be given quotations after the launch of the quotes system at the end of January) had generated five times more quotation activity than had been expected. This immediately created problems for administration because staff had to be switched from policy processing to quotation production, thus disrupting GMP installation training plans. In order to try and cope, CS also established a twilight shift to process GMP quotations.

At the same time it began to emerge that in order to boost their sales figures, Sales and Marketing were allowing their sales staff to quote contract options for the GMP product, for which the administrative systems had not been designed. Additionally, it emerged that sales staff were quoting for a number of large GMP schemes with up to 300 members, whereas the market projections and systems designs had been based on the sale of small schemes with 15–20 members.

The PM struggled to get agreement between Sales and Marketing and Customer Services over what contract features could and could not be sold. In some respects this search for agreement was rather academic for the GMP installation system had slipped yet again. In March the Steering Committee noted, 'IS sickness and other factors combined to defer the February release [of the system] until March which leaves us the almost impossible task to thoroughly test the system before it goes live.' Not only was there a problem with system testing, there also was a major problem with developing the system itself. Indeed, as more and more development work emerged in the last six months before launch, the consultant Project Manager increasingly deferred parts of the system development to the post-launch period. Thus, when the system was launched it was full of errors, had no correction facility, lacked features that had to be completed by manual intervention, and administrative staff were largely left to themselves to work out how to use it.

This deferral of parts of the system was a great worry to Customer Services for it reduced the effectiveness of their administrative procedures and put great pressure on staff. It also exacerbated the staff shortages being registered due to the difficulty of installing new policies, the higher than expected sales of the policies, and the selling of policy features for which there were no established clerical or computer procedures. All of which was further complicated by an Association of British Insurers' initiative, announced in February 1988, which changed the way GMP contracts were to be processed and which threatened to take away 20–40 percent of Pensco's potential GMP sales.

Increasing confusion and conflicting priorities coupled with the approach of the 'system go live' dates created immense pressures throughout the company. By December the IS Division was reporting that the IS team was 'stretched' (i.e. staff were working seven day weeks), that new work was constantly appearing (the amount of which 'is much greater than previously expected') and that a number of IS staff had resigned. This latter development had disastrous consequences for one of the system building blocks, the launch of which had to be deferred for first, six weeks and then, six months. By March 1988 the project was hanging on by the 'skin of its teeth'.

The Sales and Marketing Offensive

Yet Sales and Marketing, who had considerably increased their presence on the SC, were still pressing for the development of new products. In particular, after some initial uncertainty with regard to the legality of their proposal, the division's senior managers began to press for the development of a Group Personal Pension Product to go alongside the GMP product. In March 1988, with no systems to support this product, the SC agreed to develop it. However, at the March meeting where this was agreed, the Customer Services AGM relayed some very bad news to the SC. Namely, it had been 'discovered' at a meeting between CS and IS that the demand on IS resources for 1988 and 1989 outstripped supply by some 40 person years, an overshoot of 31 percent. This discovery was remarkable given the IS Division's boast with regard to its planning prowess and revealed the project to be dangerously close to being completely out of control.

In retrospect it seems that the IS resource shortfall developed because: (a) the pensions project was running considerably over budget; (b) considerable parts of the original Phase 1 systems agreed in October 1987 had been quietly slipped into a growing post-launch system schedule; (c) changes in perceptions of the market and the type and size of GMP contracts being sold required further system enhancements; (d) changes in market perceptions also now required further product development, namely the Group PPP; and finally (e) it appears that no one had considered the need to develop a GMP renewals system to be in place by April 1989 in order to process contract renewals.

The meeting where this shortfall was discussed was tense. Indeed, it broke down into a 'slanging match' at times, where tempers became extremely frayed. Its major outcome was to agree the development of the Group PPP product and the necessary adjustments to the GMP system to cater for large schemes. It was also decided to defer, yet again, the original on-line development for the executive pensions product to some time in 1989. All short-term systems developments aimed at raising labour productivity in different divisions of the company were also deferred. These developments were of great concern to the CS AGM who noted that the deferral of the on-line system would cost the company an extra £200 000 per annum in clerical costs, that the Group PPP product would be extremely expensive to administer, and that the IS resource shortfall would lead to the deferral of the major project to renew Pensco's computer system infrastructure.

SUMMARY AND CONCLUSION

This chapter provides a narrative account of the development of a market-sensitive information system. And although the majority of the systems discussed were launched more or less to date, it reveals the often chaotic process by which this questionable result (see Chapter 8) was achieved. Indeed, far from being a replication of textbook systems development method, Pensco's pension project reveals itself beneath the bluster of an aggressive and sometimes confused masculinity, to have often bordered on barely controlled panic.

The account of this project has a number of salient features. Firstly, it highlights the difficulty with which the Steering and Project Committees arrived at a fixed and clear definition of the project's aims. Throughout the project, both the products and systems to be launched changed as perceptions of markets, Pensco's systems infrastructure, and system development potential changed. This change was a condition and consequence of the shifting relative political strengths of competing factions within the company. At times an IS logic, determined to place Pensco systems on a firm footing, appeared to dominate. But this was repeatedly squashed by the force of the Marketing Department and the GM's known support for a sales maximising strategy.

Secondly, the project illustrates the way in which apparently formal and well-policed rules were tacitly or explicitly overturned when this was deemed necessary. Thus, for example, when the profitability of the project defined by Pensco accounting procedures appeared in doubt the GM simply changed the rules by which profitability was measured. Perhaps less blatantly, concern over the project's inability to stay within the company's allowable future expenses was first hidden from the Board of Directors and then satisfied by proposals that patently could not achieve the productivity improvements expected of them. This not only highlights the flexibility of apparently non-transgressable boundaries at Pensco. It also suggests a strong tension between a masculine managerial subjectivity intent on establishing controlling rules and regulations and a deeper uncertainty only made apparently controllable by the transgression of those rules and regulations and the quest for certainty and control they represented.

Thirdly, we note the tensions that dogged the project from the start. These were manifested in open hostility between different managerial functions involved in the project and are the focus of subsequent chapters (see Chapter 9 in particular) in the book.

Having here outlined the problems encountered by the pensions project through its tortured development, we now proceed to analyse the way in which the project was assessed by its different managerial, staff and clerical participants. This reveals that very different assessments of the project's success and failure were made.

8

Separate Realities: Pensco's Different Pensions Projects

INTRODUCTION

In earlier chapters we have argued that reality is socially constructed. Sometimes there is a general consensus on the reality that is thus constructed. At other times, different groups and individuals construct contrasting versions of reality that are in conflict with one another.

By now it should be clear that reality construction within the pensions project at Pensco was an increasingly contested terrain of political activity. Different departments, functions and levels of the organisation had widely differing reality constructs when it came to the assessment of the project's achievements as a major system development.

In this chapter we will examine some of these constructs. In part, we do this to show the diverse, even separate, realities that co-existed within Pensco at the same time. We also do it in order to illustrate how reality is bound up with people's position in the organisation, their immediate experiences and their identities.

The existence of apparently separate realities around the same systems development project does not imply that each of these had equal validity in the eyes of Pensco management. Rather, as we shall see, managers mobilised their substantial resources to create a dominant reality for their staff that marginalised those discordant and less comfortable understandings of the pensions project. But we will also see that while 'the management' was united around this dominant reality construct for presentational purposes to staff and the outside world, it was also deeply divided in its assessment of the project and the problems that beset it. In particular, there was considerable manoeuvring around the official management report on the costs and achievements of the project.

In some ways, this was the culmination of the blame displacement activities that intensified as the project's problems multiplied.

This chapter starts with senior management's hi-tech presentation of the pensions project and its associated products to all Pensco head office staff. We sharply contrast the slick triumphalism of this event, which was as stage managed as a 1980s Tory Party Conference, with the reality of clerical staff processing one of the pensions products on the new systems.

We then move on to examine the official management assessment of the project. The first version of this report was rejected by the senior management team and we look at the reasons behind this rejection and the subtle changes in the second version of the report that shifted the blame more squarely on to the shoulders of the IS Division. Lastly we will examine the Project Manager's own understanding of the project.

This chapter, then, is an examination of the multiple constructions of the pensions project. The emergence of these different constructs was not surprising given the problems associated with, and the intense politics surrounding, the project. It also accords with social constructionist theories of technology (e.g. Bijker et al, 1987) which argue that technologies in the making are characterised by great 'interpretive flexibility'. Thus, for example, the technology we now know as the bicycle (a two wheeled, steel framed pneumatic tyred means of transport) took a long time to emerge as different conceptions of the bicycle which were more or less appropriate to their use were developed by manufacturers. However, at a certain point technology crystallised around a consensus which defined the bicycle as we know it today (Pinch and Bijker, 1987). As such, interpretative flexibility is closed down, or at least greatly reduced. The development of the mountain bike and track bikes built out of composite materials has again opened up the interpretative flexibility of the bicycle and is a particularly good illustration of the links between technological design and new or innovative social usages.

Our case here differs somewhat from that of the bicycle or other case studies presented by social constructivist perspectives (e.g. Hughes, 1987). This is because there were no different competing material pensions systems in existence at Pensco. Rather, there was one system in terms of its actual code. But there were a number of different constructions of this system and little or no consensus was evident during the development of the system. In this chapter we see the beginning of a process of closure of interpretative flexibility around the pensions system, as an official construction of the project is fought out between different management functions and senior management mobilise, what they hoped would be, a dominant view of the pensions system.

In the case presented here the importance of organisational position and power in this process of closure are evident. This contrasts sharply with the work of other social constructivists' analyses of technology (e.g. the case in Bijker et al, 1987) which have been criticised for their failure to theorise the role of power in technology development and diffusion (Russell, 1986).

Our analysis is built around an analysis of power and politics in organisations. We differ from many critical analyses of technology and power (e.g. Braverman, 1974) by focusing on inter-managerial power conflicts (see Armstrong, 1985, 1987), more than those between managerial and non-managerial labour.

At times the disjuncture between different pension project realities at Pensco was acute. For example, the difference between the senior management team's construction of the project as a 'success' and the crisis in GMP processing was huge. This created considerable stress within Pensco and particularly within the GMP processing unit.

GMP staff and junior managers were not in a position to impose their view of the project on Pensco. Indeed, senior management did not want to hear about it. This did not mean, though, that GMP staff were powerless to act. Resistance was possible but generally indirect and, therefore, always open to alternative interpretations. However, a disproportionately large number of staff left the GMP unit through internal transfers or promotions. Junior and middles managers had less flexibility in this regard and reacted, in some cases, by prolonged absences from work. (Absenteeism through illness has always been seen as an alternative to 'active resistance' in the industrial relations literature (Eldridge, 1967) for such absences can be interpreted as a person's body 'speaking out' and resisting when other courses of action appear to be ruled out.)

MARKETING THE PROJECT

Despite the increasing panic, stress and confusion of the pensions project the various systems were launched more or less on time. As we have seen, the GMP quotation system was three weeks late but apart from this the other quotation and processing systems were launched on schedule. However, the quality and completeness of the systems launched left much to be desired.

The progress of the project had affected different divisions in the company to varying degrees. Sales and Marketing communicated considerable enthusiasm from their sales staff and regional sales managers for the idea of the project and the selling opportunities it was expected to provide. However, this enthusiasm was also tempered by the realisation within the sales force that the project was not going to plan, as evidenced in the frequent changes made to the range of products to be launched.

Within the Customer Services Division there was less enthusiasm for the pensions project. It implied retraining and reorganisation and there was a fear among managers that the division would be left to 'carry the can' with regard to the evident failings of the project in terms of the delivery of unfinished systems and a consequent failure to achieve the targeted processing times and service levels set for the division by the GM.

Demoralisation was rife among system development staff and they felt that the huge effort they were making was either being squandered or not fully appreciated, as will be seen later. The senior management team was very keen that the launch of the new products not only made the maximum impact in the marketplace but also contributed to staff motivation and commitment within the company head office and branch network. With this latter objective in mind a plan was drawn up to present the new products to all head office staff.

Attendance at this presentation, held in Seatown's largest cinema in May 1988, was compulsory for all Pensco staff and managers. Indeed, the pensions Project Manager was informed that he was to attend both presentations. Staff and managers were told to be at the presentation 10 minutes before it began, that latecomers would not be allowed entry and that their names would be taken and reported to their divisional managers.

On entry into the cinema, staff were greeted by their senior management team lined up along either side of the stairway leading up to the foyer. Young Pensco women staff had been posted as ushers to guide people to their seats in the cinema to the sound of classical music.

At 2.00 p.m. precisely the lights in the cinema were dimmed and spotlights picked out the stage set specially produced for the presentation. This consisted of three-dimensional logos of the new Pensco products and the name of the company flashed up on a large screen in electric greens and blues.

To the accompaniment of rock music the IS AGM ascended the stage and stood picked out by spotlight at the high tech podium, complete with autocue, to the right of the 3-D product logos. He welcomed staff to the presentation and proceeded to introduce and congratulate the teams who had developed the pensions projects and systems. In so doing, he showered praise on the new products, emphasised their success and the success of the core system/core contract ideal, the cost of developing them and the difficulties created by legislative and regulatory changes. A small slide show of key team members then played, with voice-overs explaining the excitement and the challenge of the project.

The IS AGM was followed by the Finance AGM. He attempted to maintain the momentum of the presentation by introducing the new contracts and their salient features. Unfortunately, he had big problems with the autocue. At times his halting presentation came to a dead stop and silence reigned in the hushed auditorium.

Thankfully, this acutely embarrassing passage was ended by the Sales and Marketing AGM taking to the podium. He had a more jovial and relaxed manner than the Finance AGM and set about addressing the assembled staff with relish. In particular, he was anxious to stress the goals of the pension project, namely to sell £50m. worth of pensions contracts by the end of the year. His speech was punctuated by a slide show that presented the company as a football team on the road to victory. At one stage in the middle of the slide presenting the Pensco team the message 'The Will to Win' was flashed incessantly at the audience.

The Customer Services AGM then introduced the improvements that had been made in the Customer Services Division with regard to service standards and made great play of the training provided for staff working on the new contracts.

Finally, the General Manager took to the stage to reiterate the wonderful products developed, the success of the pensions project and the great market prospects facing the company. His speech stressed the centrality of Pensco people to the success of the project: people were the company's greatest asset, they were the Pensco team, and it was 'all of us together' stepping forward into an era of unprecedented Pensco firsts.

The overall impact of this presentation with its mixture of sanctions (compulsory attendance), and sugary, if macho (football), team building, instrumental group psychology and high tech graphics, slides and rock music was powerful. Staff emerged from the darkness of the cinema dazed and bemused. IS staff we talked to were particularly bemused because they found it very difficult to link the presentation, which stressed the successful implementation of a carefully conceived and controlled project, with the organisational reality they had been living with day and night for the past year. Indeed, it seemed as if senior management and IS staff in the same company occupied separate worlds and realities right there on the same project. The following day the IS Strategy Manager commented: 'There are two pensions projects: the one I heard about yesterday at the presentation and the one I normally hear about.'

This sense of separateness was also very strong when a couple of weeks later we went to visit clerical staff working on the processing of the new GMP contracts. For here we did not find the bright new world of Pensco 'firsts' or the 'all of us together' attitudes mouthed by the GM at the presentation. Here we found women clerical staff surrounded by mounds of paper attempting to install the GMP policies on computer systems that were remarkable for their incompleteness.

DOWN IN THE ENGINE ROOM: PROCESSING PENSIONS

From our reading of the Pensco case different layers and functions of management often construct diverse and sometimes opposed views of organisational reality. This was clearly illustrated in the disjuncture between senior management's presentation of the systems developed by the pension project and IS staff and junior managers' experience of developing these systems. It also came to light when we visited the clerical area processing the new GMP product quotations and proposals. While the all male senior management sang the praises of the new products, female clerical staff and supervisors were struggling with the consequences of the project's deeper failings.

According to the GMP team leader, her male managers were only concerned to meet the service targets agreed between their AGM and the senior management team:

> They don't have a grasp of what's going on. They just want the figures. They don't appreciate our problems. I wish they'd acknowledge there is one. I despair sometimes.

Rather than acknowledging the very real problems with the computer system and clerical work organisation, managers were simply concerned to get the work out, to get hold of 'the figures'. Consequently staff were under increasing pressure:

> We're expected to do a lot more now. We used to be able to fight over work. Work pressures have increased and we're working lots of overtime and coming in on Saturdays.

The appalling state of the system staff were using and the fact that Sales and Marketing were selling permutations of the product which clerical staff were not equipped to administer led to a generalised feeling that 'someone has it in for us'. These pressures gave rise to a series of prolonged middle and junior managerial absences from work 'for personal reasons' in the GMP processing department. For example, the departmental manager was absent from work for over two months just after the launch of the system. The section leader was also away from the office during this period for 'personal reasons' and both team leaders were due to leave the section, one having found a job elsewhere, the other having gained an internal promotion. Clearly, the GMP administration section was an area of Pensco to be avoided at all costs in the months following the launch of the product.

These staff absences, the huge delays in processing the GMP product, and the processing time of 27 hours rather than the hoped for 14 hours, eventually created such a crisis of confidence that a senior review of the area was conducted. In a classic piece of Pensco-speak this concluded:

> The system is perceived as not reflecting the business needs, and being difficult to use. The perception may overstate the reality, but this is irrelevant in the sense that staff morale is based on the perception, not the reality.

In the garbled tongue of Pensco-speak this comment can be taken as a criticism of the GMP system. However, in its attempts to bridge the yawning chasms between the different worlds of the clerical staff, the IS system developers, and the Steering Committee, the authors of the review highlight the difference between GMP staff 'perceptions' and a Pensco 'reality'. In effect, the statement says: clerical staff perceive the system to be bad. However, this does not mean the system is really bad. But given that this perception is the clerical staff's reality it has definite consequences for labour productivity in the section due to poor morale, prolonged supervisor absences and staff and managers leaving the department. Thus, although clerical staff's perception of reality is not 'real' it has real effects of which senior management need to take note. This management did, but the General Manager, desperate to restrict the growth of staff numbers at Pensco, refused to allow the recruitment or transfer of staff to work on the mounting backlog in the section.

AN OFFICIAL ASSESSMENT

In June 1988 we spoke to the IS AGM, who held overall responsibility for the project. He tersely stated that the project has scored 7 out of 10, that he was unsure if the concept of the reusable systems building blocks would work and that his major concern was to ensure that the necessary post-launch and renewal systems were developed by the end of 1989. The extent of this work, the pressing problems with regard to the company's long-term system plans and the massive gap between IS resources available and demands upon them had forced him to scrap completely the second phase of the pensions project.

The IS AGM was unwilling to be drawn on a more detailed discussion of the project and appeared ill at ease. Perhaps this was because plans were under way to present a paper to the senior management team on the achievements and costs of the project. This paper, written by the IS Project Manager, was initially presented to the team in September 1988 and rejected. The minutes for this meeting tersely note that this version of the paper was 'withdrawn and referred back to the Steering Committee'. In a slightly different form the paper was re-presented in October 1988 and 'duly noted' by the management team.

These Costs and Achievements documents are the most official and senior assessment of the pensions project to take place and they make fascinating reading. In particular, it is revealing to examine the difference between the first and second versions of the paper presented to the senior management team. The first version of the paper was written by the Project Manager; the second by the PM and the Management Sponsor, the IS AGM.

Here we refer to these documents as Take I (the first version) and Take II (the second version). We use this language, with its allusion to film making because the documents can be seen as a potted history or film of the project, that is, as an attempt to construct and define its reality. And, like firms, the positioning of the camera and the form of the script make subtle differences to the way that reality is constructed.

Both documents were written within a set Pensco standard: a summary, achievements versus the plan, costs, and a series of appendices with more detailed information. These included a clear breakdown of project costs and made very visible the percentages by which different divisions exceeded their allocated costs. In overall terms, costs were 8.6 percent greater than estimated. The real damage, though, was revealed in the 27 percent overshot by IS. In sharp contrast, Sales and Marketing and Customer Services actually underspent by 9 percent and 10 percent respectively.

The subtle differences between Take I and Take II regarded the manner in which Take I glossed over the costs of the project while boasting its successes. In particular, Take I made light of the particular problems encountered in the IS Division and in so doing minimised the IS AGM and Project Manager's pain.

Take I begins:

> Overall, this development was very successful in that all the products, literature and key systems required on the launch date were ready when required.

It continues by noting that the only objective 'which will be missed' is the on-line system for the executive pension. This is a considerable gloss on the way the project progressed and the systems were launched. For example, one vital sub-system of the GMP system was launched six weeks after the launch of the product and many parts of the system were simply deferred into the post-launch period.

Take II does not address these omissions directly but rather modifies the claims of Take I. Thus, the same opening sentences are used with the following changes: 'very successful' has become 'successful' and 'which will be missed' has become 'missed'. Now these changes may seem largely insignificant but for the managers involved they signalled a considerable defeat. In order to soften the pain of this defeat and legitimise the less than 'very successful' conclusion of the project, two face-saving paragraphs are inserted in Take II after the above sentences. The first stressed that the project was the biggest undertaken by Pensco and involved the equivalent of 110 person years of effort which included 14 000 hours of overtime, half of which was unpaid. The second was an appeal for special circumstances to be taken into consideration. It said:

> Achieving what we did proved to be no easy task. This was partly due to the sheer size of the undertaking and also because changes to the legislation were still occurring up until February 1988.

The summary was followed by an assessment of Achievements versus The Plan. Take I noted, 'it is pleasing to report that all the products, literature and installations systems required on the launch dates were ready when required' thus achieving four of the five objectives documented in the October 1987 Board paper. The qualifier is added that, due to events beyond the company's control, 'some systems facilities originally planned, but not essential, for launch were installed on a phased basis until October 1988'.

In Take II we find that the 'pleasing' discovery of Take I has been considerably toned down. The Project Manager and his Management Sponsor are no longer 'pleased to report'; rather, they are now able to 'draw some satisfaction' from the project's achievements and they have been forced to admit that a number of post-launch system enhancements had not been completed by October 1988. Indeed 'some are still outstanding [and] this has resulted in an adverse knock-on effect to the development of computer systems for GMP renewals'.

Again, these changes may seem insignificant but Pensco managers rarely talked publicly about 'adverse effects', even if these could be attributed to events beyond the company's control. These changes, then, were a source of considerable pain and embarrassment to the two men (the IS AGM and Project Manager) with the most at risk from the senior management assessment of the pensions project.

The reports continued by detailing the costs of the project. Take I revealed an overspend for the project as a whole of 8.6 percent with an overspend for the IS division of 27 percent. In Take II the same figures are presented but a note has appeared under them. This reveals that if the cost of the on-line executive pensions system is removed from the estimated cost of the project, as this was never developed, then 'the adverse variance becomes –39% for Information Services and –13% for the overall project.' However, it is unclear which figure is to be taken as the more 'real'. Suffice it to say that Take I did not give its potential reader the possibility of exercising this magnitude of interpretative flexibility.

The three reasons given for the occurrence of the overspend are: legislative and marketplace changes, underestimation of GMP on-line development times, and the underestimation of the time needed to test the project sub-systems and ensure that they fitted together correctly.

There then followed more detailed figures for the various under- and overspends recorded in the project. Here we find the greatest overspend is the GMP development. This was estimated at 583 person weeks and ended up requiring 966 person weeks, a figure that does not include the considerable amount of development work pushed into the post-launch period. The explanation for this overshoot is as follows:

> Severely underestimated as very little information on which to base estimates. In addition, business requirements were not agreed and some were not fully understood before development began. The subsequent changes caused extra work. Few staff had an understanding of group pensions business.

Nearly all other areas of the Information Services side of the project suffered overspends with the exception of the team developing the 'stopgap' personal pensions project, which eventually accounted for over 400 person weeks of effort. The explanation for the majority of the overspends appears to be problems with estimating, relations with users and to a lesser extent changes in the legislation. This is interesting because in the main body of the paper the overspend is largely attributed to events beyond the company's control. In the more detailed analysis it appears that overspends were generated within the company, rather than from without. For example, the amazing 885 percent overrun on overall system testing was put down to the fact that the 'technique to test that all the developments fitted together had not been thought through in September 1987'.

The last appendix in the documents lists the amounts of overtime worked by the various departments in the project. Sales and Marketing present the astonishing figure of 40 hours of paid overtime and 2250 hours unpaid overtime, and added that the hours of their three top managers had not been included in this figure. Customer Services recorded 3000 hours of paid overtime and 1400 of unpaid, while the IS Division worked 4487 hours of paid overtime and 1392 hours of unpaid overtime. In addition, the Project Manager estimates that he worked 700 hours of overtime on the project, of which not one hour was paid at overtime rates.

It is possible to interpret these overtime figures in a number of ways. On the one hand, they seem to be used to show how devoted the managers are to the company. On the other, they illustrate the number of free hours the company has managed to obtain from its workforce.

As already mentioned, the second version of the Costs and Achievements document was 'duly noted' by the Senior Management Team. It represented a considerable dilution of the project's much trumpeted 'success' and reflected unfavourably on the IS Division.

A PROBLEM OF TECHNIQUE?

We now turn to a consideration of the Project Manager's rather less public analysis of the project and problems it encountered. This analysis was presented in two documents and revealed in our interviews with the Project Manager.

By the end of 1987 the Project Manager seemed worn out and devoid of enthusiasm. One felt that he was ready to accept the inevitable accusing fingers pointed at him even though he knew that he was being made a scapegoat. His manner of speech, his false laughter and his forced yawns, betrayed a sense of detachment and distance from the project and his role in it.

When Pensco was forced to hire the consultant Project Manager to save the pensions project, the General Manager asked Pensco's Project Manager to write him a letter detailing the problems besetting the project. In this letter the Project Manager identified two key problems. The first concerned his own managerial role in the project; the second raised the thorny issue of system development estimates.

The Project Manager identified his dual role in the project, as both Project Manager and Project Committee representative for IS, as the first major problem. This dual role came to be referred to as the 'two hats' problem and caused considerable resentment and unease among IS staff and other personnel working on the project. The Project Manager believed the 'two hats' role led him to lose sight of his departmental role; that is, his role as the representative of the IS Division and, more particularly, the Pensions Business Systems Department within IS. This division of his loyalties had considerable consequences for his colleagues. However, this was not the

Project Manager's major concern. He thought that by losing sight of his departmental role he had allowed prevarication over key decisions to delay and then compress the time schedules to which his systems personnel were constrained to work. This failing caused the project to 'sink'.

> Sink, not sink but cause us great problems. We all got sucked one level down [We] took our eyes off the completion date and overall plans; what should have been done in mid-June 1986 was still dragging on into early August; by the time I picked up and responded to it, it was already too late.

The second problem identified by the PM concerned the system development estimates. In his view these had gone 'haywire'. This was in part caused by the inherent and recognised difficulty of estimating system development times and costs. But it was exacerbated because the PM and his colleagues did not realise that one product (the Group Money Purchase pension) was fundamentally different from another (the Executive Pension Plan). Consequently, they estimated the development time for GMP and its attendant systems by taking the estimated costs for the Executive Pension Product and saying, 'it will be like that plus a bit'. This resulted in a huge underestimate of the resources required to develop the systems.

With regard to the estimating problem the PM commented with resignation:

> One's got to say, one's [yawns] got to find a better way of estimating. Thank you very much [big laugh]. Easier said than done.

This tendency to underestimate was common at Pensco and in many system development projects and is usually explained by reference to insufficient knowledge and communication or absence of technique (see Sharrock and Andersen, 1993), although estimating is also an area of political activity. The underestimate had a number of consequences with regard to the pensions project. In the first place, it caused planning problems because plans were forever being rescheduled as key decisions were missed or delayed. In the second place it gave the project an increasingly bad image as more and more IS personnel were 'sucked in' from other projects. Indeed, the project was viewed as a bottomless pit, a 'black hole' into which energies, personalities and careers were fast disappearing. IS staff did not want to work on the project. Its ill-defined and ever-changing contours created the sensation that it had no sharp edges and that it was devoid of manageable bits 'you could get your arms around'. It had taken on a life of its own and an insatiable appetite for IS resources.

In his letter of contribution to the General Manager the PM suggested that the 'two hats' problem could have been solved by keeping a check on the overall progress of the project at all times: a responsibility that, although he refrained from mentioning it, perhaps lay with the project Steering Committee and the Management Sponsor as much as with the PM. Indeed, it was the IS AGM's determination to maximise his control of the project as management sponsor that led to the 'two hats' phenomenon in the first place.

In a later document detailing the 'lessons' of the project for the IS division, the PM returned to consider the problem of estimating. Now he no longer blamed the difficulty of estimating on to some inherent problem with all estimating. Instead, analysis focused on specific events at Pensco. In particular, he returned (perhaps under the influence of the consultant PM) to consider the setting of business requirements, system specifications and IS schedules. With regard to business requirements the PM noted:

> There is no standard structure for specifying business requirements [at Pensco]. In particular, a 'top down' approach should have been adopted whereby the key requirements affecting system design were identified first.

This absence of a formal method of collecting and analysing business requirements gave rise to a situation where 'IS did not really analyse'. Instead, the IS staff on the project, *'tended just to ask the users what they wanted and then program it'*. This surprisingly informal manner of working might have been sufficient on a small, well-defined and stable project. However, the pensions project was large and unstable. And when new products were required of the project, the full implications of these changes were not examined. Thus, for example, the document stated that when the GMP product was added to the list of products to be developed:

> We should have stopped the IS design work and specifically assessed the impact of this new item on the key requirements.

For anyone labouring under the illusion that systems development at Pensco was an exact or even inexact science, embodying an infallible rationality, this assessment will have come as a shock. Estimates were not accurate at Pensco, according to the PM, because IS staff neither knew nor analysed what they were supposed to be developing in any detail. Instead, they asked the users what they wanted and then programmed it!

This allowed prevarication over the setting of these requirements such that the necessary time to develop the systems required was increasingly compromised. The documents make this point in the following fashion:

> IS and CS lost their way from April to August '87. IS said they could not produce a [systems development] schedule until they had the business requirements from CS. Without a schedule it was very difficult to establish when the project was becoming impossibly tight. Future projects must insist on IS doing a schedule to launch, albeit at a very high level, so that everyone is aware of when the key business requirements need to be defined by.

Evidently there is chicken-and-egg problem here. On the one hand, IS needed to produce a schedule that in effect estimated the time and resources required to produce a particular system. On the other hand, it appeared difficult, if not impossible, to produce such a schedule without estimates based on a detailed specification of the systems development work required. Yet without this schedule there was the danger that the business requirements setting process would drag on to such an extent that the time left to develop the necessary systems would be compromised. In effect, it seems that the development of an IS Division systems development schedule was an important political device, that is, it would have established the date by which business requirements had to be tied down if the necessary systems were to be developed by the project's completion date. But IS did not want to produce this until CS had given them the business requirements from which they could have begun to estimate the resources and time needed to develop specific systems. In effect, IS would not commit themselves until CS had committed themselves. And CS probably did not want to limit their room for manoeuvre by tying themselves to tightly defined business requirements when these were likely to change unexpectedly. One consequence of this situation was the 'sinking' of the project as it drifted down through uncharted waters.

Part of the problem here lay in CS and IS ignorance of GMP products and the systems needed to support them, as the PM's 'lessons' were at pains to point out. However, at the time the PM and his senior project leaders appear to have been unaware of this lack of experience because they failed to enquire as to the difference between a group and individual pension scheme. Instead, they simply continued to design their systems without analysing the impact of the inclusion of a group pension scheme. And if this were not enough to threaten the viability of the project, we then learn that no system specification was developed for the GMP processing system. Not surprisingly this resulted in the omission of 'various items', such as data validation, from the systems development schedule which were later and unexpectedly to emerge from the 'woodwork' of the project in the final months before the launch of the products.

The version of the project explicated by the PM for more limited circulation in the IS Division is surprisingly candid and differs considerably from that presented to the senior management team. To an outsider the PM's analysis looks like an admission of failure and incompetence stripped clean of extenuating external circumstance.

For the PM the problems outlined above had two significant consequences: firstly, the system lost some of its hoped for flexibility; secondly, the credibility of the IS Division within the company suffered. This had a negative impact on the morale of hard pressed IS staff.

In late 1987 the PM was well aware that his staff were upset but he was not sure how upset they were. He thought that IS staff were thinking, 'you don't really know where you're going sort of touch'. But he was not sure. He wanted to ask them. He would have loved to ask 'the troops' what they felt. He did not because,

> They don't always give you the right answer. They give you the wrong vibes. The vibe coming through is: 'we don't really know what we're doing'.

So although the PM wanted to ask 'the troops' he did not because he was afraid of what they might say. Instead, he relied on his ability to 'pick up vibes' which suggested his staff felt at a loss and out of control: the 'you don't know where you're going sort of touch'. As we shall see later, this was indeed the case.

A STRATEGIC SUCCESS

Success is clearly a relative measure in organisational life. Success is also a crucial attribute of the competent manager and was a particularly valued resource at Pensco. The arrival of the new General Manager had placed managers under great pressure to produce tangible successes. Indeed, in the new performance-related assessment of senior and middle managers there was no room for failure; nor was there a sense that mistakes were inevitable and part of an important learning experience. It is not surprising then that the pensions project was hailed as such a success by managers united in their fear of failure. Hence 'facts' and 'figures' were constructed in their most favourable light within the predominant accounting rules at Pensco and a bright gloss was painted over the omissions, deferrals, and expanding post-launch systems schedule.

The secret of success lies in the fact that if enough people believe something is a success then it really is a success. At Pensco it was vital for the company and for managerial careers that the pensions project was a success. And, hence, it was. It may not have been a complete success, but 7 out of 10 was not bad.

As researchers we are perhaps not in a position to say what does or does not constitute a success. However, in this last section of the chapter we are interested in constructing a different reality of the project's success which is less flattering to Pensco and its managers, based as it is on the perceptions of other less privileged actors, in particular, IS staff and junior managers at Pensco.

One of the new GM's primary concerns at Pensco was to introduce tight planning procedures, divisional budgeting and strategic management. In so doing he hoped to 'bed down' his new senior management team. Allied to this was his concern to drive Pensco towards a marketing-led approach in order to protect the company's reduced market share in key pensions markets.

In the middle 1980s following the Fowler White Paper the GM determined that Pensco would do all that was necessary to capitalise on the anticipated boom in the personal pensions market. Thus he pushed through a decision to drop the development of a Universal Whole of Life product in favour of pension product and system development. As such, short- and medium-term strategy focused around the launch of a new range of pensions products in early 1988.

To the outside world this strategy objective was achieved amidst a carefully orchestrated fanfare of publicity. The senior management team also attempted to convince Pensco staff that the pensions project was nothing if not a success. As we have seen this view was promulgated by compulsory attendance at the product presentation ceremony. Even within the senior management team, strenuous efforts were made to sing the glories of the pensions products and their associated systems while playing down, ignoring or simply being unaware of the project's 'real' and potential long-term costs.

To the outside world the pensions strategy met its first objective. That it could only do this by breaking the rules established by the self-same GM with regard to profitability and allowable expenses was a less widely reported cost. Furthermore, it was only by the massive shifting of launch to post-launch systems development that the project, as least from an IS perspective, could be seen to have reached its objectives. With regard to the latter point the transfer of masses of development work into the post-launch period also served to obscure the real financial costs of the project. Junior managers in the IS division were unsure if the GM was cognisant of this situation. Said one manager,

What I don't know is how much the General Manager is aware of the post-launch work … Sometimes I wonder if he realises that although the budget and timetable are being met the amount of actual ballast that is going to be in his bucket when he gets it is going to be a great deal smaller than he thinks. And there will be this rather unpalatable time when he realises, and possibly the Board realises, that the amount of stuff in post-launch is enormous and far greater than ever intended.

Of course, the pensions strategy not only aimed to get front-end computer systems established in time for the launch of the new products. It was also intended to embody a new product and system philosophy based on a flexible core contract and reusable systems modules. This, it was hoped, would allow the rapid development of products in the second phase of the project. However, as we have seen this second phase was eventually scrapped.

In later chapters we will enquire further in this area. Suffice it to say here that it was unclear if the core contract as envisaged was ever developed. Staff and managers were sceptical of this and even the Project Manager did not appear convinced that it had been. Similarly, it is doubtful if the objective of creating discrete systems building blocks applicable to a range of products was achieved. The IS AGM, usually one to stress the positive, could only say that it 'remained to be seen' if this objective had been achieved.

Beneath the apparent success of Pensco's strategy in the pensions area lurked a number of failings. This is hardly surprising given the constant changes taking place in the legislation and the project's inability to decide about, and stick to, a range of products when confronted with changing views of their potential markets. Indeed, in our interviews with other insurance companies many IS managers commented on the massive strains imposed by senior managements keen to exploit the new market opportunities offered to them by the Government.

What we find striking, if not surprising, is the manner in which within Pensco management invested such energy into the manufacture of the successful outcome of the project. This, of course, concerned the substantive work of developing software, sales literature and proposal forms, etc. But it also concerned a particular way of constructing the successes and costs of the project. This at times acknowledged problems but on the whole these either did not come to light within the management team or were buried. From our understanding of managerial practice, we would expect this to be the case but were surprised at the actual extent to which problems remained concealed or deflected. It cannot be said with confidence whether or not this was peculiar to Pensco. We would suggest, however, that the particular managerial style invoked and enforced by the GM was inimitable to the 'open' discussion and assessment of the more intractable problems facing the company. And this was compounded in the systems area by a particular style and politics pursued by the IS AGM, who ensured that he tightly controlled the assessment of the project emanating from the IS Division.

If anyone had bothered to ask the IS 'troops' about their assessment of the project they would have encountered serious opposition to the 'success' thesis promulgated elsewhere within Pensco. Indeed, the Project Manager was right when he said that he thought that IS staff were unhappy.

By the end of 1987 staff in the IS Division working on the pensions project were bearing the full weight of the mistakes made earlier in the project. They were working long hours under intense pressure to meet milestones in a situation characterised by hostility and recrimination between the different divisions involved in the project. The manager for IS personnel commented:

> It's been a bad year. You think all the time: in three months it will be better, in three months it will be better, we won't be working overtime. But you don't because this morning we heard that Pensco is going to enter the mortgage market and instead of feeling excited you feel: Oh God, it's the whole thing over again.

One of the major problems staff commented on was the absence of a sense of achievement among them. What had started out as a prestigious project had become a monster out of control. At the end of 1987 many IS staff and junior managers thought that the systems being developed were neither 'wonderful' nor 'quality' systems but rather systems that would simply be able to 'cope'.

Staff and junior managers felt angry at the way the promise of the project had been compromised. A project leader commented:

> They set out with great intentions and ended up bodging something in. They lost the design stage; I don't know where it went. And now they're paying a very big price. The system was supposed to be building blocks but now it just goes down the quickest route from A to B for launch day. We've missed our big chance to by-pass the old systems.

Missing the big chance to bypass the old systems offended some IS members' sense of efficiency. This, combined with the constant changes in the project, led one senior analyst to comment:

> It's the waste at Pensco that gets me so. They've got good people. We waste so much time and effort and get things wrong.

This waste and the failure to achieve satisfying results was undermining staff motivation. IS staff had 'no sense of achievement. [They] can't be proud about their involvement.' Rather, 'people feel it's not really worth doing anything properly because it's going to be shelved at some time or change direction.'

This sense of demoralisation was blamed by some staff on the general lack of professionalism in the IS Division, the remoteness of middle and junior managers, their apparent disregard for the welfare of their staff, and their tendency to sell the division's interests short.

One female senior programmer who had joined the company two and a half years previously illustrated this more general situation. She saw the major problem at Pensco as a managerial one. That is, senior management in the IS Division did not listen and were unwilling to recognise the problems before them. She also considered there to be major weaknesses in middle and junior management: the middle managers were intent on pushing the new 'marketing driven' line rather than saying what they believed in and many of the junior managers were only concerned to create a semblance of competence. She wanted to get a transfer away from the pension project because she was told by her project leader,' Don't mention the fact you can see problems just get on and do the tiny bit you've been told to do.'

This approach offended this programmer's sense of professionalism for she regarded herself as 'quality-minded'. She wanted to do the job 'properly', to gain a sense of achievement and to be affirmed in her work. Instead, she found she was getting no recognition or affirmation. She said:

> I found it really distressing to go from a position where I was very highly thought of [in the Home Office] … to here where whatever I try doesn't seem to be enough and where I'm never given the feeling that they actually think you're doing a good job.

It was a common sensation among IS staff that it was not possible to do enough to achieve recognition for one's work and that middle and senior managers did not really care about their staff. Staff not only felt aggrieved because they were not getting enough 'well done, chaps' from their senior managers; they were also angered by the continual compromises and bodges they were forced to make in pursuit of the IS AGM's conception of software quality. Indeed, 'bodging' seems to have become a way of life at Pensco during the pensions project. One project leader commented:

Everything you do you're always pulled off to do something more urgent. You never finish. You never get a chance to tidy up. So you end up bodging and paying the price building on other bodges and there are only certain people who have knowledge of those bodges and they move on.

This comment is interesting in the way in which it gives the lie to the appearance of tightly controlled technical efficiency generated by the plethora of data presented at pension project Steering Committee meetings. For underneath this appearance was the constant use of 'bodging', of 'string-and-sealing-wax fixes', of 'frigs', and the prevalent practice of 'wallpapering around the corners'. And as the quote above clearly points out, this method of working had direct consequences for the quality of the systems produced and their 'maintainability', that is, the ease with which they could be enhanced.

This interviewee was particularly annoyed at the way system quality was compromised. Programmers wanted to do the job well but everything was working against them: design specifications were non-existent, the documentation for existing systems was very weak and there was not enough time to test the systems properly. She went on to assert that:

> People aren't bodgers because they want to be bodgers. They have to get things done by a certain time. They know how to do it properly but it takes twice as long and they don't have that time. There's not enough documentation and it takes the next person to work on the system weeks getting into it. Then you find it doesn't do what you thought it did and that leads to another round of bodging.

IS staff, therefore, were not very happy with the pensions project. They felt undervalued and maligned by their own managers and other divisions. They were aware and scornful of inadequacies of technique within systems development but they believed that the pension project's problems originated elsewhere. In their anger and frustration the more outspoken IS staff and junior managers we talked to pointed the finger directly at management. In particular, they pointed the finger at their own IS managers who were unwilling to listen or bring problems to their superiors' attention. IS staff believed that this unwillingness to reveal the 'truth' about the systems being developed within the pensions project had fatally compromised those systems as managers had chosen expedient, although ultimately costly, ways of creating the success demanded of them by the IS AGM and the General Manager. A consultant working on part of the project commented:

> Pensco is very good at meeting and monitoring costs but I get a feeling that to meet budgets they axe contract staff and cut corners so that they can report: Yes sir, we're on target for our costs. Yet cutting out [development] work may have a much greater effect than overspending by ten percent.

Before drawing to a conclusion, let us quote one IS project leader who hilariously summed up the success imperative at Pensco.

[The pensions project] will go down as a success. It is doing 142 hours of overtime a week. Somehow that will be painted as a success. There will be branch notices saying how well we've done. Everyone will be patted on the back. We don't have any method of measuring failure here; everything is a success. We never have failure; we never give up on a system; we never say: Oh, it's too expensive and drop it. Once we start we go on. If it's four weeks late, four months late, four years late we go on to the end. Everything's a success. Nothing's a failure. There are degrees of success. There's an over budget success. There's an under budget success. But everything is a success. *Because it has to be really for the people on the project. They know it's not a success but at the end of the day they'll soon forget.*

CONCLUSION

In this chapter we have examined the different constructions of the new pensions systems at Pensco. And, as we saw, despite opposing constructions of the systems, senior management was able to mobilise its superior forces to encourage closure around a 'successful' construction of the project.

This process of competing constructions of in-house computer systems bears some resemblance to that of social constructivist work on the emergence of technologies such as the bicycle or bakelite (Bijker et al, 1987). In particular, during its construction the pensions systems appeared to possess considerable 'interpretative flexibility' in that different actors had different views of what those systems should be and what they were. As the project progressed senior IS managers invested more of their time in self-conscious attempts to construct a positive reality of the pensions systems.

This was challenged by other senior managers as they fought shy of taking responsibility for those system shortcomings that could be admitted. But, by and large, senior managers, galvanised by their General Manager, were content to bury the hatchet of this inter-managerial squabbling in order to present a success to their own staff and the insurance marketplace.

As such the interpretative flexibility of the pensions systems was closed down. This did not mean that Pensco IS staff and GMP processing staff believed the view of the project as an unqualified success. Rather, their view of the project was marginalised, received no official recognition and, if mobilised, was likely to be seen as an individual act of 'carping' or a malicious or confused representation of 'reality'.

Power, resources, hierarchy and politics were crucial aspects, therefore, of the social construction of reality at Pensco and we will examine these phenomena in greater detail in Chapters 9 and 11. Here, we wish to reiterate the importance of these concepts in the field of information technology research and practice. And, in particular, as should be abundantly clear by now, we insist that IS managers and staff cannot be regarded as above or beyond the reach of power, politics and hierarchy, as is often implied (see, for example, Willcocks and Mason, 1987). Indeed, with regard to systems development in a 'user relations' phase of computing, it would seem that IS managers have the most to gain and lose from the way in which systems successes and failures are constructed within and outside organisations. At the same time, however, they have never been under more pressure to relinquish control of their resources and their ability to steer and massage the construction of systems development into necessary successes.

This chapter also illustrates interesting aspects of gender relations at Pensco. As we saw, the struggle to achieve a successful interpretation of the project was largely carried out by men whereas it was women using the system who had to deal with the project's shortcomings. Surfacing these difficulties was not easy. Male managers just wanted 'the figures' and did not want to acknowledge or own problems. Managers sensed that 'the vibes' were wrong but they were not keen to explore these. Instead, they appeared intent on securing their own organisational and masculine identities as successful and competent men and managers. This and the following chapter give us some idea of the time and energy expended in constructing and sustaining these identities in conditions that threatened to undermine them.

9
The Politics and Pain of Managing Information Systems[1]

INTRODUCTION

Through further discussion of the empirical case study of Pensco, a principal objective of this chapter is to demonstrate how the development and use of information technology (IT) can be as much a source as a resolution of specific organisational problems. While this particular study was undertaken within a life insurance company, the problems and attempted organisational and technological resolutions of them, we believe, are relevant to a variety of situations. Not least this is because the design of, and demand for, information systems are not in themselves tied to specific uses; moreover, they are frequently subject to the conflicts and tensions associated with inter-divisional and specialist occupational career pursuits—that is, of organisational politics which are a feature of all organisations.

Our case study merely provides a particularly vivid example of the centrality of politics in organisational life. For example, in Pensco the only promotion of inter-divisional communication was through highly masculinist analogies with sport:

> 'but it's so competitive, it gets nasty, fierce … people say: 'I'm really gonna get them.' It's like we are a different company. (Organisation and Methods manager in IS)

As was indicated in Chapter 2, the political process within organisations assumes a diversity of forms and intensities depending on the

---

[1] This chapter draws heavily upon Knights and Murray (1992).

degree of change internal or external to the organisation and the extent to which the political process has become institutionalised around an agreed set of normative conventions, standards or rules. Radical change is currently experienced by most organisations in what may be described as increasingly competitive conditions within socio-political and cultural boundaries that are in continuous flux in postmodern global economies (Jameson, 1984; Featherstone, 1991; Lyotard, 1994).

This was especially so at Pensco not least because of the strategic replacements in the senior ranks as a result of the appointment of a new General Manager who had explicitly declared his intention to rid the company of its 'sleepy' and paternalistic traditions. But the pace of this demand for internal change is forced by a rapidly changing environment created by deregulatory and re-regulatory pressures stemming from government and competitive challenges in the industry and beyond (Knights and Willmott, 1993).

Within this dynamic context, proliferating demands and transformations in the use of information technology may seem comparatively mundane, but it is our view that the tensions and conflicts surrounding instability and change in Pensco often found their expression in systems development. This is because much had come to depend on delivering information technology systems that could meet the ever changing demands of an organisation seeking to retain a viable place in a dramatically shifting and uncertain economic and political marketplace. And as has been argued (Zuboff, 1988), computerisation with its dual capacity both to automate and to informate has substantial implications for the way that organisations function. Potentially, at least, it produces a more organic and interdependent set of learning relations that are incompatible with traditional imperatively structured hierarchies of control (Zuboff, 1988, p.394).

While the development of information technology is only one condition for the possibility of such dramatic organisational changes not their determinant, there is little doubt that in conjunction with other pressures for greater flexibility and learning in organisations (Piore and Sabel, 1984; Zuboff, 1988), it is disturbing the institutionalised rules and expectations and thereby intensifying political energy and uncertainty. Add to these changes, of course, perhaps the worst recession since the 1930s and the measure of difficulties facing this, as so many other organisations, is considerable. Clearly, then, the political climate in Pensco was fairly intense but no more than we would expect to find in organisations more generally as they confront dramatically changing markets, cultures, technologies and global politics.

Our focus in this chapter, then, is upon the internal politics of career and resource competition as a medium and outcome of IT management in general and systems development in particular. As we have argued throughout this book, one theoretical inspiration for our research is what may be termed the 'processual' perspective in organisational analysis (e.g. Mintzberg, 1978; Pettigrew, 1985) which can be traced back to such classics as Dalton's *Men Who Manage* (1959) and Burns and Stalker's *The Management of Innovation* (1961) and is clearly influenced by the negotiated order (e.g. Strauss et al. 1963; Day and Day, 1977), the strategic choice (e.g. Child, 1973) and the power (e.g. Crozier, 1974; Lukes, 1974; Clegg; 1975, 1979) literature.

This processual approach distinguishes itself from the 'rationalist' perspective (e.g. Hage and Aiken, 1970; Zaltman et al, 1973; Porter, 1980) in arguing from empirical case study research that management decisions are rarely as deliberate or intended as is implied by such literature (Mintzberg, 1978, p.945). In focusing upon the internal political processes which are a condition and consequence of decisions and activities in organisations, the processual approach provides also an alternative perspective to much of the conventional research on the development of IT in organisations and industry. For when applied to the insurance industry, where our case study has taken place, this literature is especially prone to account for the development of IT as a 'natural' trajectory (Barras and Swann, 1983; Rajan, 1984, 1987) from the early stages of data processing, characterised by relatively inflexible batch processing, through to the more recent on-line and distributed processing developments.

While at a general level, the follow-my-leader tendencies of insurance executives render this form of account plausible, it provides only a superficial analysis of the relationship between IT and organisational change. These analyses are simply retrospective accounts of events and historical change reconstructed to meet with some notion of smooth development or inevitable progress. When examined in more detail, these trajectories often turn out to be neither smooth nor inevitable (Law and Callon, 1992) but the 'product of heterogeneous contingency' (Bijker and Law, 1992, p.17). Alternatively their evolution may be explicable in terms of more broad ranging contextual stabilities (Murray, 1989b, p.293)—factors which largely account for the trajectory of the early use of IT in UK insurance as documented by Barras and Swann (1983) and Rajan (1984, 1987).

It may be thought from this brief introduction that what follows is just another organisational case study of processual change. While at one level there are strong parallels with both the processual and the firm-in-sector approaches, what we seek to do is draw upon the analytical framework presented in Chapter 2 both to illuminate our empirical data and challenge some of the limitations of these models of organisational change. In short, we want to develop these approaches to organisational change in directions that they have not yet travelled. One is to extend their empirical target more directly to embrace the study of information technology and organisational change where it has only been limitedly involved (see Pettigrew, 1973, 1980). The other is to probe more deeply and theoretically into the processes of change in an organisation to explore not just the political negotiations and career concerns of the actors but also the relations of power and identity or what might be termed the 'politics of subjectivity'.

This chapter is organised as follows. We begin with a fairly brief theoretical statement which partly develops further the points we have been making before turning to an analysis of the Pensco pensions project. Following this, a discussion of centrifugal managerial forces seeks to develop a more coherent analysis of the data from a perspective that sees definitions and interpretations of technology as intrinsic elements of the politics of career and resource competition. The chapter ends with a summary of the main points arising from the analysis of inter-managerial competition around IT, concluding that 'politics and pain' are inextricably involved in the management of IT regardless of ideologies which would seek to render such processes 'purely' technicist in content.

THE POLITICS OF SUBJECTIVITY

We have already indicated that our theoretical approach draws on the political processual literature within organisation theory. However, our concern is to broaden the scope of this analysis to examine management and organisational change in the context of the development and use of information technology. In particular, we seek to demonstrate how the management of IT can only be fully understood through an analysis of relations of power and identity that supplements the politics of process.

Drawing partly on Foucault's (1980, 1982) analysis, we suggest that the exercise of power not only appeals to, but also constructs, definite identities and subjectivities such that individual (or groups of) managers begin to *attach* themselves to certain practices and definitions or constructions of reality in respect of, for example, technology, markets and organisation. Quite clearly, as the processual literature would declare, these attachments are related to the pursuit of material and career advantages that may derive from supporting or creating specific policies or strategies (Burns and Stalker, 1961; Burns, 1977; Mintzberg, 1978; Pettigrew, 1985).

However, such a perspective neither explores the conditions which render strategic behaviour both possible and probable nor examines fully its effects on specific managerial identities. Our objective is to show how strategies are often accidental in their formation and neither a direct reflection of market forces (as much of the conventional strategy literature suggests) nor a simple negotiated outcome of political struggles (as processual theorists argue). Rather, they are a complex product of both these features but not in the planned and consciously designed way that may be intended by practitioners seeking to control IT, the market and their own careers. More often they are discontinuous, fortuitous and unpredictable in their realisation, as the Pensco case illustrates.

Another sense in which our perspective differs from but contributes to a processual approach is in recognising how technology and the market can be constructed by practitioners as either externalities over which the organisation has little control or as open to negotiation internally. It is these constructions to which the strategic and the processual approaches respectively respond but, in so doing, they take a particular management interpretation as given and thus reproduce it as reality, rather than reflect critically upon its power-infused construction.

By seeking to examine power and identity more closely, we intimate that these constructions of an externally determined or an internally negotiated reality are precisely the tools of politics. Once such constructions are drawn upon or created in the exercise of power, they generate practices which transform individuals into subjects who secure a sense of identity, meaning and purpose through a commitment to those realities (Knights, 1990).

Nonetheless, in so far as there are competing practices and definitions as, for example, with regard to assessments of Pensco's project (see Chapter 8) then, struggles within the managerial labour process will take place and individuals' careers and a department's or division's claim on resources will be heavily dependent on their outcome. Definitions of, and prospects for, the use of information technology are especially prevalent in these political struggles since IT commands considerable resources and enjoys a 'progressive' image in contemporary organisations. Trading on the 'halo' effect surrounding new technology, IT managers will frequently seek to impose decisions upon organisations that they regard as inevitable. However, increased computer awareness and usage combined with user-friendly software packages is involving non-specialists in debating the issues more virulently and the effect for IT managers inexperienced in political bargaining is often painful (Murray, 1991). Not that politics can ever be painless for it always involves struggles over interpretations of significant realities and competitive demands for resources and career positions. At times of rapid change which our case study company is presently witnessing, the pain can be particularly acute as struggles over particular competences, positions and resources intensify and managerial identities are made vulnerable by the instability of continuous threats and challenges.

This threat is particularly acute because, as we argued in Chapter 2, managerial identities are also linked to gender identities and may be mutually reinforcing. Thus, for example, managerial concerns to gain and maintain control of organisational processes and render them predictable are closely bound up with the predominance of men and a control-oriented masculinity within management. The pain of failure and anxiety generated by uncertainty play on deeper fears of a loss or dilution of a masculinity, that is both condition and consequence of contemporary management, which celebrates absolute control and the aggressive exorcising of uncertainty.

Organisational struggles are not entered into from a position of equality. Some enjoy specific advantages by virtue of their position in the organisation; others in relation to what is becoming the conventional wisdom concerning, say, technology or the market. Until recently, IT specialists in insurance companies held considerable sway because of the overwhelming importance of securing efficient computerised administrative systems. It seems that they did not use their position politically to ensure a strategic role in the exercise of power more generally and perhaps, as a result, IT management is now often the subject of widespread debate and conflicting demands within an organisation. And, as we saw in Chapter 7, particular pressures stem from those who claim to have an expertise in markets and whose definitions of the latter will rarely be questioned by non-marketing managers. But we must beware of assuming that information systems work is merely the target of other management controls since the boundary between control and production in IS, as increasingly elsewhere in post-Fordist organisations (Lipietz, 1992), is diffuse (Scarborough and Corbett, 1992, p.3):

> Not only are IS workers to some extent self-managing in their work practices and their careers, but even at the highest level, management in the IS area generally shares a common occupational background and skills with lower level workers (Scarborough, 1992).

As was observed in the previous chapter, however, the IS AGM in Pensco tended to subscribe to both hierarchical and coercive lines of authority, believing his own career to be best served by subordinating the IS Division to the demands made upon it. So despite organisational transformations occurring all around IS, the Division was subject to a traditional hierarchical mode of management. This added a further dimension to the political instabilities and struggles within the organisation but perhaps meant that the IS Division had to compete with one hand tied behind its back.

Inequality, of course, also derives from forces outside the organisation such as the educational structure and class and gender privileges but these advantages in material and symbolic status rarely free their holders from the tensions and conflicts of resource allocation and career competition. For it is precisely through such conflicts and struggles that their privileges both inside and outside the organisation are reproduced. Nonetheless, in so far as we are focusing on managers, a fair degree of such privilege may be presumed from the outset.

THE PENSIONS FIASCO

As we observed in Chapter 7, the Government's intention to revolutionise pension provision by encouraging citizens to contract out (of SERPS) and purchase private, personal or company pensions created much excitement in the pensions and insurance industry.

After an initial rather hesitant start, due largely to the uncertainty surrounding the new legislation, Pensco began developing systems to support a new range of pensions products. While the IS AGM was Management Sponsor of the project, he appointed his head of Pensions Systems as overall Project Manager. As we have already seen, this turned out to be somewhat problematic as the latter had to combine these responsibilities with those of managing the IS Division's input into the project. The Project Manager then established a multi-divisional team with day-to-day responsibility for co-ordinating the project. The task of initial product specification in the pension project was delegated to two members of the project team—both of whom were 'high flying' young managers from the professionally dominant Actuarial Division. They produced a number of papers outlining possible product features and the alternative mixes available between new products and on-line administrative systems to support the new and existing pensions products. These papers were then presented to, and discussed by, the Steering Committee. It is noteworthy that, in contrast to an earlier systems development for a new product, the GM did not sit on this committee and that, despite the project's espoused strategic importance for the company, membership of the Steering Committee and of the project team changed continuously during the period of product development.

The first paper which the actuaries presented proposed the idea of products based on 'core contracts'. These would consist of a generic 'parameter driven' contract (i.e. a table of variations of different product profiles to be selected as required) for the full range of pensions products (i.e. personal, group and executive) offered by the company. They argued that this concept would provide vital product flexibility in the new market conditions and give 'neat and tidy' reusable products.

For purposes of legitimising their proposals, the actuaries produced competitor analysis which revealed that 10 life companies had been using the 'core contract' idea since 1983. In our interviews it emerged that this analysis was based on a survey of life company brochures carried out by an actuarial student. And, as if in self-criticism, one of the actuaries involved in promoting the 'core contract' commented in late 1987:

> If we were starting again we'd look at our six closest competitors and see what they're doing ... when we started [the pensions project] we just took a general view of the market.

In short, the actuaries drew upon what they themselves admitted to be a less than adequate market analysis to mobilise support for the development of the 'core contract' concept. Having established the legitimacy of the 'core contract' they then presented a second paper outlining particular product development options. In this, their 'high risk' strategy advocated the redevelopment of Pensco's group money purchase and personal pensions products. Their 'low risk' strategy concentrated on developing on-line facilities for the existing executive pensions product which previous systems development constraints had prevented, resulting in it being one of the most expensive to administer in the whole industry. A compromise half-way strategy involving an on-line new personal pensions product and on-line facilities for the executive pension was approved by the Steering Committee early in 1986 although the Sales and Marketing Division preferred to take the high risk option. Looking back on this period a year later, an assistant divisional manager from marketing who was brought in to the project to communicate views from the field sales staff argued that:

> The actuaries were putting things forward that were not very sensible ... we shifted the actuaries quite a long way to a position more in line with our competitors. Sales and Marketing should have been organised sooner to prevent the Actuaries going down their own theoretical rather than practical alleys. We got there in the end and we won most of the battles, which is part of the healthy debate, but it had gone too far.

Another critic of the actuaries expressed anger with finance for selecting young part-qualified actuaries as project leaders, which then resulted in delays in getting charging structures for products approved because they do not have the ear of the Finance AGM. Also he criticised their inherent conservatism:

The actuaries are as happy as sandboys if all we're doing is developing a product that stretches back 20 years and other companies are doing the same. They're quite happy because original creative thinking isn't called for. (S&M junior manager on the project)

Although at first glance it appears that decisions are flowing from 'market requirements' which are assumed to derive from the external environment, it is clear that particular distinctive views of the market are mobilised by different managers as indicated by the view from Marketing expressed above. In part, this mobilisation is an attempt to legitimise specific divisional and career interests by couching them in projects which are claimed to be coincident with the corporate objectives. In the first instance the GM attempts to create a consensus around his sales maximising pensions product strategy. However, once the Steering Committee attempts to implement this broad decision a number of supplementary and crucial decision-making processes are set in motion. They reveal a lack of consensus with regard to views of the market and some fairly intense, if often explicit, jockeying for professional and career positions. We have already seen the competition for supremacy between marketing and actuarial managers from the Finance Division, but this extended to other divisions. So, for example, Marketing were convinced that IS were too powerful, as illustrated by a high flying manager from the former division:

IS has too much power in the organisation at the present time. We are working to change that. Sales and Marketing should drive the organisation. ... But I can't get away from the view that IS still dictate what the company can and can't do. Once the pensions systems are in we'll have to use IS properly. (S&M manager on the project)

One explanation for this feeling of comparative subordination to IS could be the late reorganisation of the Sales and Marketing Division and therefore their difficulties in getting into the corporate driving seat. But there was also the technical difficulty of questioning the resource costs of new systems which echoes issues raised in Chapter 5: 'How can a layman question it when they [IS] say that it will take 8 man years to develop a system? You can't challenge them' (ibid.). Resentment stemmed also from a feeling that IS enjoyed rather comfortable surroundings and that getting 'a 'grotty' system from people in luxurious furnishings doesn't help' heal inter-divisional wounds (ibid.). As a systems analyst on the project put it, the relation with users has been at times 'very much us and them'.

Such conflicts and rivalries existed between all divisions but a particular problem for IS was that of getting business requirements tied down especially with Customer Services (CS). As a senior systems analyst put it:

> There's such a lack of IS knowledge in the CS area that when they design their business requirements they are obviously going to miss things out. The problem is that there is no one from our area who's got the right sort of knowledge to put to them the right sort of questions.

As a result of the absence of detailed communications, things were forgotten or assumed to be one way when in fact another. Consequently, business requirements were arriving as late as the final stages of the project.

In the end this senior systems analyst resigned out of sheer frustration at the failure of IS and CS to understand one another. While acknowledging that IS is a service department, she argued that it cannot respond to a changing marketplace unless it has the tools and resources and this means the systems infrastructure, the staff, the development methods and techniques as well as adequate staff training. She also felt that CS and S&M had to be made to consider the IS implications of their requests at an early stage. Then

> if it's impossible for IS we shouldn't say: 'OK, we'll have a go.'

But the attitude in IS has tended to be:

> we'll have a go but throughout the project we've been aiming at a target we can't hit and when we get close to it we think: 'No, we can't hit it.' So we change it and even that's not very realistic (ibid.)

One reason why other divisions did not consider the implications of their demands upon IS was that they were not made accountable for any mistakes. So, for example,

> if CS change their minds they don't get penalised or anything ... we've got to make the changes because they've got to be able to make it work. (ibid.)

But another reason was that, although autocratic and aggressive in managing his own division, the IS AGM sought to curry favour with his GM by appearing to deliver everything demanded of IS. Accordingly, he forced his division into a subservient role in servicing the other divisions and thereby put them under enormous stress. This was because though the demands proliferated, the timetable and the deadlines for the final delivery were rigid due to the importance attached to being in a position to distribute 'government approved' products from the day set down by the legislation. While professing to have an 'open door policy', the IS AGM, and in turn the GM, created a climate of fear and apprehension in which a failure to complete the pensions project to deadline could not be contemplated. Yet the project budget was a woeful underestimate of the resources required and pushed the divisions into intense competition over the share of resources for their respective systems requirements. Added to the uncertainty of the changes occurring both within and outside the organisation and the usual rivalries between individuals, groups and divisions, this competition dramatically increased the intensity of political activity as institutionalised ways of consensus management (i.e. the old regime) began to break down.

Not surprisingly, costs soared, botch-ups proliferated and a number of staff left the company from IS. As the IS consultant brought in at great expense to salvage the project put it:

> Pensco doesn't listen to its good IS people and they don't have a vehicle for expressing their ideas.

The senior systems analyst quoted above is a case in point, for she was:

> a very good analyst and she'd come through very fast for Pensco but, as far as she was concerned, it was too slow. She'd got ideas but she couldn't influence [senior management]. She couldn't get on with what she wanted to do so she left. (ibid.)

Despite the speed of external changes in the industry (the approach of the Financial Services Act and changing pension legislation), the fragility of the GM's control of centrifugal managerial forces made it impossible for a single all-embracing view of the market to gain consensus among those responsible for the development of the pensions project.

By the middle of 1986 the absence of a consensus was becoming clear, but by September the increasingly assertive Sales and Marketing Division had mobilised sufficient pressure to overturn the initial product/system mix.

> Sales and Marketing didn't have a clear enough idea of what they wanted initially. (project leader, Sales & Marketing).

This led to delay in product specifications. However, the shift in favour of group personal pension plans was unforeseeable, according to this project leader: it was largely brought about by changes in the Superannuation Funds Office rules.

But all rules are open to interpretation and it is again by asserting a particular view of the market, legitimated by an appeal to a change of opinion being expressed in the specialist financial media, the Sales and Marketing Division was able effectively to advocate the necessity of developing a group pensions product.

Divisional tensions came to a head in September 1986 when the Steering Committee 'away day' was arranged, and a 'compromise solution' was claimed to be the outcome. However, there appears to have been little compromise or agreed prioritisation of the objectives arising out of the new situation. Rather, it was agreed that the development of a revamped group pensions scheme and accompanying on-line data entry system would simply be *added* to the commitments already undertaken—namely, the personal pensions product, and on-line administration for the executive pension. The IS Division did propose a 'fall back' position in case of problems in which the administrative system for the executive pension would once again be deferred.

At this stage, the Steering Committee appears to have thrown caution to the wind in that they expanded the product plan to include two product and two system developments: an option not considered to be a feasible risk by the actuaries eight months earlier. To the great frustration of their staff, the project's management sponsor (the IS AGM) and the Project Manager, seemed unwilling or unable to raise obvious and cogent objections to the multiplicity and diversity of demands being made of their division.

Beneath the plethora of Steering Committee papers, automatically generated project reports and the constant monitoring of milestones achieved, the project appears at this stage to have been largely out of control. Undoubtedly the reasons given for the apparent chaos—the Government's prevarication over the launch dates for the pensions legislation, and the uncertainty in respect of new financial services regulations and Internal Revenue rule changes—were not without foundation. However, they served as something of a gloss on some of the fundamental problems associated with IT and the Fowler Project and provided a ready rationalisation for the failure to meet deadlines and budget targets. For in the end, the project went considerably over budget, the 'core contract' concept was virtually abandoned and the executive pensions on-line administrative system was postponed for two years imposing extra clerical costs of £200 000 per annum. In addition there was a loss of key system development staff through illness or departure, and the deferral of all but the most pressing systems functions to a rapidly expanding post-launch development.

A project leader in IS recognised that it takes courage to get up and say 'we are in an awful mess' but someone needs to do it. She was not to be the one to do it either, other than indirectly by leaving the company. Another senior analyst in IS was completely demoralised by the 'dreadful' pensions project. Her reasons for leaving were a combination of being shunted around from one part of the project to another with little or no notice or consultation and the lack of co-operation and understanding between IS and Customer Services.

Overall, her view was that IS lacked the tools and resources in terms of the systems infrastructure, the staff, the development methods and techniques and the training available for them to respond properly to a changing marketplace. New systems were continually compromised by being 'bodged in' and 'bolted on' to old and insecure systems and often would be launched, as in the case of the group pensions scheme, full of faults and with no correction facility.

The growing disparity between the appearance of order and a significant loss of operational control was successfully managed until mid-1987. By September, tensions were increasingly apparent and the IS AGM was forced, belatedly in the view of his development staff, to bring in a consultant (at a cost of over £100 000) to try and salvage the project. By organising the release of *minimal* systems for the product launch dates (which could not be postponed because it would mean an enormous loss of new business falling to competitors), the consultant managed to retrieve the situation sufficiently to escape disaster.

By late 1987, the GM had become increasingly concerned and demanded an explanation from the Project Manager. The latter replied by letter arguing that the most important problems were the dual role he had been given as Project Manager and the Manager of the IS Division input into the project and the fact that the project estimating process had gone 'haywire'.Resigned to his fate, the Project Manager accepts much of the responsibility for the failures rather than criticising the entire project and, by implication, senior management.

The IS AGM, a more powerful and politically aggressive operator, claims that the situation has always been under control. He said in late 1987:

'I suspect at the beginning we aimed too high and with hindsight it probably wasn't on anyway. We knew what our fallback position was and we had to activate it.'

A common theme that emerges here is that despite the problems caused, revealed, and in places exacerbated, by the pensions project, and articulated by IS development staff, these problems do not 'emerge' in senior management discussions. In this regard the role of the IS AGM as a technical and political gatekeeper who presents a heavily dissembled picture of projects 'under control' is crucial.

THE CENTRIFUGAL FORCES OF MANAGEMENT

The Pensco case study illustrates the centrifugal forces characteristic of management practice in contemporary organisations. In particular, it shows the strength of these forces in situations of considerable uncertainty. And, as we have seen, this in itself creates considerable managerial conflict. This renders the development of software problematic particularly when this involves the construction of market-related systems. This is not to say, however, that IS managers and staff are simply victims of these conflicts and struggles. Indeed, they are an important agent and product of them.

The major axis of these forces in the Pensco example emerged between the IS, the CS, and the Sales and Marketing (SM) Divisions. Sales and Marketing were specifically concerned to have the range of products and front-end systems necessary to meet their ambitious sales targets. They thus tended to push for the maximum number of products and product variations possible. This implied the development of a flexible core contract and quotations systems able rapidly to deliver new product variations to the market. SM representatives on the Steering and Project Committee had little direct interest in the cost of processing, or the profitability of the products their staff sold. After all, they were not judged by profit or cost but sales volume.

The Customer Services AGM on the other hand was particularly concerned to secure the back-office systems necessary to meet his divisional objectives in terms of service standards and staffing. The CS representative on the Project Committee said:

> One of my main objectives is to keep fighting our corner to make sure we get as many new systems as possible in April [1988] because the [CS AGM] is obviously concerned about the staff explosion at Pensco and one of the ways to solve that is to computerise.

In this project, however, the CS Division appears to have lost out to the marketeers. It did not get its on-line executive pension system although this had been included in the project specification from the outset. Nor did it get the new accounting system meant to ease the processing of variable premium payments. And when its clerical staff took belated delivery of the GMP new business system this was only half-finished and full of major faults. Furthermore, these problems were compounded by poor communication between branch and head office staff and the discovery that sales staff were selling permutations of the GMP product for which there were no established computer or clerical procedures.

One junior pensions administration manager rather accurately summed up this situation. He likened the systems developed for the pensions project to a film set façade. That is, it was largely front-end, market-oriented systems with little solid administrative back-up. And he bitterly commented, 'The systems to get the business in are there and Pensco will throw people at the administration side to process it.'

The CS AGM appeared philosophical if concerned about the future of administration at Pensco following the revelation of the shortcomings of the project. In response to the question: how long can Pensco continue to develop products at the speed evidenced in the pensions project, he replied:

> I would say it's got to come to an end very soon. We had no choice with the pensions project. We were in a position where 80 per cent of our market was changed so we had to change 80 per cent of our products...You've just got to adapt to the market place. ... We're reaching a point now where we've got to take a rest for a few years and spend some time putting the infrastructure in place. ... We've got to a point where we've got to say: Stop and no more.

This comment is reminiscent of the Thatcherite belief, current at the time, that you could not 'buck the market'! However, as we have been at pains to point out, the market is constituted by its actors who are able to mobilise particular views of it in support of their objectives.

In this situation, one might view the IS Division as hapless victims struggling to reconcile competing demands on its finite and over-stretched resources. To an extent this was the position of junior managers and IS staff stuck at the sharp end of the project. But the IS AGM was not only a victim of these circumstances. He helped both to perpetrate and reproduce them by his tight control of IT organisational politics at Pensco.

The Pensco case, then, clearly shows the importance of controlling and channelling the centrifugal forces of users' demands on the IS resource in the financial services industry. At Pensco these appeared to take a particularly strong form due to the GM's determination to alter radically the management style, culture and practice of the company. Senior managers' fear of the GM may have contributed to their unwillingness to look over the parapet of their divisional walls. With regard to these tensions an old hand in the IS Division commented thus on the senior management team:

> There's this awful feeling that they do as they're told. AGM teamwork is a bit hollow. They don't dissent in public but I'm not convinced they're a team at all. I wonder if that affects the way we do our developments. They're scared stiff of the General Manager.

The force of centrifugal forces may also have been exacerbated by the divisional structure of the company and poor communication and accumulated hostility between divisions. Furthermore, the management of the project and its stress on individual responsibility is unlikely to have fostered more collegiate and co-operative forms of management practice.

Our research clearly illustrates the potential for conflicts and tensions to arise around the use of information technology. As an organisational resource, IT developments emerge from and reproduce complex political processes. In our case study, these processes reveal the importance of organisational power and certain definitions of the market and other priorities as a means by which to mobilise and advocate particular IT strategies.

In seeking to transform the organisational culture and the strategic potential at Pensco, the GM made significant changes (e.g. the reorganisation of IS and a large number of strategic replacements) to the organisation's structure and power relations. But, as we have seen, his exercise of constrained domination (Hickson et al, 1986) also produced unforeseen and not entirely beneficial consequences.

Confusion about the general direction of the market combined with the absence of a 'strategic recipe' (Child and Smith, 1987) for success has created problems for Pensco's GM. He has simply tried to shape the senior management team around his sales maximising ambitions but without being entirely clear which sales and products should be pushed in both the short and long term. While in the first corporate strategy plan, product diversification was identified as essential, the result of the pension legislation forced its abandonment as their best selling pensions contract had to be revised in order to meet the demands of contracting out from the state scheme and the intensification of competition that was anticipated (Knights and Willmott, 1988). As we have seen, the absence of a common or definitive view of the market, combined with a diverse and competing set of divisional priorities (e.g. the core contract, containment of administrative costs, and pensions product diversification) resulted in an uncontrolled proliferation of demands on the IS Division at Pensco.

Had Sales and Marketing perhaps been in a stronger position they might have been able to push through an uncompromising product diversification strategy. However, Customer Services was able to insist on the importance of having new business systems on-line for reasons of administrative efficiency. Information Services, in the figure of the IS AGM, attempted, quite unrealistically as it turns out, to accommodate all demands made of it. Indeed, in interviews IS project staff complained of both the IS AGM and the Project Manager's tendency to sell their divisional and professional interests short. The reasons for this appear to be two-fold. Firstly, the IS AGM was not made aware of the extant systems problems and their potential damage to the project partly because his aggressive style invoked fear and a reluctance to bring 'problems' to the AGM's attention. Secondly, he appears to have tried to subsume his divisional interests to the GM's market-driven approach. This aggressively supine attitude opened the floodgates to competing demands on IS resources and had a most deleterious impact on the quality of systems produced and the morale of IS staff.

Our analysis of the pension project suggests as a preliminary conclusion that however 'coherent' and 'rational' is the image of systems development, there will tend to be unforeseen circumstances that cause serious disruption to IT strategies. It could be argued that the disruption of the 'rational' development of systems in Pensco is a reflection of continuous processes of change, and a comparatively 'poor' understanding of the potential and limitations of IT use by executive business managers. Within financial services these problems have been exacerbated by the combined effects of political regulation and economic deregulation. The uncertainty in financial services has tended to engender an incrementalist or 'wait and see' approach to systems development that leaves companies with an inadequate processing capacity to meet their administrative demands. Certainly, Pensco is not alone in suffering from imperfect IT systems becoming overloaded (*Financial Adviser*, October 1989). These also continued more than two years after the big legislative changes. One leading life company, for example, was in major conflict with its agents on administrative inefficiencies and recently had to stop all direct communications with its head office pensions in order to regain control over administrative backlogs (*Financial Adviser*, 1 November 1990). Another has had continuous problems in seeking to meet systems demands whether as a result of increased business stemming from the pensions boom or their becoming the tied agent of a major building society. As late as 1993 this life company was struggling with a backlog of policy processing in one of its product lines forcing it to send letters of apology to new clients.

While acknowledging that the industry has experienced increased pressures as a result of externally induced change, it is our view that much of the problem revolves around internal rivalries and power struggles between distinct specialist and professional groups. As we have already argued, in examining these features of organisational life the processual analysis (e.g. Mintzberg, 1978; Pettigrew, 1985; Peters, 1992) provides a much more realistic account of organisational life than when internal political processes are denied or discounted as is the case in 'rationalist' accounts of technology and strategic management (e.g.

Hage and Aiken, 1970; Zaltman et al, 1973; Porter, 1980). But the process-ual perspective fails to analyse this politics in terms of a theory of power that links it to the formation of specific personal identities or subjecti-vities (i.e. categories of subjects). Nor, as was argued earlier in this book, does it recognise power and politics as the 'life blood' of the organisation. Rather, it sees political struggles and conflict as viruses to be purged and, in this sense, the processual perspective remains wedded to a function-alist paradigm wherein the body of an organisation is not sustained through, but rendered sick by, political contest and competition. As may by now be clear, it is our view that organisations do not exist except as continuously changing outcomes of political contests and power struggles.

In order to understand the chaotic pressures besetting the develop-ment of systems at Pensco, it is necessary to focus on the unintended as well as the intended consequences of the exercise of power and the pursuit of identity by participants. Take, for example, the IS AGM whose identity was clearly tied to his perception of the GM's faith in his capacity to transform the organisational culture from its paternalistic and slothful past towards a dynamic, professional and commercial future (Knights and Willmott, 1987). However, his aggressive way of doing this left him uninformed about systems and skills difficulties and constraints as subordinates dissembled in order to protect their own identities against his expected wrath. Ignorant of the impending chaos, the IS AGM simply absorbed all the demands on his division from a plurality of political and career strategies emerging in other divisions of the organisation. Only the intervention of an external consultant could salvage the operation and prevent the myth of success from being exposed. Not that he had no politics to play and identity to protect but the consultant will tend to provide the paymaster (i.e. the IS AGM) with the solutions that at least are capable of being presented as successful.

This way of analysing our case study could be seen as merely a modification of the processual approach simply involving an elabora-tion of the analysis of the socio-political processes. But because we view politics as central to the reproduction of organisations, what the process-ual theorists define as their disruptive impact we simply understand as an aspect of organisational change that has a diverse range of productive and disruptive effects variable as and between different groups and individuals. Another difference in our approach is that the pursuit of individual or sectional interests and the broader structure of inequality that is its condition and consequence can no longer be taken for granted. Accordingly, the GM and the IS AGM may be seen as seeking to remain or advance within a hierarchy of status and prestige that extends beyond the confines of their own organisation. In effect, they are imprisoned within an identity and system of inequality over which they have only limited control. From this perspective, information technology, the market and other 'realities' are both tools but often also obstacles to their 'designs' on the world, as is the case for many others who seek to advance their positions within the organisation and the broader society.

Few processual theorists would probably disagree with this account even though they do not themselves pursue the analysis of power and identity quite so far. But in so far as identity or subjectivity (Knights and Willmott, 1985, 1989) and the conditions of its possibility remain unexamined, processual analysis tends to reproduce the perspectives on technology and the market which organisational members themselves use as a resource in their political contests. Frequently this involves treating the market and technology as forces *external* to the organisation in which their effects are managed. However, technology and the market are themelves social contructions both inside and outside any particular organisation and the interpretations that define them are intimately tied to the constitution of subjects and the practices with which they identify and feel comparatively secure. In short, the 'reality' of markets, information technology and other aspects of organisation are intimately tied to the development of, and pursuit of security through, particular identities.

This is not always clear from analyses which following the grounded theory of Strauss and Glaser (1980) and its concern not to *impose* meaning upon respondents, reproduce organisations' tendency to treat the market and IT as 'externalities'. Admittedly, processual theorists will recognise that these 'externalities' are brought into the political arena as individuals interpret them to suit their career objectives. But they do not see the market and IT as internal constructions which are central to the exercise of power and the development of identity.

By contrast, our examination of the politics of organisational change in Pensco suggests to us that diverse groups in competition with each other for scarce material and symbolic rewards are continually constructing technology and the market in ways that allow them to secure advantage. Prior to our arrival it would seem that technology was treated by most divisions as an 'externality' that was beyond their technical competence to understand. Consequently, demand for IS services were manageable though not providing the company with a competitive advantage. The replacement at the top encouraged a change of perception which was also reinforced by a growing awareness of IT use created partly by the impact of personal computers and user-friendly software. IT became an internal construction that was subjected to the demands of a Marketing Division made increasingly confident by virtue of the perceived backing of a marketing-oriented GM. They insisted on treating the market as an 'externality' to which information systems must respond in order for Pensco to remain competitive. Aware of the GM's position and possibly as insecure about challenging marketing knowledge as the latter had traditionally been with respect to IT, the Systems Division simply accepted the demands despite their often conflicting and contestable nature.

What we have been arguing is that the way in which technology and markets are constructed, defined or interpreted, whether as externalities beyond question or as internalities subject to negotiation, is itself a part of the politics of organisation. It enables senior members of the organisation to incorporate staff into an official ideology which commits them to a view of technology and the market either as a challenge through which to transform the organisation or as a threat to its very survival. In short, this has the effect of transforming individuals into subjects who secure a sense of reality, meaning and identity (Knights, 1990) through meeting the 'demands' of technology and the market as defined by their seniors.

The pressures and the uncertain future the life insurance sector presently faces calls for careful co-ordination of, and internal coherence in, managerial actions. Yet senior management is also being called upon, perhaps as never before, to make strategic and, maybe as Pensco's GM says, 'entreprenuerial' choices. These choices are sometimes 'sporadic' having a tenuous link with clearly expressed and coherent requirements and 'vortex'-like in that they bring latent conflicts into the open and often imply considerable shifts in the distribution of organisational power and career prospects (Hickson et al, 1986).

In the past, managements in financial services have recognised which performance criteria figured in satisfying structural imperatives to profitability. The arena of action in which they needed to constitute their identities and social practices in order to be regarded as effective and competent managers was also easily identified. As a result of the various upheavals in this sector, it is now much less clear what is required by consumers and institutional shareholders and how managerial competence is to be constituted, although the predominance of corporate and IT strategy discourses give some clues (Morgan and Knights, 1991).

SUMMARY AND CONCLUSION

In the introduction to this chapter we argued that the relationship between organisations and technologies is a fluid one requiring the exercise of managerial choice. Thus, technologies do not determine organisational forms and labour processes, nor is their design and use simply a reflection of a managerial imperative to control wage labour. Rather, technologies, and the inherent flexibility of information techno-logies in particular, open up specific ranges of possibility of develop-ment, design and application, within particular socio-economic contexts, that require active management. This, in itelf, is hardly a stunning revelation yet it is a point worth reiterating given the powerful appeal of simple deterministic frameworks of technical change.

We further argued that processual analysis has made a significant contribution to the analysis of the organisational politics of change but that it tends to obscure the way in which the reproduction and transfor-mation of micro-organisational power relations are constituted and sustained within both specific identities/subjectivities and broader pol-itico-economic markets and inequalities. Furthermore, the intentions of significant organisational actors are often taken as given rather than linked to the development of specific managerial identities and particu-lar exercises of power surrounding certain resources such as IT—pro-cesses and strategies wherein the very definition and interpretation of technologies/markets and their application/ threat involve an exercise of power and the development of specific practices that secure individ-uals' identities, meaning systems and realities.

In our case study, we argued that tensions and conflict around the management of the organisational IT resource occurred as a result of different managers and operating divisions perceiving and pursuing distinct IT priorities by invoking particular constructions of 'markets', 'technology' and 'organisation'. And, as alluded to earlier, these phe-nomena are not merely a force to which actors respond but, rather, they are constituted by the power and practices of key personnel within the organisation.

In our analysis of Pensco's pension project we saw how the General Manager and the Marketing Division invoked particular views of the life insurance market to legitimise their plans for sales maximisation. This meant defeating opposition and resistance to these objectives by the virtual replacement of the whole senior management team, the reorgani-sation of operating divisions, and the introduction of new control mech-anisms through the instrument of strategic planning.

In particular, the GM appears to have felt it necessary to bring the IS Division firmly under his control by reducing its hitherto relative auton-omy from the business. This has been attempted through the replace-ment of the AGM and the restructuring of the division on product-oriented lines. The AGM has in turn rigourously applied the tight control mechanisms of strategic planning in an overtly aggressive and intimidating manner.

Having apparently secured the control of the IT resource as such, the GM began to make his particular demands of it in terms of product-related systems development. But, as the pensions fiasco only too clearly illustrates, the generality of these demands and the lack of cohesion of his management team around particular IT priorities, led to a proliferation of demands on the IT resource that, although accepted by the IS AGM, could simply not be met. This situation led to a growing disparity between the appearance of an apparently well-ordered and controlled software development project and the chaos, and frantic efforts to displace blame, that characterised the project.

We have argued that this chaos, and the failure of the project to meet its original objectives is probably typical of systems development projects rather than an exceptional case. This is due to the character of managerial labour processes and markets, the tensions between individual and collective goals, and the very uncertainty that managers reproduce through their practices as a result of particular concerns with career advancement, management control and subjective identity. At first glance, the prescriptive literature which advocates 'IT strategies' and greater 'communication' between systems users and developers, would appear to bolster the semblance of purposive–rational managerial technique in the use of IT. In our view, though, it tends to reproduce and yet obscure the tensions and contradictions that underlie the problematical character of IT management.

That is to say, the management of IT first and foremost can be understood as a process of organisational and extra-organisational politics responding to, and acting upon, perceived imperatives that are generated through, yet serve to reconstitute 'markets', 'technologies' and 'organisations' as socially contructed phenomena. These phenomena appear to take on a life of their own, and the individual confronts them as a constraining or facilitating reality. The asymmetrical distribution of power, as access to and possession of material and symbolic resources, allows certain individuals, groups and classes to dominate a socially constructed development, design, use and management of particular technologies. However, the tensions and contradictions generated out of prevailing patterns of social action, conditioned in our case by market mechanisms and managerial labour processes, will always place limits on the notion of a singular purposive–rational use of information technologies. Although the development and use of IT involves certain complex techniques and methods, management practices surrounding IT are best understood as particular social constructions arising out of unequal and dynamic power relations. They cannot be regarded simply as a concern with 'technical problems' looking for 'technical solutions'. But even when management practice assumes such a technicist stance, it does not escape the politics and pain in managing information technology.

In conclusion, the account of the pensions project at Pensco has examined in some detail the considerable fluctuations that occurred throughout the project with regard to product definition, the systems to be delivered, perceptions of markets and perceptions of the project itself and its success. We believe that these fluctuations at Pensco were registered to a greater or lesser extent in other UK life insurers in this period of market and regulatory turbulence.

As already indicated, the pensions project represented novelty in a number of areas for Pensco. And in the account presented we have seen how that novelty in terms of size, the simultaneous development of product and process systems, and the battle between divisions with vital interests in the outcome of the project created a series of debilitating problems for Pensco. Nevertheless, as we have also seen, the project was construed as a considerable success that more or less met its ambitious objectives. We are not, of course, in a position to provide strong evidence to question this interpretation although many less senior members in the organisation did so. But we can point out the divergence between senior management's objectives and their claims to have met all of these. However, as we have already hinted, very different assessments of the pensions project were in circulation in Pensco. That these were largely subterranean attests to the competence of senior managers in suppressing alternative constructions of the project's reality and putting in their place a successful version of events.

10

Constructing Technology Context at Pensco: Systems, Staff and Systems Practices

INTRODUCTION

In this chapter we examine Pensco's 'technology context' a concept that was elaborated in Chapter 2. By the term 'technology context' we mean not only the organisational structures, practices and cultures that characterise technology-related activities at Pensco, in particular the IS Division, but also the way in which actors understand and construct those structures, practices and cultures within the organisation. For, as outsiders, it seems to us that the development of Pensco's pensions project systems had been attempted under the influence of a minority, but dominant, construction of this technology context. This downplayed or wilfully ignored other constructions that drew attention to the serious constraints imposed by Pensco's existing systems infrastructures on the pension project's ambitious plans.

In their study of a US insurance company in the 1970s, Kling and Scachi (1982) argued that computer systems were embedded in a particular organisational and sectoral context. While not according sectoral context a great deal of importance they did notice that an organisation's past history of commitments constrained its current technology choices. With regard to computing they revealed that past system developments were liable to constrain current choices. The incremental addition of new systems and facilities at their case study company tended to become more complex and costly as the web of interacting systems in operation grew in size. Additionally, IS managers found it difficult to recruit and retain IS staff to work on old core systems that were neither exciting nor liable to furnish skills and career credentials saleable in other organisations.

In this chapter we draw some similar conclusions to those reached by Kling and Scachi (1982). In particular, we will explain how Pensco's old systems not only required increasingly costly maintenance but also severely compromised the implementation of choices taken regarding future systems development. But we also want to go beyond research that emphasises the constraints imposed by 'sunk costs' in technology (Littler, 1990). In particular we want to examine how it was possible for IS managers at Pensco not to raise the problem of the company's old systems more vociferously in the face of the General Manager's demands for new pensions products and administration systems. Indeed, it is remarkable that so little was said about Pensco's old systems as a constraint on the pensions system as it progressed. One reason for this appeared to lie in part in a desire to please both the new General Manager and the IS AGM and the embarrassment IS managers felt with regard to the costs of maintaining and enhancing their systems. The problem lay in the conflict between spending IS money on new core systems, with little immediate demonstrable cost- saving or revenue-producing capacity and the immediate demands of those able to produce profitable new business. As we shall see, the latter demands always seemed to displace projects designed to renew the core systems. This, despite (as we saw in Chapter 6) these claims to profitability on new business being rather weak and requiring changes in Pensco accounting norms to pay for the development of the pensions systems. Lastly, and rather ironically given the ever expanding pensions project, the IS AGM was keen to avoid large risky projects that might jeopardise his standing in the company. That is, he did not want to attempt a core system conversion while developing new business systems.

In this chapter, then, we will examine Pensco's technology context and the manner in which this came to constrain and subvert the pension project's grand objectives. In so doing we will also look at the way in which this context was socially constructed by IS managers in such a way as to minimise it as a 'problem' likely to create difficulties for the pensions project. This is not to say that there was no opposition to the emergence of this view of Pensco's old systems problem. Rather, those opposing views were kept in check or ignored by managers with greater access to resources than their supporters.

This chapter, then, examines three aspects of Pensco's technology context and the manner in which these were constructed within the company. Firstly, we look at the constraints represented by Pensco's existing system infrastructure and a surprising lack of managerial cognisance of this potential problem. Secondly, we examine the Pensco IS Division in terms of its managerial and staff capabilities and the potential brake these imposed on the highly ambitious pensions project. And, thirdly, we briefly examine the culture of the IS Division before and after the reorganisation implemented by Pensco's new GM and IS AGM.

SYSTEMS RENEWAL AT PENSCO

As we have already seen in Chapter 3 a major problem facing many financial services companies in the late 1980s concerned the rapid technological ageing of their computer systems. This ageing occurred for three reasons. Firstly, the hardware upon which systems were being run simply wore out. This could of course be patched up but in an effort to persuade their clients to upgrade hardware and move to new generations of mainframe and mini-computers, major suppliers have a tendency to stop supporting ageing generations of hardware.

Secondly, computer systems have a specific life cycle of birth and eventual death (Duffy and Assad, 1980) that in part results from the problem of maintainability and enhanceability. That is, the great majority of systems are developed throughout their life rather than merely being developed during the 'development phase' and then used (Friedman and Cornford, 1989, p.174; Kling and Iacono, 1984). This continuous development occurs for many reasons: the elimination of bugs and bad programmes arising from the 'development phase'; enhancements to improve system performance; and changing user requirements. Indeed, system maintenance and enhancement is the primary activity of most IS divisions: a recent survey of UK insurance industry IS divisions concluded that as much as 70 percent of programming effort is accounted for by system maintenance alone (Sturdy, 1989).

Continual enhancement of systems aims to improve them in terms of the user needs they meet. However, such constant changes can render the underlying structure of the systems increasingly complex if it does not undermine their original design entirely. Thus, further enhancements become more difficult and costly. This is especially the case if the original systems and enhancements made to them have not been clearly documented. If such documentation is not generated, knowledge of particular systems comes to reside in the heads of particular analysts and programmers. This has two potential consequences: firstly, IS personnel may regard this knowledge as their personal property; and secondly, the simple size of one system and its multiple interfaces with other systems may prevent any single IS specialist understanding the whole system. IS personnel attempting to enhance such systems will experience great difficulties as they struggle to understand the systems and the implications of even minor changes to them.

The third way in which computer systems 'age' is caused by the rapid development of computer technology itself and the diffusion of these innovations into organisations. That is, even though a system may function quite adequately managers within a given organisation may consider it necessary to develop new systems that are able to facilitate service levels or product development possibilities that their competitors appear to have achieved through major systems or hardware upgrades. This is the case, for example, with the search for competitive advantage through the use of client-oriented databases which have only been made possible by advances in relational database design and continual increases in data processing speeds.

These three factors—physical decay, software decay and technological innovation—in large part explain the periodic occurrence of major systems and hardware renewal programmes in many IT-using organisations. These renewal programmes imply large investments in new hardware and software and represent a major risk in that a switch to new systems can threaten to undermine, at least temporarily, an organisation's activities.

The design, management and timing of system renewals programmes is then a crucial matter for senior management. Often though, such programmes appear to offer little benefit to senior managers. They represent high risks and large expenditures and may be perceived as little more than a necessity in order to keep a company running. It is perhaps for this reason that senior managers will try to put off the day when they need to renew their computer systems particularly as the cost of running old systems may be largely obscured from their view. System conversion can also be delayed because there is no manager who is willing to take responsibility for the conversion.

We would expect that perceptions of the desirability, costs and opportunities implied by a major systems renewal will differ considerably depending on the particular location of actors within an organisation, and their perception of and involvement with the systems in question. These differing perceptions may lead to considerable latent or open conflict around the issue of systems renewal. This appears to have been the case at Pensco, as we shall now see. In particular, the issue of system renewal was given some urgency by the decision to renew and extend the company's pensions products and systems. For this decision was taken with the specific recognition that the pensions project would use a new product and system 'philosophy' to build flexibility into product designs and 'reusability' into systems modules. Here we argue that the project did not confront the question as to whether its ambitious plans were remotely feasible without first renewing the core Pensco computer systems with which any new system would be forced to interact.

In the middle 1980s Pensco had a number of different computer systems, most of which were integrated with one another. At the centre of these systems was the accounting system and the master data file. These stored and transacted financial and policy data. The accounting system carried out functions such as the calculation of premium and commission payments while the master data file stored relevant client policy data. The latter was connected to front-end systems like the new business system and the business movements system (the system that records alterations to policies in force, such as changes in address, premium payments, etc.).

These systems were first developed in the early 1970s using batch processing technology. In the early 1980s the IS Division implemented a strategy to renew many of these systems and bring them on-line. This strategy was pursued until the middle 1980s through the renewal of the On-Line New Business System. It had as its central aim the improvement of service levels to customers and financial intermediaries and was driven by IS and CS senior managers. In the middle 1980s the new General Manager began to make different demands of the IS Division. In particular, he was more concerned to develop systems to support new products rather than completing the on-line system renewal project. In effect, he was willing to sacrifice long-term cost savings for what he hoped would be increased sales and a protection of Pensco's falling market share. Thus in 1983 and 1984 there was a considerable shift of IS resources away from systems renewal towards the development of a new executive pensions product. The General Manager let it be known that this was very much 'his baby' [*sic*] and if it did not meet its launch date it would do so 'over his dead body'. When this product was launched it did not have an on-line processing system and, although it proved popular, it was one of the most administratively costly products on the market according to confidential figures produced by the Association of British Insurers.

When questioned about this state of affairs, Pensco's internal IT Strategy Consultant, appointed in 1988, commended the initial on-line conversion strategy. However, he commented that once the obvious high cost benefit systems had been converted, the strategy had 'lost its way' as the General Manager mobilised his demands for product development. In 1987 considerable conversion work remained to be completed. However, this concerned the 'old and less glamorous' housekeeping systems, the expensive update of which appeared to offer few immediate benefits to senior managers. Consequently, the renewal of these systems was put towards the end of the IS Division's long backlog of systems development, described as 'quite horrendous' by the General Manager.

In the late 1980s during the pensions project Pensco's system infrastructure then consisted of a mixture of relatively modern on-line processing and product systems running alongside and integrated with old accounting and central database systems. The latter database system had been subject to a limited conversion in the mid-1980s whereby part of this had been switched from tape to disk storage. However, this conversion was not completed and consequently a tape-based system was running alongside the disk-based system.

One project leader estimated that having to write duplicate programs to communicate with this dual database system increased programming effort by as much as 40 percent. It had been planned to carry out the necessary and costly alterations to the master file to bring it all on to a disk-based system but this plan was deferred in favour of developing the pensions project.

At the centre of Pensco's computer systems, then, there were major constraints caused by the dual structure of the master data file. This not only increased the cost of developing new systems but also imposed considerable limits on the design of those systems. For example, the structure and number of data fields that could be set up with regard to a new product was restricted by the existing structure of the database and its manifest inflexibility.

Added to this problem was the general state of many of these systems and some of the later systems developed during the on-line renewal project. In 1988 Pensco systems were described by a relative newcomer to the company in CS in the following terms:

> The systems that are there are so shaky; they're creaking, over-complicated, out of date, ill documented and far too reliant on what's in people's heads, and no major revision is planned.

A senior system analyst echoed this point of view when she said of the Pensco system infrastructure:

> It's a huge meshed system where you can't touch anything without affecting everything. It's quite a challenge really. There are half a dozen IS staff who know what to do; most don't have a clue.

And a system analyst with the company for two and a half years commented:

> Even the most minor changes don't seem to be simple here. The documentation is very poor and it is difficult to discover what the system does and no-one will own up to knowing what it does.

This view of Pensco systems was widespread among the IS development staff we interviewed and one staff member commented that finding someone with a good working knowledge of the accounting system, which stood at the core of Pensco systems, was like looking for gold dust. A project leader in the IS Division commented:

> With some of the system you get hold of the specification and it's all falling apart. It's had about 125 amendments to it and the original logic of the specification doesn't hold up. It's just a pile of old code. It doesn't seem to have any rhyme or reason to it.

Reading this passage it is hard to remember we are hearing about the so-called 'new technology' of the 1970s which is now summed up in this image of crumbling decreptitude. In general the quotes above reveal a number of interesting points: the 'meshed' (interlinked) character of Pensco systems where even minor changes have repercussions throughout the network of systems; the lack of good documentation; reliance on the knowledge of systems that IS staff hold in their heads; and the difficulty of accessing or finding this information that IS staff may not want to 'own up to knowing'.

The continued existence of Pensco's old systems severely constrained the pensions project both in the detail of the systems designed and the resources that were sucked into 'bodging' (integrating) the new systems into the old ones. This happened even where systems staff set out with the specific intention of avoiding such constraints. For example, the consultant system designer brought in to work on the new accounting system argued:

> The danger is that we affect the system design to fit what is there rather than what it should have. So we're ignoring what's there and specifying what we want in the future.

However, the consultant designer discovered that he could not do this in practice. This became clear with regard to the structure of the existing database on the master data file. A consequence of the database structure was that the file structures for new business were constructed in such a way that the systems would not issue premium payment demands until every piece of policy information had been entered on the system. This often took three months and in the mean time no premiums were being collected and no commissions were being paid to financial intermediaries. This was considered to be an unacceptable delay by the Sales and Marketing Division and as a consequence the consultant designer on the new accounting system felt constrained to 'start building in all sorts of tricks to get round the system ... rather than confronting the problem'. The consultant designer argued that the database file structure should have been changed during the pensions project. However, he believed it had remained in place because the senior IS staff who might have effected such a change were so used to the file structure that they simply did not 'see' the problems facing them.

Reflecting on the theme of old Pensco systems, the Technology and Planning Manager in the IS Division reckoned the pensions project was a fundamentally contradictory undertaking for Pensco. That is, it attempted to build flexible business-orientated systems on the basis of inflexible machine capacity-orientated systems of the 1970s. As he saw it, five years previously 70 percent of the IS resource would probably have been devoted to developing administrative systems with an emphasis on maximising machine use. This in part resulted from the 1970s when hardware costs were relatively greater than system development costs. In the middle and late 1980s the emphasis in IS divisions within the insurance industry was shifting away from administrative system development towards marketing-led systems. This immediately posed problems for systems developers and Pensco's 'IT strategy' because little or no thought had been given to building 'business flexibility' into the systems developed in the company in the early 1980s. Yet in the late 1980s this flexibility was considered to be an essential prerequisite for the development of a marketing-led approach to IT use. Given this situation, it is interesting to consider why the issue of Pensco's incompatible systems did not become a recognised problem at the beginning of the pensions project.

During our interviews with IS Division staff and managers a number of partial explanations were advanced to explain the failure to recognise and act upon the systems infrastructure problem. These included explanations based on expediency, lack of information, fear, blame shifting and costs and costing.

A first explanation of the continuation of the old systems problem concerns expediency and security. The ex-Systems Manager, who was promoted sideways and upwards to head up Computer Operations when the IS Division was reorganised in 1984, was one of the most vociferous opponents of the strategy adopted when developing the pensions project. He believed that it would have been possible, and in fact was vital, to complete the conversion of Pensco's old systems while also developing the pensions project. In the event, a 'more expedient route was taken by using the existing systems where it was thought it would be quicker and more sure to deliver'. This was a route that he believed would lead to continuing and expensive systems maintenance problems.

This route appears to have largely been decided upon by the new IS AGM and the Pensions Systems Manager who was to become the Project Manager for the pensions project. In the view of the Technology and Planning Manager, who had worked alongside the IS AGM at their previous employer, the IS AGM had 'a large hand' in the decision to use the existing systems. He concluded that it sounded like it was the IS AGM's idea when he had been at Pensco a short while and had an imperfect understanding of what he was taking on. In his view, the IS AGM had not realised the large differences between systems at Pensco and their previous employer.

The Computer Operations Manager largely agreed with this position in that he argued that the IS AGM 'would have taken this decision on advice because he wouldn't have known the existing systems'. In his view the IS AGM not only had an imperfect understanding of the situation, he was also given bad advice by the Pensions Systems Manager.

It is understandable perhaps that the IS AGM and Project Manager ended up taking the decision they did. This appeared to minimise the risk of the project running out of control and the collapse of Pensco system capabilities. Indeed, in 1987 the IS AGM had made it very clear that he was unwilling to contemplate developing major new product and processing systems while also undertaking system conversion work: his philosophy was 'one step at a time'. And given the General Manager's concern to launch new products, and the IS AGM's reputation as an IS specialist with a penchant for a 'marketing-driven' approach, it is perhaps not surprising that the managers in question plumped for product development rather than system conversion.

This decision was also influenced by the costs and benefits involved in the different strategies: it was relatively easy to make a case for the business-generating character of the pensions project as compared to the resource-consuming character of systems conversion. Not only was it also relatively easy to make a case for product development over systems conversion: it was also easier to produce figures for the potential profit accruing from the pensions project although, as we have seen, these were not entirely convincing. It was much more difficult to demonstrate in a convincing and recognised manner the adverse cost effects of continuing to run the old systems. This situation was summed up by the consultant Project Manager brought in to save the pensions project in the following manner:

> The problem is that continuing with the old systems is very expensive but so is replacing them. So whichever way you jump the situation is getting worse and the longer you leave it the more it will cost you. If the one generates profits and the other costs you money you choose the one that generates profits as the soft option.

A more general consideration to be taken into account when dealing with the emergence or burial of particular problems in organisations concerns the prevailing managerial culture and style with regard to constituting and solving problems. At Pensco in the middle 1980s there was a considerable climate of fear among managers as the new General Manager brought in sweeping changes and practically replaced the entire senior management team. The manner in which this style was implemented in the IS Division under the control of the new AGM created fear and resentment among managers and staff working on the pensions project. Given this adverse climate we believe that all but the most courageous or self-assured managers would not have wanted to bring difficult problems to the attention of their new senior management team, that is, unless they felt able to offer a brilliant, simple and relatively painless solution to them. Furthermore, it is unlikely that senior managers, who were made responsible for the achievement of specific key corporate objectives, would have wanted to be made responsible for corporate tasks that seemed difficult or impossible to achieve given the IS resources available and the pressures on their allocation to product development. Indeed, in the middle of the pensions project the IS AGM apparently attempted to remove the problem of long-term system architecture from the list of IS divisional key tasks for which he was responsible. It appears that it was only his Assistant AGM's furious reaction (we were told by a participating manager that he 'went berserk') to this suggestion that kept the prospect of an eventual renewal of Pensco systems on the corporate agenda.

Junior IS managers were increasingly concerned with fundamental problems in the the IS Division and Pensco's systems that were not getting the recognition they deserved. For example, one project leader was angry that the 'real' problems with Pensco systems were not being recognised and she sincerely hoped that someone would find the courage to stand up and say, 'We are in an awful mess.' However, instead of asking the question 'what shall we do' she felt that the IS AGM was more concerned to ask: 'How did we get here' in order to find someone to blame for the mess rather than trying to sort it out. In despair she concluded:

> Somebody has to accept that if we don't spend the money [on new systems] we won't be in the market. We can't react fast enough and the pensions project is costing us a fortune and it shouldn't cost that.

Another project leader thought it unlikely that someone would dare to stand up and make this pronouncement. As he saw it the 'mess' of Pensco systems referred to above was a source of constant embarrassment to IS senior management. He said:

> The Steering Committee doesn't understand this problem; they don't want to. It's an embarrassment for IS; the IS AGM is constantly embarrassed by the fact that it costs us so much to do what appears to be a fairly simple problem.

Rather than increase his embarassment the IS AGM and his senior managers appear to have preferred to play down, ignore or bury the problems posed for the pensions project by Pensco's old systems.

IS STAFF

In the 1980s the buoyancy of IS specialist labour markets in SE England in which Pensco was located (see Chapter 4) was favourable to IS career strategies based on job hopping from one company to another (see Friedman, 1987a). Such strategies tended to broaden IS specialists' knowledge through an experience of different technology and business contexts. However, they caused major problems for organisations eager to recruit and retain these scarce staff.

These general labour market conditions had a considerable impact on IS recruitment and the staffing profile of the Pensco IS Division in a period of rapid expansion. (The systems development section of IS doubled its headcount from 35 in 1979 to 70 in 1985.) In particular, there was a large gap between a predominance of time-served Pensco IS senior and middle managers and relatively young programming and analyst staff, half of whom had been with Pensco for less than two years.

The IS manager with responsibility for recruitment recalled that when she had arrived at Pensco in the early 1980s there had been no IS staff turnover whatsoever in what she regarded as a 'closeted environment'. She was amazed to find that:

> No-one looked for another job or read the computer press. I couldn't believe it. Where I came from you spent 50 per cent of your time looking for jobs.

The relatively stable IS environment at Pensco was in part responsible for the creation of a skills gap where there was a group of 'oldies' in middle management and a 'huge chunk of new people'. Further, she considered it 'quite odd that everyone stayed on in IS to become middle management' and suggested that domination of the IS Division by these 'oldies' generated a conservative culture that was apt to shy away from radical IT solutions.

The ex-IS AGM gave two reasons for the tendency for some IS staff to stay with the company despite opportunities elsewhere. Firstly, 'Anyone who is any good goes up [the IS structure] very quickly...there are shortages at every level.' Secondly, the company had developed a policy for holding on to staff:

> We tie them in with mortgages and things like that which appeals to the family man. We now give it to single people...so you can give enormous mortgages or far more than the same salary would hold down outside. It means they can only move to another finance organisation...*we have to trap them in.*

This lack of turnover in the early 1980s in the IS Division and the subsequent promotion of time-served men into middle managerial positions in the IS Division (during our work there were no women in middle management positions in the division) gave added weight to the creation of a systems development culture that enjoyed considerable autonomy from the rest of the organisation and was marked by an *ad hoc* and informal managerial style. This embedded culture, and its strong allies in IS middle management, had important consequences for the pensions project. These were articulated by the consultant Project Manager brought in to sort out the project. In his view the pensions project had an ambitious 'but not unreasonable' timescale. However, in order to have achieved this ambitious timescale Pensco required IS skills not at its disposal.

The consultant PM believed Pensco had serious problems in its IS Division. These concerned the relatively high percentage of trainees and IS specialists with little experience in the division: a situation the consultant PM attributed to the insurance industry's lack of 'IT image' which has made it difficult to attract the cream of the IS specialists, 'the high fliers'. Thus, Pensco had not been able to attract the senior system analysts and project leaders and managers it required to control and co-ordinate the pensions project.

At the same time all of the IS Division's middle managers had been with the company for a long time and were to an extent stuck in a rut:

> Certainly if you work in two or three places you manage to pick up the best techniques and learn the lessons from other installations. Whereas if you've been in one installation for twenty years you don't make the basic comparisons; you can't say: Oh, they're making that mistake because I've seen it made somewhere else.

From this line of thought the consultant PM concluded that the problem at Pensco was not 'technological' as such. It was rather a problem of organisational and system development technique. With regard to staff he argued that Pensco particularly lacked the middle layers who become the high fliers of the future. This lack of staff with a broad IT experience and detailed business skills was particularly felt due to the competing and changing views of the markets in which the pension products were to be sold and the generally high level of contextual uncertainty surrounding the project. Said the consultant PM:

> If you know exactly what you want to do you can implement a system very satisfactorily with average calibre staff. *If you have uncertainty it requires people with a great deal of experience in that industry, who also have a degree of creative flair to come up with flexible solutions which can accommodate uncertainty.*

As will be recalled, 'flexibility' was a major concern of the pension project in its early days when the guiding idea was to create flexible products and flexible systems able to cater for changing client needs and changing product market requirements. This desire for flexibility coupled with market and legislative uncertainty put a premium on broad and in-depth knowledge of different approaches to systems development and the insurance industry.

The consultant PM argued that in order to build flexibility into systems this could either be achieved in an *ad hoc* or planned fashion. With regard to the former he said that it was possible to try and add in flexibility as you went along. However, it was preferable to have a long-term vision of the type of system architecture a company was trying to build. At Pensco the pensions project attempted to build flexibility into the systems in an *ad hoc* manner as the project developed. The attainment of this objective was massively hampered by the size of the project, the constant changes within it, the calibre of IS staff at Pensco and the state of Pensco core systems.

SYSTEMS DEVELOPMENT CULTURE

The culture of the IS Division at Pensco in the early 1980s was based on strong personal loyalties, considerable divisional autonomy, and informal and *ad hoc* methods of systems development. In those days, looked back to with a certain nostalgia by older members of the development staff, 'jobs took as long as it took to finish them'; staff worked in 'small, very comfortable friendly teams'; and many of them felt a strong personal loyalty to their AGM. As one older member of staff put it, 'he was the sort of guy you'd walk through walls for'. Senior management's paternalism, and tendency to hold itself responsible for everything, placed few pressures on individual managers to perform and there were few checks on progress.

In the early 1980s the IS Division was in a strong organisational position. Pensco was dominated by the actuaries who were financially conservative and had few general or 'professional' managerial skills whereas IS managers had received considerable managerial training and were accustomed to planning and monitoring operations. In the IS Assistant Divisional Manager's opinion, this gave the division an 'unduly influential' position in the company. As a consequence IS managers 'were able to drive, with very little control over what they were doing, more or less in the direction they wanted to go'. With the arrival of the new General Manager, and the growth of the Sales and Marketing

Division, the influence of the IS Division was on the wane. The IS Assistant Divisional Manager (in 1985) felt all right about this development:

> Um, I'm personally pleased because I think that essentially whilst we can add to the general direction of the company, broadly we are here to provide a service first and something over and above that second. You can't buck your general managerial responsibilities but primarily we're here to allow other people to do things.

IS managers' ability to 'drive in the direction they wanted to go', at least in part, was responsible for the huge project to update Pensco's batch administrative systems to on-line systems. This project dominated the company between 1980 and 1985 and focused on using IT to improve service quality to Pensco's financial intermediaries and customers. As such, it was a process-driven application of systems that concentrated on upgrading systems that made a direct contribution to service quality. Within this strategy there was also the intention of renewing Pensco's core accounting systems but, even at this time, it was difficult to cost-justify this on top of the spending already undertaken to complete the on-line conversion work.

IS staff worked in a relatively relaxed *laissez faire* atmosphere. The on-line developments suffered budget and time overruns but nobody seemed particularly worried until the new General Manager arrived. One middle manager in IS went so far as to say of these days, 'Senior management might have set targets but if you missed them you knew damn well most probably no one would worry about it.'

This IS culture, and the methods of system development it favoured, appeared to work when the division was relatively small and concentrated its activities around one major project. But these conditions were rapidly changing: IS systems development headcount rose from 35 in 1979 to 70 in 1985; IT began to be used in a product-driven manner as technological and market possibilities changed; and the new General Manager and his fierce IS AGM were about to appear on the scene. The old IS culture and methods were not suited for this new business climate and the IS AGM set about with a will to transform them.

New IS staff were critical not only of the meshed and confused systems but also the systems development methods. They criticised the absence of a formal business requirements format and signing-off procedures. Such procedures would have allowed IS staff to, as one project leader put it, 'screw down the users'. Their absence added to increasing tensions between IS and CS staff as the latter division 'bunged everything they could think of into the business requirements'. In response the former 'chucked out what they considered to be non-essential': a situation that created a much commented on 'us and them' tension between the two divisions.

Another point raised in the interviews regarding system development techniques concerned the absence of a technical design. This resulted in the practice of 'designing as we go along' and exacerbated senior managers' apparent inability to recognise the problems that the periodic reviews of the project they commissioned might have brought to light. For example, when the Technology and Planning Manager reviewed the project in September 1986 he found that those in charge of the project 'weren't acknowledging that the problem [with the business requirements] existed and nothing was being done about it'. This 'failure to acknowledge' the problem was commented on by many IS staff. However, rather than 'failures' as such the marginalisation and mystification of these problems may have been intentional strategies pursued by managers anxious to limit the proliferation of difficult and threatening problems around the pensions project.

CONCLUSION

In summary the problems created by Pensco's old systems' infrastructure were well known and acknowledged by IS staff working on the pensions project. Nevertheless, a number of factors combined to minimise this problem and led senior managers to attempt to build the pensions project's new 'flexible and reusable' product systems on the basis of the existing system infrastructure. These factors included considerations of expediency and security under conditions not of the organisation's making, a lack of information flowing up to the IS AGM, and his and the IS system manager's reluctance to 'own' the systems infrastructure problem. In addition, there was the difficulty of assessing the quantitative and financial implications of the problem and convincing the senior management team, and the General Manager in particular, that the problem merited immediate attention and the expenditure of considerable resources.

Thus the problem of the technology context at Pensco was more than a strictly material one concerning the organisation's system legacy. Undoubtedly this legacy placed restrictions on the realisation of the pensions project's ambitious plans but, as we have seen, the manner in which it did this was complex. That is, senior managers do not appear to have been aware of, or did not want to privilege, the problem of the old systems and the manner in which it might impinge on their objectives. Rather, there seems to have been little eagerness to 'problematise' the systems legacy and bring it to senior management's attention.

If Pensco's system legacy was a heavy burden in the face of the desire to radically alter company culture and practices so too were the existing staff, particularly managers, and practices within the IS Division. This was particularly apparent with regard to the dominance of the systems development area by Pensco 'oldies' and the development methods they favoured.

Evidently the new GM and IS AGM had hoped speedily to sweep away these old practices and their associated culture. To this end the head of the division, who commanded considerable staff loyalty, was pushed into the Customer Service Division while his lieutenant was moved away from the strategically important systems area.

The IS AGM then attempted to institute a range of new reporting procedures to increase control and surveillance of his division. His heavy handed and aggressive management had the effect of inducing considerable fear among middle managers. However, they quickly learnt to sing the new corporate tune and produce the kind of quantitative paper results the IS AGM wanted to see. But beneath the figures and managerial reports that were intended to please and placate the IS AGM, a different older world existed uncomfortably and subterraneously beside the new imperatives from on high. This was the 'pure Pensco of old' referred to by the Technology and Planning Manager.

This 'oldness' was deeply rooted in the practices and culture of the IS specialist collective and its individual members. Many of these latter had made considerable investments in time, energy and identification with these practices and so long as they continued to be the organisational and cultural norm at Pensco, individuals' positions and identities were relatively secure. Furthermore, new members of the division with new ideas and different IS experiences found it extremely difficult to make their voices heard. And, as we have seen with regard to the old systems problem, systems developers new to the division were constantly forced to compromise their previous ways of working in order to accommodate Pensco's peculiarities. As such, new recruits, particularly those with little or no commercial systems development experience, were likely to be rapidly 'embedded' within the predominant Pensco way of building systems.

In this chapter we have examined the ways in which past decisions and practices are embedded within Pensco systems and the manner in which these constrained the pension project's aim of creating flexible and reusable systems. These were the specific technological conditions of possibility at Pensco but they were differentially articulated by IS managers. We concluded that, for a variety of reasons, the IS AGM and Project Manager could not or did not want to 'see' the problem of Pensco's old systems. Other actors such as IS project leaders and analysts could 'see' or construct this problem but they were not in a position to make it an organisational issue. Someone had to stand up and say, 'Pensco systems are in a terrible mess' but IS staff and junior managers could only say this to their IS superiors and these managers did not want to hear this 'bad news' nor convey it to the General Manager.

From this we concluded that it is important not only to look at the constraints and opportunities represented by technological conditions of possibility but also to examine the interplay of organisational politics and the process of socially constituting these conditions. This is an aspect of IT research that has until now been largely neglected, even in those accounts of systems development that have usefully highlighted the constraints often implied by existing systems and IS cultures (e.g. Kling and Scachi, 1982). That is, systems development is more than a mere technical activity. Rather, it is a process of constituting the meaning, or developing a particular understanding, of an organisation. This concerns not only the constitution of the meaning of an organisation in terms of its objectives and activities with regard to a particular system development but also in terms of the conditions of possibility faced by that system development.

The process through which one construction of those conditions of possibility comes to be established is crucial for systems development projects. This is because the aims and objectives of such projects will be required to take account of, or perhaps subvert, that construction of organisational reality. In the Pensco case there appears to have been relatively little organisational reflection on the technology context in terms of the company's existing systems infrastructure and systems development capabilities. Even in the assessments of the 'completed' pensions project, Pensco's system infrastructures and staff were not recognised as a constraint on the project—a fact perhaps not unsurprising in that these assessments were largely led and controlled by those very IS staff who constituted part of the 'problem' of Pensco's technological conditions of possibility.

Increasingly, large users of IT are having to confront the problem of the huge 'sunk costs' represented by earlier generations of systems technologies, methods and cultures. As we hope is apparent from this chapter, the way in which this problem is constituted within organisations is itself not immune from the interplay of organisational politics. Therefore, it cannot be taken for granted that the currently dominant understanding of an organisation's systems constraints and opportunities is necessarily the best or most appropriate one with regard to assessing the potential success and cost of planned systems development projects.

If this is so it suggests organisations may need to develop different ways of considering their conditions of technological possibility. These might be well served by mechanisms that encourage the open contrast of different constructions and interpretations of these conditions. Whether or not this is possible in organisations where the identities of the participants are so closely tied to a favourable interpretation of their past actions remains to be seen.

11
The Politics of User Relations: The IS Division

INTRODUCTION

As discussed in Chapter 1, certain recent sociological studies of technology have been concerned to understand the social 'shaping' or 'construction' of technology. In so doing both these schools of enquiry have expressed an intention to look within the hitherto unexplored 'black box' of technology. In effect, though, social shapers (e.g. MacKenzie and Wajcman, 1989) have tended to focus on the forces, such as class, gender and political economy, that shape the black box of technology. Social constructivists, such as those represented in Bijker et al. (1987), have tended to look in greater detail at the contents of the black box of technology. As such, they examine a range of detailed conditions of technological and social possibility and their interactions. Unfortunately, though, in the process they almost totally ignore the broader social conditions of possibility privileged by the social shapers (Russell, 1987).

In the previous chapter we looked into the black box of technology inasmuch as we examined in some detail the constraints on systems development represented by Pensco's particular conditions of technological possibility (systems, and IS staff and culture). In this chapter we want to take this further by exploring a range of technology practices at Pensco.

In a recent collection of essays coming from one faction of the social constructivist school centred around Rank Xerox's Cambridge Euro-PARC, previous research using this framework is taken to task for not looking sufficiently closely at the work processes of technological innovation or systems development (Button, 1993). In Button's collection different contributions focus on a detailed examination of system user/developer interactions and work processes by employing an eth-nomethodological research methodology (see, for example, Harper and Hughes, 1993; Sharrock and Anderson, 1993). These generate interesting accounts of the 'content of technology' by attending to the fine detail of work processes and the search for mutual understanding between users and developers. However, these are rarely located within a broader context of these specific situations and practices. Not only are the macro-social relations of market economy, race and gender discounted but also these accounts fail to theorise or explore the internal operation of power and politics within the organisations that represent their research sites.

This failure raises a fundamental issue as to what is meant by 'the contents of technology' or the 'black box'. Synthetically speaking, social shaping theory understands the content of technology to mean macro-social relations, where these concern the exercise of power and control, as they are operationalised at particular sites of technology development or use. Social constructivists, on the other hand, understand 'the content of technology' to be the detailed interactions between a web (Pinch and Bijker, 1987) or network of actors (Callon, 1987, 1991). In these approaches the primary concern is understanding the activation and establishment of social relations around the crystallisation of particular technology solutions.

Our definition of the 'contents of technology' draws to some extent on each of the approaches outlined above. As already mentioned, we define 'technology' as more than an artefact. Technology is represented by artefacts but includes the skills, techniques and cultures of technologists. Therefore, the contents of technology's black box concerns the practices, techniques, culture and personnel of those engaged in particular sites of technological activity. However, and this is where we differ from the various social constructivist approaches, we insist that these particular sites of activity must be placed in their broader conditions of possibility in terms of macro level social relations, organisational specificities and technological contexts. Furthermore, as we have argued throughout this book, these conditions of possibility are associated with particular distributions of rules and resources, the exercise of power, and the pursuit or preservation of particular identities.

While agreeing with the social shapers on the centrality of power we have attempted to develop a more explicit analytical perspective for understanding power and politics within organisations, in general, and the management of information technology, in particular. This, we hope, moves beyond that notion of power underpinned by the legacy of Marxism inherent in the social shaping perspective. That is, we see relations of class, gender and the market as broad conditions of possibility of human action rather than as acting directly, in a unilinear and almost autonomous fashion on sites of technological activity. Rather, these macro levels of possibility are overlayered by organisational and micro levels of possibility that have a profound and enduring impact on technological innovation and development. Additionally, we have insisted on the importance of linking power to notions of identity and subjectivity and the manner in which subjects become tied to, and struggle to maintain, particular organisational and specialist identities as managers.

Thus far, we have argued that the social construction, mobilisation and interaction of these possibilities is played out through the process of organisational, or inter-organisational, politics. It follows, therefore, that for us an essential part of the 'contents of technology' concerns that political process. As such, the interactions of actors involved in technological activities are both a condition and consequence of that complex and multi-dimensional process.

In this chapter we want to employ this approach with regard to the content of technology processes within Pensco's IS Division. Here our focus differs somewhat from the bulk of sociological writing on systems development which tend to privilege user/developer relations (see, for example, Sharrock and Anderson, 1993; Harper and Hughes, 1993). Rather than looking at systems design and analysis our concern here is on the detailed organisational and functional divisions that render systems development possible. In particular, we examine the embeddedness of systems development within the specific hierarchies and career concerns of Pensco's IS Division and the practices that emerged out of these during the pensions project.

In some respects, this bears a resemblance to an analysis of the labour process of systems development (Friedman and Cornford, 1989). However, it differs in that we are not only interested in the tensions between labour control, co-ordination and competition within systems development. We are also interested in the way in which IS managers attempt to construct, through various social and political mechanisms, a favourable reality of their endeavours. As such, we would suggest that managing the labour process is an attempt both to control and to co-ordinate labour power and construct a particular, localised and temporally limited interpretation of organisational process that reflects favourably on those in charge of that labour process.

The, much neglected, notion of managerial practice as attempts to control and channel the construction of meaning casts a new light on Pettigrew's (1973) notion of the 'technological gatekeeper'. In his study, Pettigrew theorised the gatekeeper as an actor with a monopoly control of scarce information regarding technological possibilities. Certainly, IS managers have been in a position, although weakened in recent years, to exercise this control of information. But we would argue that IS, and most other managers do more than control information. Rather, they are in the business of constituting the meaning of their activities and those of their subordinates. For example, we have already seen the way in which the IS AGM and Project Manager attempted to create a favourable interpretation of the pension project.

In this chapter we focus on the details of managerial activities around meaning constitution within the IS Division. Specifically, we examine the position, role and tactics of the IS AGM and Project Manager in their efforts to act, to borrow a phrase from Callon (1991), as 'obligatory passage points' through which both the activities and meaning of the pensions project had to pass and thereby be controlled.

We then go on to look at the way in which marketing-led IT use was practised at Pensco and the way in which the IS AGM mobilised IS practices to discipline his managers and staff by, firstly, taking on impossible systems demands and, secondly, instituting a 'milestone mania' that individualised responsibilites and disciplinary pressures.

TOWARDS USER-LED COMPUTING

In earlier chapters we have discussed the onset of the so-called 'user relations' phase of systems development. In Chapter 5 we went further and examined the ambiguities of power relations in a user-led systems development project at another financial services company. In this we saw how IS specialists have resisted user incursions into their organisational domain while at the same time embracing the rhetoric of IS-as-service-provider.

It will be recalled that the emergence of the user relations phase of systems development is associated with a number of key developments. Firstly, an increasing number of users are interested in the IS resource as IT applications spread through organisations. Secondly, the process of systems development and the management of the IT resource become more complex as applications multiply and there is an increasing focus on business and market-sensitive systems. Thirdly, this complexity is associated with a more intense relationship with users, who increasingly lead systems development projects. And fourthly, the position of IS managers becomes both more public and vulnerable as IS applications become central to organisational strategies (cf. Friedman and Cornford, 1989).

In the financial services sector these developments have had their own particular features, one of which has been the emergence of a powerful and assertive marketing specialism much favoured by the rhetoric of Thatcherism, chief executives and industry advisers alike.

The rise of this specialism has been associated with a shift in the emphasis of IT applications away from 'back office' administrative systems towards product and, latterly, distribution systems (see Murray et al, 1992).

In Chapter 10 we examined the significant problems Pensco senior management faced in introducing a regime of marketing- or business-driven IT use. The IS Division was a world unto itself, dominated by time-served Pensco-trained male IS managers somewhat out of touch with new ideas regarding systems development. They had broken their teeth developing administrative systems at a time when maximising hardware usage was at a premium. Systems methods were suprisingly informal and relaxed and there appears to have been little sense of urgency within the division. This was to change dramatically with the arrival of the new General Manager and his IS AGM.

In this section we examine the changes that the IS AGM tried to implement within the IS Division. These had two primary and explicit objectives. Firstly, the IS AGM wanted to tie IS developments more firmly to Pensco's General Manager's marketing-driven priorities. Secondly, he wanted to raise IS staff productivity. Bringing about these changes was not straightforward due to the embeddedness of IS practices and cultures and the ambiguities of a 'user relations' phase of systems development. We also believe the IS AGM had a third, less public, objective. This was to ensure that he controlled and directed assessments of his division's performance and success.

The arrival of the new General Manager and IS AGM signalled important changes at Pensco. The General Manager was determined to introduce tight planning and monitoring procedures involving strictly quantified targets and deadlines in his mission to protect Pensco market share and professionalise its management team. He was also keen, given his acknowledged strength in marketing, to focus the company's attention outwards to look for new growth opportunities and keep a closer eye on competitors. In particular, this meant responding to the new opportunities created by market and technological changes to launch an extended range of life and pensions products.

IT strategy at Pensco switched, therefore, during this period from a process driven approach to a product driven one that responded to the General Manager's concerns to maximise Pensco sales in expanding and diversifying markets. This strategy, such as it was, was directly fed by the company's product launch schedule and, as we saw in Chapter 9, paid little attention to longer-term systems infrastructural problems.

Instead of a long-term and proactive strategy the General Manager's and IS AGM's main concern was keeping up with the competition. So the size and direction of Pensco IT use was a follow-my-leader affair determined by competitor IT use. On this point, the General Manager said:

> Competitive pressures drive you to make not commercial judgements per se but *intuitive judgements*. For example, are you going to link the hardware in your biggest branches to the mainframe. The answer is: every other bloody life office is doing it so we're going to have to.

This copycat approach was espoused by the IS AGM who believed that Pensco was not spending enough on IT. He therefore persuaded the General Manager to set up the monitoring of IT spending by competitors in order to make sure that Pensco matched it.

The IS AGM was in a difficult position. On the one hand he was keen to prove his worth to the General Manager as a 'switched on' marketing-driven IS man. On the other, he was responsible for sorting out Pensco's system 'mess' and the day-to-day running of systems development. As such, the IS AGM was caught between his desire to promote user-driven IT use (particularly when the user was the General Manager) and his concern to maintain control of IS resources and systems development practices. The IS AGM could only square this tricky circle if he could both create the impression of full-blooded marketing driven IT use and maintain a tight control on manufacture of systems and systems development successes. The IS AGM attempted to do this by imposing rigid controls over the IS Division and systems development while embracing the rhetoric and structures of user-led computing. This he did in an aggressive and openly political manner which contrasts sharply with struggles for IS control of systems development analysed in Chapter 5.

Reorganising the IS Division

The IS AGM recruited by the new General Manager was in stark contrast to his predecessor. This latter manager had been shunted sideways to head the Customer Services Division. He was a gentle, easy going man who inspired fierce loyalty from his staff. The new IS AGM was a highly ambitious and aggressive operator keen to make his mark on Pensco. He was perhaps keenly in tune and nourished by the re-emergence of an intransigent macho management style closely associated with the years of Margaret Thatcher's governments, most graphically represented by Ian McGregor's aggressive management of the National Coal Board during the miner's strike of 1984–85.

On arriving at Pensco, the IS AGM promptly sacked three members of the IS Division and within a very short time he had IS managers 'shaking in their boots'. For example, one IS project leader observed that at IS divisional meetings departmental managers visibly shook when they read out their weekly reports, and engaged in overt blame-shifting attempts if they ran into problems.

By the late 1980s this fierce managerial style had created 'a really closed environment [where] people were running around in fear of senior management'; according to the IT Strategy Manager. This was particularly noticeable in the systems departments of IS where managers were particularly concerned not to 'step out of line'. The IS AGM's punitive managerial style invoked fear and made managers very anxious to avoid mistakes. This meant that managers were inclined to tell the IS AGM what he wanted to hear. It also had implications for vertical communications within the division. For example, within the pensions project one IS project leader commented, 'everything that goes to the Steering Committee goes up through various levels and various levels will change it. I'll say [to my departmental manager]: we missed this because we underestimated. By the time it gets to [the IS AGM] it will probably be: we missed this because we didn't get the requirements.'

The thrust of the IS AGM's reorganisation of the division was to introduce much greater direct senior and middle management control over the day-to-day running of the division. This was done by placing great emphasis on reporting mechanisms to him and the clear setting and monitoring of numerical targets. These changes had a significant impact on managerial practices in the division. They also changed the definition of what it was to be a competent IS manager at Pensco.

One of the IS Business Systems Managers expressed his concern over this development in 1985. Before the new General Manager arrived Pensco had a reputation for being a cosy company that was a good place to train as an actuary or become an IS manager, as many actuarial students did. With the establishment of the new regime, initially he felt confused and anxious because the company culture was obviously changing but 'nobody had told you how the ground rules had changed'. In particular, he felt more accountable and more closely observed in terms of performance—it was a harder, sharper, and more demanding surveillance than before—yet he was unsure exactly what he was accountable for. And he was worried that if he did not perform, 'you could find yourself eased out of the company'. This was not his paranoia: the General Manager had 'eased out' most of the existing senior management team and the IS AGM had sacked IS staff in the early days of his appointment.

In the old days, this manager said, you 'knew where you stood'. But now there was a new breed of managers: visionaries who wanted to 'make their mark and shape the company'. This new breed seemed to lack sensitivity:

I'm not saying there's anything wrong with the new breed. It's just a bit difficult to take on board. ... I tend to think they think people should help themselves by managing themselves better.

Two years later this IS manager clearly knew where he stood. Now he was full of praise for the new system and the IS AGM's insistence on hard hitting and hard facts and milestones. His earlier anxiety had disappeared and his concerns for 'sensitivity' seemed much allayed. He declared, with macho pride, 'If IS isn't pulling its weight you need to give them a right rollicking.'

Other managers appear to have undergone similar conversions at least in rhetorical terms. A long serving project manager in another part of the division believed the IS AGM had not fundamentally changed the way people in IS worked. Rather, he had simply made them work harder. This 'top down pressurisation' had allowed him to exert greater pressure on his own staff, a fact he appeared to relish, particularly as this pressure came to settle most intensely on those towards the bottom of the IS hierarchy.

With regard to the setting of IS system development priorities these were now to be established through consultation with user departments. To facilitate this, and the IS AGM's control of the division, the systems development side of IS was split up into three sub-units comprising Life Insurance, Pensions and General Business systems (see Figure 11.1). Each of these was headed up by a Business Systems Manager. IS priorities were then set by each user department relaying its key system development requirements to these managers. They would then negotiate between themselves, with IS AGM as arbiter, until systems development resources were divided up between them. This method of system prioritisation was supposed to rationalise the distribution of IS resources and greatly improve IS responsiveness to business needs. However, as we have already seen, it did not prevent the rapid overloading of the IS resource during the pensions project as new systems requests were taken on by the division.

The effects of 'letting the users in' to the IS Division were ambiguous. On the one hand, it was now impossible to drop a system once it was written into the company's plans, particularly if the General Manager had an interest in seeing that system developed. On the other hand, IS still retained a good deal of control of the systems development process, particularly in its later design and programming stages. Indeed, one Business Systems Manager still felt IS had too much say on what was and was not developed.

The IS AGM attempted to increase this control. Having been given responsibility as Project Sponsor for the pensions project he then chose an IS middle manager to be the Project Manager. According to the IS Assistant Divisional Manager, prior to the arrival of the new IS AGM in

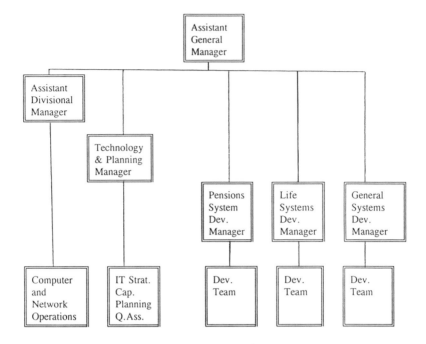

Figure 11.1   Pensco's IS Division Organisation Chart 1989

1984 project managers were considered to be corporate representatives without divisional responsibilities. On his arrival the IS AGM declared:

> I want project management to be an IS function, and we will have IS PMs and they will report to the IS AGM and they will develop the IS bit [of the project].

The Assistant Divisional Manager felt this would make the pensions project 'look like a computer led project and it may end up a computer led project'.

Given the overtly political character of the IS AGM's *modus operandi* at Pensco we would suggest that he insisted on this move in order to control as tightly as possible the 'politics of technology' surrounding systems development. That is, the IS AGM, who had worked under Pensco's General Manager at another company, appeared very keen to live up to the General Manager's expectations of him. This was relatively easy with regard to the area of Computer Operations which was amenable to the kind of quantitative monitoring and analysis favoured by the General Manager. However, from past experience the IS AGM was well aware of the uncertainties surrounding systems development. Thus, the IS AGM would seem to have reasoned that if IS were to be implicated in systems development projects, where it usually had the largest input, it would be advisable that he and his, generally subservient, managers should act as gatekeepers and exercise the maximum control of these projects and assessments of them.

Asked how he saw his role as management sponsor in 1987 the IS AGM replied:

> My role is to make sure people are working in their various divisions, ah ... [pause] taking the decisions and taking them at the right time I can't ... [pause] OK, I've got to comment on decisions, the key decisions come through to the Steering Committee where we jointly take them. As project sponsor I back up the Project Manager and ensure the decisions he's taken ... [pause] and help him make sure that decisions are being taken in the requisite time and people are recognising what the big decisions are, as well as taking an overview for making sure things are happening.

This somewhat disjointed speech was typical of the IS AGM and reflected his constant self-monitoring to ensure that he spoke with the necessary diplomacy. Despite this he nearly let the cat out of the bag when he started to say that he saw his job as backing up the Project Manager's decisions. Immediately, he back-pedalled away from whatever he was about to say and in more diplomatic language suggested that his was merely a supervisory, rather than controlling, role.

New Systems Methods

Despite the IS AGM's efforts to change IS culture in 1989 the Technology and Planning Manager in the division detected, with some disappointment, 'pure Pensco of old'. That is, despite the rapid growth of the company and the IS Division, in his view, its work culture was still based on 'informal mechanisms and everyone knowing each other'. This had worked in the past but with the growth of the company:

> things weren't getting done and when they weren't people said: We'll do it tomorrow and nobody will really mind. That was fine five years ago but it's bad news today. A small organisation can pull all the stops out to get things done but a big organisation has more commitments and less flexibility.

The IS AGM had recruited the Technology and Planning Manager, from their old company, to sort out this situation. In 1988 the TP Manager was rolling out a programme to introduce a new system development framework, a new project management framework and new system development methods. At the time he was under great pressure from the IS AGM to do this as quickly as possible. He preferred what he termed a 'softly, softly' approach but nevertheless issued IS staff with a 150 page system development framework in the middle of the pensions project. The reaction from his hard pressed staff was perhaps predictable. Said one voluble critic:

> It's a load of crap. No one on my team will use it. You can't give someone a document that size and say, 'Start using it'. They'll work if we are given time to make them work. As soon as schedules are tight ten chapters will go aside.

As well as introducing this raft of new frameworks and methods the Technology and Planning Manager was also setting up planning, quality assurance and IT strategy functions in the IS Division. The purpose of these was to rationalise systems development planning and monitor and measure IS productivity.

Overall, the new IS AGM had attempted to reorganise the IS Division to make it more responsive to user needs and more amenable to tight controls. He was aware of the need to transform both IT strategy and systems development methods and had moved to change these. However, his initial intiatives had been hampered by the complexity of the problems facing him, in particular the tensions that lay between the conflicting desires to maintain a tight control of IS and encourage greater IS reponsiveness to business needs.

DISCIPLINE AND MEANING IN THE IS DIVISION

In this section of the chapter we look at the way in which marketing-led IT becomes a disciplinary mechanism for IS managers and staff. Allied to this was the IS AGM's insistence on tight, personalised monitoring of the progress of the pensions project through the so-called 'milestone mania'. Lastly, we examine the IS AGM's tight control of assessments of IS divisional performance through the reporting procedures he established and the absence of a discursive forum where divisional problems and alternative representations of the division and its systems could be raised and aired.

When an IS Manager Just Cannot Say No

There was considerable criticism from within the IS Division of the so-called 'two hats problem' (where the Project Manager of the pensions project was also its IS representative), which was seen to be compounded by the fact that the IS Division also occupied the position of management sponsor within the project. One systems analyst argued that the evident over-representation of the IS Division in the management of the project caused the PM to try and overcome his IS bias by 'going the other way'. She also felt that the IS AGM should have 'push[ed] more for the division' rather than allowing it to take on the 'impossible'. For this analyst, the failure to reject any demands indicated a lack of professionalism within the division and an inability to think through the IS implications of developing particular systems. She went on to say:

> If it's impossible for the IS division we shouldn't say, 'OK, we'll have a go.' The attitude is: 'We'll have a go'. But throughout the project we're aiming at a target we can't hit. When we get close to it we think: No, we can't hit it. So we change [the target] and even that is not very realistic.

Criticism of this prevailing 'have a go' attitude, or what may be seen as a masculine 'heroism' (see Chapters 6 and 7), within the IS Division was echoed, with considerable irony, by one of the project leaders. He said:

> We never turn anything down. We never say no. We like to take on what seems impossible for us to do. We like to say to ourselves: 'We only had two months to do this and what we did seemed all right in those two months. We did this and it was a success given that we only had two months.' We'd rather do four or five bodges than one thing properly.

Here we note the apparent inability of IS senior and middle managers to say 'No', which suggests that the division had little power to influence the systems commitments that it took on. If this was the case it was not a view widely shared in the IS Division or the company. For example, senior Sales and Marketing managers felt the IS Division had 'too much power' and that they had no way of challenging the 'figures' it produced with regard to systems development estimates and costs (see Chapter 8). Furthermore, a number of managers within IS felt the division exercised too much influence over systems development. This was expressed in the following manner by one of the Business Systems Managers:

> The pensions project we ended up doing was perhaps not the one we started out doing. There are elements of what happens to the rest [of the project] and we [the IS Division] are in there saying: we feel we've got to do A rather than B—and all the time there isn't a body to argue against us and I think we have more influence than we should do on what we do next.

Drawing upon the three quotes above we can make an important distinction between the exercise of IS power at Pensco within the systems development process. On the one hand, there was a perception within the IS Division that senior divisional managers' had a predilection for 'having a go' and taking on the 'impossible', particularly where quality was sacrificed for quantity ('four or five bodges [rather] than one thing properly'). This is taken to be a sign of weakness and disregard for IS junior managers and staff who are charged with 'realising the impossible'. On the other hand, the IS Division is perceived to have too much power, particularly once development projects have begun.

From this apparent dichotomy we draw the following conclusion: the IS Division at Pensco in the late 1980s had lost the influence it once exercised with regard to the quantity and character of system development commitments it took on. In this sense, its first wall of defence had been breached. This invasion of the division by user imperatives had however been facilitated by the IS AGM and PM who in a sense opened the outer doors of the divisional castle and let the other divisions in. That is, they not only did not know how to say 'no' but also openly espoused the rhetoric of a 'marketing-led' use of IT that saw as legitimate the explosion of user demands on the IS resource.

However, while the IS Division may not have been able to control the quantity and character of strategic system development decisions, once systems development projects were underway it was still able to exert considerable influence over the quantity and quality of the actual systems developed and delivered to the users. This situation was clearly illustrated during the pension project when the IS Division was gradually loaded up with an impossible burden. Once loaded, IS managers then set about the task of either jettisoning bits of that burden altogether, with or without user agreement, and deferring (by consignment to the post-launch phase) or scrapping other parts of it. This was particularly prevalent in the design and coding stages of the project. In this manner the impossible was rendered possible, although at often considerable personal cost to staff tied into the project. This tendency to jettison or off load parts of a system was epitomised by the consultant PM brought in to salvage the project. At the end of 1987 as the project entered its most frenetic period he said:

> We're in a position now where we have no option but to discard things. Either we have to persuade the users they don't need it, give them a cut down version, or give them a temporary frig: a bit of chewing gum in the hole rather than replacing the panel. Fortunately, I know enough about insurance so that when a problem does arise I know if that really must be solved rather than having to go back to the users who are going to say they want it. I can decide if they must have that or if they can do without it for a month. So I make a phone call and say—I'm sure you don't need this. *It's the only contingency they've got: if the boat sinks a bit further they throw a bit more luggage overboard.*

In effect, the IS AGM's initial inclination to let the 'enemy' into the IS castle was an effective way of scaring the living daylights out of his managers and staff taking refuge in its inner keep which was a bastion of 'pure Pensco of old'. That is, the IS AGM was able to utilise user demands as a disciplinary mechanism ('top down pressurisation') within the division to increase productivity by simply 'making people work harder'. This cast him in a good marketing-led light and allowed him to shine in the senior management team. However, it also posed a considerable threat to the IS AGM. That is, he was caught between his desire to show that he was a trustworthy prince loyal to his king, the General Manager , and his concern to maintain effective control of the resources in his charge. The IS AGM and Technology Manager's longer-term strategy to develop the tools and techniques of the state-of-the-art systems development (namely, formal IT strategy, quality assurance and system developments frameworks and techniques) can in part be inter-preted as a concerted attempt to reconstruct, in the guise of profession-alism and formality, the breached walls of the old IS castle. That is, by mobilising a discourse of IS 'professionalism' they appeared to be in the process of refixing inter-divisional and inter-personal power relations that had begun to threaten their organisational positions.

There appears to be here a kind of exchange mechanism in operation where the IS Division gives with one hand only to take away with the other. Ground is ceded in one quarter ('taking on the impossible') only to be regained in another ('jettisoning'). This process also takes the form of saying one thing in public, thereby often taking on the impossible, and another thing in private, thereby making it achievable.

Once back within the safe walls of the IS Division the impossible is pared down to the doable by strategies such as 'jettisoning', 'the inele-gant fix', 'the bodge', 'the frig', and the 'transfer of ballast' from the project timetable into an ever-expanding post-launch phase.

These practices may have allowed the IS Division to maximise the short-term manufacture of 'successful' systems development projects. This was good for the IS AGM although the 'success' was often peri-lously thin. During the pensions project this sleight of hand was pulled off, with questionable results, by taking on user needs and then signifi-cantly paring them down during the systems development process. In order to ensure success here it was vital that definitions of the project were constructed in such a way that the full extent of post-launch work was obscured from the view of Pensco's senior managers.

The preceding analysis perhaps errs in its tendency to attribute the practices of the IS Division to Machiavellian plotting by the IS AGM. It is unlikely that this was the case. In the first place, even the IS AGM did not exercise enough control to implement such a plan. And secondly, these practices more probably emerged in the day-to-day running of the division and were more a response to contingencies than the exercise of an iron will. The IS AGM's overall control of IS, and the fear he inspired in his managers, made it in everyone's interest in IS to obscure the full extent of the project's problems.

The IS AGM's lack of confidence in the second phase of the pensions project was considerable. Indeed, he was very keen to hand over his sponsorship role once the first 'successful' phase of the project was over. He presumably hoped to hand over the 'frigs and fixes' to another manager who could then carry the can for the bloated post-launch system work still to be done.

Discipline and Punish: The Onset of Milestone Mania

One of the striking aspects of the general reorganisation of the company under the leadership of the new General Manager was the manner in which the constraints of his formalised system of top–down, strategic management, involving cascading responsibilities, impacted upon the managerial labour process. Budgeting constraints and the demands for quantification and strict monitoring generated a constant need to justify expenditure in the present and future, and to plan rigorously the alloca-tion of resources between estimated needs. As such it created a huge amount of work for managers. Further, as well as creating work it continually imposed formalised constraints on expenditure, on key task completion dates, and individual responsibilities that, given the state of pension market perceptions within the company, were in a state of almost continuous flux. Thus, the vast amounts of energy that were expended on constructing these planning, budgeting and monitoring mechanisms were further added to by the effort then spent in obscuring or justifying the transgression of these constraints. This was clear, for example, in the many papers written in order to demonstrate (uncon-vincingly) the pension project's potential profitability. These were later rendered redundant by the General Manager's decision to write off part of the project's expenses.

The pension project was no stranger to these planning and monitoring mechanisms. These had been established to hold the project on a tight course within the constraints constructed around it. In particular, indi-vidualising systems of control and responsibility were established through the development of the 'milestone mania'. They were also the consequences of similar disciplines operated by the General Manager on his AGMs at monthly strategy meetings.

In the early days of the project, each Project Committee member was given responsibility for achieving action points by certain dates. This form of control was then further refined so that each Project Committee member was responsible for project milestones which were even smaller subdivisions of the project. Further, at times of particular crisis, Committee members had to report to the IS AGM on a daily basis in order that he could monitor and control the completion of crucial milestones.

On the face of it this seems to be one more or less rational way of organising a large project involving the labour of many different specialists spread across the fractured divisional structure of a medium-sized company. By arranging software production in this fashion, progress was potentially made highly visible and amenable to centralised control. This form of project organisation also conformed with the existing structures of the company and therefore did not challenge interests invested in the maintenance of those structures. At a more particular level, we know that the IS AGM had first hand experience of large projects running out of control and that his preference was to dispense with large projects by using software packages where possible.

Lastly, this form of project organisation and control may have recommended itself to IS managers by virtue of the fact that there were project management software packages that had effectively inscribed this particular method of system management into the apparently objective technological artefacts available on the business systems market. One such package was used in the latter part of the pensions project.

However, whereas on the face of it this method of project management appeared to have a commonsensical rationality it was also strikingly resource expensive. For example, each Project and Steering Committee report included pages of milestones, their projected completion dates, and slippage that had occurred. And the minutes of these meetings were peppered with the admonishments and the threats of the PM and the Management Sponsor to Project Committee members who fell behind with their milestones. Yet there was an almost continuous slippage of milestones which necessitated the time-consuming rescheduling of development plans. Admittedly, this was minimised by the use of a project management system that was programmed to carry this out automatically.

However, the real cost of this system of control appeared to lie: firstly, in the emphasis it placed on a definition of software quality that was largely quantitative, that is, delivering software on time and to budget; secondly, in the way in which it further exacerbated inter-divisional tensions by assigning milestones to individuals within different divisions so that there was rarely any joint responsibility for project tasks across divisions; and, thirdly, in the stress it created for those controlling, and being controlled by, this particular disciplinary mechanism. In part this was caused by the constant need to 'chase' individuals with regard to their progress. It was also due to what we suspect was the considerable amount of political and psychic energy devoted to the legitimation of milestone slippage and the avoidance of censure and public humiliation in project meetings.

In Friedman and Cornford's terms (1989) the form of project management employed at Pensco is characterised by a managerial strategy of direct control, or one of 'low trust relations' (Fox, 1974). An unintended consequence of it was the diversion of potential labour power into organisational politics, the demeaning of specialist labour and junior managers, and the creation of an onerous progress chasing responsibility on the Project Manager who, as a partial consequence of this attention to detail, lost track of the project's overall development. It also appears to have contributed to the serious problems of co-ordination and antagonistic organisational politics from which the project suffered. Thus, as mentioned above, it increased the potential for inter-divisional hostility and buckpassing. As one project leader put it:

> Everyone's dead scared of doing anything wrong. While you're waiting for something you're alright because it's someone else's fault. No one here works at the company level.

As a particular control mechanism the 'milestone mania' also heightened problems of project co-ordination by fragmenting the project between divisions and between staff within the divisions. The problem then was how to ensure that the separate tasks being carried out were assembled in a coherent overall plan. This was clearly missing and created major problems towards the end of the pre-launch period of the project when no one was quite sure what extra development work was next 'going to crawl out of the woodwork'.

This form of punitive, bureaucratic work organisation also prevented the development and exchange of collective skills and knowledge within and between divisions: a consequence that may have had particularly deleterious effects given the level of mutual ignorance and indifference that characterised much of the project.

However, an advantage of this form of work organisation, which was strictly controlled through the formal managerial hierarchy on a vertical and horizontal axis, was that it minimised the development of challenges from below to the assessment of the project's progress. This it did in a number of ways.

Junior and middle managers, for example, generally felt extremely constrained by the imperative to meet milestones. One project leader decried the new managerial style in the division. He felt the new IS AGM did not 'care'. He added, 'He just wants the work done.' Gone were the days when senior management were in touch with staff and gave credit where credit was due. Instead, this junior manager experienced his middle and senior divisional managers as remote and demanding. And rather than being given more 'pats on the back' the PM would simply tell him, 'Here's a job, get it done at all costs and I don't care if you have to work 24 hours a day to do it.'

For this manager, meeting milestones had become the overriding objective of his working life. For, he argued, if milestones were missed 'then the boot comes out and you get kicked ... the only motivation is your target to meet and the threat of a kick'. Clearly this man did not relish the thought of being 'kicked' by his Project Manager and, even less by his AGM.

The above project leader freely admitted this method of working resulted in poor programming: simply 'getting as much done as you can' did mean that milestones were achieved but the 'usability' of the systems thus developed was seriously compromised. However, it was all this project leader felt he could achieve, and even this he found extremely difficult. Caught in this disciplinary mechanism with the constant fear of 'being kicked around', the project leader had no time or energy to protest. Even if he had we suspect that such individual protests would have been dismissed as a sign of personal failure and rancour rather than a symptom of a deeper collective malaise. Similarly, the eventual nervous collapse of this project leader, and the more public breakdown of his predecessor were apparently regarded as a sign of their inability to cope.

For the major part, then, passive resignation appeared to dominate over active resistance to milestone mania. This gave rise to a kind of privatisation of the anxiety and pain of the project; when at certain points the apparent control and order of the project collapsed, a number of staff suffered nervous exhaustion and began to be absent from work. However, these collapses served to discipline further other staff while they provided convenient scapegoats on to whom could be piled the blame for the project's failings.

Some project leaders and senior analysts were more openly critical about the prevailing project control mechanisms. For example, one project leader noted that you missed milestones 'at your peril' and that if Friday came 'and you've missed a couple of milestones you don't sleep easy through the weekend'. He continued:

> I don't care if I miss them. I'd rather get the grief from upstairs than rush the bloody thing through. To me that's where we go wrong [by] rushing things through to meet deadlines.

However, this rhetorical belligerence was in part a substitute for concerted or collective action against the prevailing and punitive use of milestones and the 'grief from upstairs'. Indeed, the above interviewee admitted that he had 'put in quite a bit of effort at weekends to keep us on schedule'. Other staff fed up with the 'quantity = quality' definition of software quality simply left the company.

Primarily, then, the control mechanisms discussed here appear to have been geared to the individual control of managers and the rigorous control of costs. This strategy generated unexpected and unacknowledged consequences that had considerable costs for the company and people working for it.

It is not particularly surprising that there was little concerted resistance from junior managers to the 'unbearable' pressures to which they were being subjected. For while perhaps deploring the goal-oriented style of the new IS AGM they were dependent on him for their future employment and career unless they were willing to leave Pensco. Further, there was a widespread feeling among IS junior managers and staff that senior managers would not listen to staff grievances or ideas for improvement. Indeed, it was believed that middle managers would so 'massage' any information flowing up the managerial hierarchy that it would be rendered politically palatable or impotent by the time it reached the IS AGM.

CONCLUSION

This chapter has argued that the apparently technical domain of systems development is as much influenced by the play of organisational power and politics as other organisational practices. In the past the IS Division had carved out a relatively protected and autonomous position within Pensco. This allowed managers within the division to determine to a considerable extent their systems development objectives and software development practices. These were characterised by an *ad hoc* and informal approach which stressed the development of administration-related systems. The arrival of the new General Manager and his IS AGM threw down a challenge to this orientation and way of working.

In the first part of this chapter we suggested that the IS AGM and his Project Manager were willing to take on an 'impossible' number of systems demands. This in part resulted from the sheer pressure users were able to place on the division and perhaps the Project Manager's unwillingness to disappoint any user demands for new systems. It also appears to have been used by the IS AGM as a disciplinary mechanism through which to put increasing pressure on his managers and staff.

One result of this was the massive overload of the available system resource. In order to render the project doable managers adopted various tactics to reduce the systems they developed. Hence there was a widespread use of bodging, fixing, frigging and jettisoning in order to meet the IS AGM's declared objective of producing quality software. Inasmuch as the pensions systems were mostly launched to date with a nominal budget overrun of 13 percent, managers were able to claim the project was a relative success. IS junior managers and staff had a different assessment of the project but this did not achieve a widespread legitimacy.

The first section of this chapter examined the shifting balance of power between the IS Division and other divisions in the 'user relations' phase of systems development. The initial parts of the second section continued this theme while the last one, on the 'milestone mania', examined shifting balances of power within the division itself. In the first half of the chapter we revealed how the shifting pressures of senior and user managers affected IS Division autonomy in an adverse manner. This led to the taking on of impossible commitments that were then pared down behind the walls of the division's near monopoly on systems development skills. However, this method of working created considerable disquiet among junior managers and IS staff. They were distressed to see their work being squandered on the development of poor software that they felt could not meet the ambitious targets set for it in terms of flexibility and reusability.

We then went on to analyse some of the ways in which senior and middle managers kept the lid on this discontent and the alternative perception these actors had of the quality of the systems they were producing. This was done both by the use of tight monitoring of development work through the milestone mania and the effective silencing of a collective voice of dismay and disquiet.

As already mentioned the imposition of milestones had a number of unintended consequences. For example, they tended to exacerbate inter-divisional hostility and the overall disunity of the project. Nevertheless, they achieved their purpose as a control device in that IS junior managers were sufficiently scared of senior management to put in long hours of overtime to meet targets. Furthermore, by individualising performance appraisal, they effectively fragmented internal opposition to the manner in which the project was being run.

This silencing of opposition to the progress of the project and the assessment of the software it was producing was further achieved by the manner in which the IS managerial hierarchy functioned. Firstly, this was set up in such a way that staff and junior managerial views on the project did not get a hearing. This in part resulted from the lack of a forum in which such a voice could be articulated and mobilised. It was also a consequence of middle managers' fear of their IS AGM. In effect, they were unwilling to challenge his view of events preferring to present him with the data he required in their regular meetings with him.

At the beginning of this chapter we argued that sociological studies of technology need to examine the 'content of technology'. However, as we saw, advocates of social shaping and constructivist perspectives disagree between and among themselves as to the definition of the 'content of technology'. We argued that the content of technology was as much to do with the organisational politics of technology processes as with systems analysis, design and coding as discrete 'technical' operations. Indeed, these 'technical' procedures cannot be abstracted from their social and political contexts. In addition, we suggested that the development of technology is as much about the constitution of meaning and knowledge as it is of artefacts.

The politics of technology at Pensco in the middle and late 1980s was dominated by the new GM's managerial style. This aimed to be marketing-driven, goal oriented and tightly controlled by a vast array of quantitative monitoring and reporting procedures. Given this style, managers perceived performance standards to be judged by their ability to meet specific goals within the costs and time constraints decided by the Senior Management Team. This particular form of controlling the managerial labour process placed considerable emphasis on quantitative measures and achievements. As a consequence, the underlying quality of work being done was often hidden from the GM's gaze. This disciplinary mechanism also engendered considerable fear among managerial staff. In this regard a recent junior manager recruited to the company commented:

> People can't admit things have gone wrong. You're running at 100 miles per hour just to stand still and covering your back to make sure nobody has found out what might have gone wrong. [There is] a really closed environment, people are running around in fear of senior management. And people are telling me it's wonderful.

And he continued by criticising the systems department and its three business systems managers who were, in his view, unable to make decisions because they were 'afraid of stepping out of line'.

More specifically, the IS AGM attempted to dominate Pensco's politics of technology during the pensions project through his control of technology-related resources. Given his position and the situation, it seems plausible to argue that the IS AGM had the most to gain and the most to lose with regard to the definition and assessment of Pensco's technology opportunities and problems.

The politics of technology largely concerns the struggle to control the manner in which 'technology' is made socially meaningful in an organisation. This concerns the way in which the meaning of particular technological opportunities or developments is generated and privileged so as to become an undeniable reality, the social construction of which is lost or forgotten. Thus, the politics of technology of the pensions systems projects largely concerns the manner in which the developing pensions systems are perceived, assessed and explained.

Managerial survival depends on reproducing assessed stature or a respected status in an organisation. This confers legitimacy on the actor involved and allows her or him to mobilise effectively the available resources behind objectives that she or he can claim as legitimate. Without that positively assessed stature, the manager in question may formally control resources but find it extremely difficult to use those resources to achieve the results she or he wants.

The IS AGM at Pensco had the most to lose from the failure of the pensions project. This was because he was the management sponsor of the project and he had set it up in such a manner that it was perceived to belong to the IS Division. This was achieved in his choice of a Project Manager from the IS Division.

There were in effect two key elements that the IS AGM had to control in order to ensure that his status or assessed stature was not undermined by the pensions project. In the first place he was ultimately responsible for the control and co-ordination of the resources invested in the project. That is, he was responsible for ensuring the project produced the material output required, in the form of computer systems, training and sales literature, etc.

A second key element in protecting his reputation as a competent AGM was to ensure that the project was given a successful profile. In effect, he had to try and control the way in which the system was understood throughout the organisation, the manner in which perceptions of the material value and symbolic significance of the project were formed and diffused, and the way in which problems with the project were constructed and then explained away in the public and private domains within and outside the company.

If it is the case that computer systems are no more significant than the meanings attached to them as a result of socially constructed definitions of their value and use, those charged with bringing them into being are likely to take a sharp interest not merely in the production of the system as a set of machine codes, formal methods and material outputs. They are equally likely to feel compelled to ensure that the 'reality' for the systems in question, or how they are perceived and understood, reflects favourably upon themselves and thereby reinforces and advances their position in the organisation. This is particularly so where they feel that their sense of identity is closely bound up with 'successes' in the area of systems development.

Subjects take an interest in the social construction of reality or rendering 'things' meaningful not simply because their reputation within an employing organisation may be at stake. They are also concerned to maintain their own sense of purpose, meaning, self-esteem and identity. For example, a system developer attached to her or his occupational identity will feel compelled to produce 'successful' systems, or explain away 'unsuccessful' ones by finding a scapegoat outside their control.

12
Conclusion

In this book we have argued that organisational and technological realities are constructed, reproduced or changed in and through the exercise of power and the identity securing strategies of individuals and groups. This process takes place through the contextually specific process of organisational politics. Further, we argued that the development, deployment and use of IT is in no way immune to this pervasive process of politics. Indeed, because IT represents considerable complexity and uncertainty and is associated with the rise of new and powerful trade, specialist and managerial groupings, it has often been productive of particularly intense organisational politics.

This political process is enacted in specific conditions of possibility. These socially constituted conditions make certain courses of action feasible while constraining or ruling out others. These concern both local and general conditions of possibility. Local conditions are constituted by organisational structure and subjectivity, technological possibilities and sectoral specificities. General conditions concern the global conditions of capitalist market economies and class, gender and race relations within them.

These conditions of possibility are neither 'facts' nor 'objective realities', although they are often mistaken or portrayed as such. Rather, conditions of possibility are socially constructed. In a situation of relative stability these conditions may take on the appearance of objective conditions immune to change. At times of uncertainty and change these predominant conditions are open to challenge by alternatives. Thus, within a given organisation the construction and mobilisation of local conditions of possibility is also part of the political process at the centre of organisational life.

This organisational political approach distinguishes itself from other perspectives on technological change in a number of important ways. With regard to technological determinism, it argues that technological possibilities are but one condition of organisational change. Furthermore, the way in which such possibilities are constructed and mobilised within an organisation is part and parcel of a broader political process. These possibilities cannot be simply 'read off' the IS Division wall like a series of tyre pressures to fit different car models. However, we note the utility of processual approaches emanating from within the functionalist tradition that begin to dissect the practical actions of managers, albeit from a perspective that usually ignores those larger contextual conditions that are a condition and consequence of such action.

We have distanced ourselves from Marxist and 'radical feminist' approaches arguing that technological change processes cannot be explained as merely the direct product of capitalist or patriarchal interest. While dominant property and gender relations are important conditions of technological change, the construction of interests and objectives is a complex and conflictual process involving a range of issues not least of which, as we have indicated, is inter-managerial competition. Moreover, it is also important to acknowledge the unintended consequences, and unplanned and accidental processes of organisational change to which Marxists and radical feminists concede little.

Lastly, we have criticised constructivist and actor network approaches due to their unwillingness to bring into consideration general socio-economic conditions and theorise the basis of power in contemporary society. However, we have drawn upon their close analyses of the social achievement of technological innovations through the construction of webs or networks of actors. We also value their insistence that technologies are constructed through social process comprising accident, fortuitous circumstance and self-conscious political action. In examining these different perspectives to technological and organisational change we proposed a two-dimensional framework that differentiates theoretical approaches by their analytical focus (general v. local) and their view of politics (abnormal v. normal).

Within this framework we position ourselves in the segment that combines a focus on localised events and that regards politics as an essential feature of organisational life. Of course, as with all such frameworks, the complexity of the fuller picture is obscured in seeking provocative differentiation. Thus, while arguing for a localised analytical focus we see such local sites of social process as part and parcel of the global relations that condition and are reproduced or incrementally changed in those localities.

Our analysis has, then, identified organisational politics as the motor of organisational life. This political process concerns the struggles of individuals to pursue careers and achieve a measure of security in uncertain and competitive market conditions. For us, political process is not an aberration or pathological condition. Rather, it is the dynamic process at the heart of organisational life played out in conditions of considerable inequality. This challenges functionalist organisation theory which, in a variety of forms, views the organisation as a rational and objective entity. It also challenges the over-rationalised versions of organisational process that managers readily give to their actions.

There is, however, an important paradox within the realm of organisational politics, which in part results from the continued dominance of overly rational views of organisation process. This paradox is that while political process lies at the heart of organisations, this is normally obscured from view. Thus, we have argued that managerial activity can be seen first and foremost as a political process that constructs a reality of management that denies its own political character.

To admit of this politics would be to acknowledge the often arbitrary and unintended consequences arising from the conflict and resolution of competing career and identity-securing strategies. It would also be to disclose the ways in which managers learn to perform in order to curry favour from superiors. In short, it would be to attack and weaken management's claim to embody an 'objective', rational and competent, let alone 'one-best-way', of management. For when politics is placed at the centre of managerial and organisational process and the role of unintended consequence and accident is revealed, the activity of management becomes a much less precise and planned activity than is often believed, or claimed by those with aspirations to 'professional' competence. This challenges the predominant belief that management is a privileged repository of a singular organisational good sense. The 'one-best-way' of managing can then be seen as one of many alternative ways of co-ordinating social and economic activity. Further, the 'one-best-way' can also be seen as a particular localisation of events connected to a specific, and socially constructed, set of conditions of possibility.

Our stress on the importance of organisational subjectivity and identity plays an important part in this development of an organisational politics approach to technological change. For we argue that managerial activity is also a process productive of particular managerial and non-managerial identities. That is to say, people make organisations but organisations also make people.

In this process of 'people making', managers, specialists and office and shopfloor workers internalise codes of behaviour and identification through a range of discourses that have powerful effects upon identity.

The sense of identity thus developed is vital for the way in which subjects secure a psychic place within an organisation. It is through our identity that we make ourselves known to ourselves and others in organisations. We become a particular gender, a particular manager in a particular organisation doing particular things. This subjectivity 'fixes us' in a potentially infinite sea of choices and possibilities. Our actions, mores, responsibilities and commitments become a known quantity. But as we bind ourselves to that identity, organisations have a way of shifting and changing. A new boss arrives, the share price falls, new techniques and discourses emerge. Just when you think you are safe, home and dry, the world tilts—maybe only slightly but enough to throw into question that sense of identity, of completeness, so laboriously achieved.

In our discussion of Pensco we saw how the reorganisation of senior management upset established rules and boundaries. Managers in IS no longer knew how to 'play the game' of organisational politics. They ran around shaking and trembling, terrified by exemplary sackings and the threat of a public and humiliating verbal 'going over' by their new boss: a boss himself struggling to bring off his identity as a 'switched on' IS chief.

Such struggles to maintain and secure identity in constrained and competitive circumstances are the less acknowledged, more painful part of organisational politics. Organisations 'make' people but, as we have seen, they also 'break' them, exposing and exploiting their vulnerabilities and weaknesses'. People 'wobble and fall over', they crawl into work in agony slurring their words, they go into prolonged absences, into a black hole of non-existence, their desk a poignant reminder of their broken identity.

Organisational subjectivity is a vital ingredient of our analytical framework, because it helps us understand how people become tied into positions in organisations and how they will struggle to maintain those positions, or change them, in the face of threat and competition. This concern with identity suggests that resistance to change is far from irrational. People in organisations often have very good reasons to fear change, particularly when this threatens the way in which they make sense of themselves. This fear in part explains the difficulty of 'open communication' in organisations, which increasingly is a prerequisite of effective information systems development. That is, when faced with growing complexity and uncertainty individual anxieties, especially those associated with masculinity, are aroused and exacerbated. Organisation subjects become wary, possessive, controlling, tight fisted and tight lipped. As a new information system is conceived and constructed, a strange kind of dance begins to evolve.

Users and developers constantly re-position themselves as they change their interpretations of the project and its chances of success. Here a few user requirements are withheld, here a few added (supported by the 'dictates' of the market), here a few parts of the system are quietly shelved, here a few fixes are bodged in, here a few 'implications for future system flexibility' are ignored, and here a few of the rules governing definitions of success and failure are subtly changed.

The dancers step in and step out, and on and off the brightly lit dance floor. They swop partners, weigh up contenders, or rest at the bar watching and waiting, watching for a chance to step back into the spotlight. And the question asked in those quiet moments is: What are we giving birth to here? Will it live? Will it die? Will it reflect well on me? Do I want to be there at the birth, a proud parent, or miles away, otherwise engaged, out of reach? Just to indicate that the metaphor is not too far fetched, one project leader at Pensco claimed: 'Systems successes have many parents. Failures have none. They are born orphans!' This organisational dancing has major implications for trust relations in organisations and systems development to which we will return later.

Having developed this critical framework of organisational politics we went on to examine in greater detail the management of technology and the conditions of its possibility. In so doing we noted that political process varies over time with regard to its intensity, its degree of institutionalisation, and the self-consciousness of organisational subjects. With regard to the politics of IT, we suggested that this is likely to be particularly intense because IT has yet to be normalised as an organisational practice. This is due to the growing complexity of IT management issues, the conditions of which are the increasing range of technology applications and actors involved in technology-related decisions, and the speed of technological and market change. This trend is likely to intensify as information and, increasingly, communication technologies are mobilised to change organisational structures (Zuboff, 1988; Hammer, 1990).

The adoption of discourses of IT strategic management is one response to this growing complexity. These have promised a resolution of problems and conflicts through a rationalised process of planning and priority setting. However, we warned against an innocent reading of these techniques, arguing that they were part of a particularly intense phase of organisational politics rather than a solution to intra-organisational conflict and uncertainty.

The IS specialism has too often been seen as an independent arbiter in political process issues around IT management and systems development conflicts. Indeed, partisan commentators and our culture of technological progress have raised IS specialists above the 'hurly burly' of organisational politics and imbued them with a neutrality and omniscience unimaginable in practice. For clearly, the IS specialism exercises considerable power in contemporary organisations and has increasingly been drawn into or sought to intervene in, the mainstream of organisational life.

This has particularly been the case with the emergence of a user-relations phase in systems development which has intensified conflicting pressures on the IS resource and IS managers and staff. Drawing on empirical material from the financial services industry we examined user/developer relations from an organisational political perspective, concluding that these remain highly ambiguous and often characterised by 'low trust' relations. Astutely, IS specialists have mobilised 'technical–rational' discourses to block the incursion of users into IS domains, but the dilution of their monopoly control of IT knowledge has rendered systems development increasingly vulnerable to user controls.

IS functionaries not only exercise power as a specialist occupational grouping; they also happen to be predominantly white and male, particularly within the ranks of management. This fact has important consequences for systems development and the reproduction of gender inequalities. That is, the predominance of men in technology areas infuses technology practices and discourses with the concerns of dominant forms of masculinity. As such technology is not only 'politicised' by organisational politics but also 'masculinised' due to the dominance of men in powerful positions in organisations. Furthermore, we have argued that there is a strong and enduring symbiotic relationship between social definitions and understandings of masculinity and technology. Thus a masculinity obsessed with issues of control and rationality and profoundly 'alienated' or distant from the emotional aspects of human life, finds solace and mastery in a technology that appears to be 'free' of the uncertainties and fears of everyday social life. In this way technology has often come to be defined as synonymous with male or masculine activity and elevated to a superior status, as a result. However, where women have been predominantly involved in using technology (e.g. domestic 'white goods' or office equipment), the activity is denied the accolade and rewards associated with 'technology' occupations.

The promise of a disembodied and asocial world offered by conventional definitions of technology may even attract and foster a masculinity that has felt threatened or a failure in other areas of social life. Thus it may be that the IS specialism sustains and develops a 'harder' and less flexible masculinity than prevails in other male dominated occupations. In our case study companies this was characterised by the 'have a go' attitude in which an aggressive obsession with control and a refusal to contemplate 'failure' blinded management to the tremendous social and political complexities involved in developing software under tight constraints in changing markets.

The mobilisation of this masculinity certainly contributes to the continued exclusion of women as well as the more feminine values and sensibilities from IS managerial positions. This could be seen to have a deleterious impact on systems development practices generally. For a sensitivity to others and to the contingent and precarious nature of life is ordinarily absent in masculine discourse and practice where a linear 'progressive' conception of goal-achievement predominates. Consequently, attitudes, beliefs and behaviours (e.g. an ability to listen, empathy, openness, non-careerism) that are important in managing situations of uncertainty and unpredictability are effecively excluded from the lexicon of systems development, or confined to the margins of IT management process. These skills, however, are likely to increase in importance as flexibility and complexity are even more prevalent in the user relations phase of systems development. It remains to be seen if these 'softer' skills will be 'masculinised' or whether they will infiltrate and undermine the gendered character of technology processes, largely defined by a dominant masculinity that eschews emotional self-reflexivity and marginalises women and femininity as a result.

Our examination of the politics of organisational change at Pensco suggests that diverse groups of managers in competition with each other for scarce material and symbolic rewards are continually constructing technology and markets in ways that will allow them to secure advantage. Prior to our arrival at Pensco most divisions treated IT as an 'externality' that was beyond their technical competence to understand. But as IT became strategically important in all divisions, it became a subject of increasing competition and controversy. As such, IT's interpretative flexibility was opened up and it came to be an internal construction, no longer taken for granted or left in the hands of IS personnel. In particular, the Marketing Division, encouraged and backed-up by the General Manager, launched a growing offensive on the IS Division through the mobilisation of the supposed dictates of the market with regard to new product-related systems requirements. This eventually led to the massive overburdening of the IS Division and chaos in the pensions project. The situation was only recovered by the dramatic, but largely hidden, jettisoning of large parts of the system development into an almost mythical post-launch phase.

The development of information systems is, then, a political process. This concerns the way in which 'technology' or a particular system, is made socially meaningful in an organisation. In particular, this involves the manner in which the meaning of particular technological opportunities or developments is generated and privileged so as to become an undeniable reality, the social construction of which is lost or forgotten. This is illustrated by the competing interpretations of the pensions project at Pensco as managers jockeyed for position and sought to blame the project's shortcomings on other divisions. The need to ensure a construction of the project as a success, and the resources mobilised behind this version of events by senior management, largely obscured from view the competing interpretations of the project.

Pensco's IS AGM had much to lose from the project. Much managerial time and effort was consumed in protecting his reputation as a competent manager. This he did by attempting to control the manner in which the perceptions of the material and symbolic significance of the project were formed and diffused and how the eventual systems were understood throughout the company.

We have argued that computer systems are no more significant than the meanings attached to them as a result of the socially constructed definitions of their value and utility. Thus, it is not surprising if those charged with bringing them into being are engaged in more than the production of the system as a set of machine codes, practices and material outputs. They are equally likely to feel compelled to ensure that the 'reality' of the systems in question, or how they are perceived and understood, reflects favourably upon themselves and thereby reinforces and advances their position in the organisation. This is particularly so where they feel their sense of identity to be closely bound up with 'successes' in the area of systems development.

Subjects take an interest in the social construction of reality concerning activities in which they are engaged not simply because their reputation within an organisation is at stake. They are also concerned to maintain a sense of purpose, meaning, self-esteem and identity with regard to these activities. At Pensco this became increasingly difficult as the pensions project proceeded. The disparity between the future oriented 'flexible' systems under construction and the company's ageing technology infrastructure made the achievement of successful and satisfying systems a near impossibility. This was not an apparent concern of senior managers who simply wanted to see 'the systems there on day one' in time to meet the market opportunities provided by the new government legislation. But for IS staff the continuous inelegant compromises and bodging were a source of growing dissatisfaction. The ageing architecture also has long-term implications for the organisation's ability to operate and adapt in a fast-changing market. For a systems infrastructure that was in continuous need of maintenance and enhancement was hardly likely to be flexible enough to meet the multiplicity of diverse demands made of it.

The case study of Pensco has focused on an important paradox. This is that IT management, and systems development in particular, have frequently been seen as predominantly 'technical' processes in contemporary organisations and thus amenable to the most rational and scientific forms of management. Yet, as we have argued, the area of IT management and systems development is one of the most intensely politicised and masculinised areas of management. If this is the case, what implications do these findings have for technology management in contemporary organisations? We have already hinted at these implications. In particular, they have to do with communication, trust, gender, power, politics and change. They concern both the field of organisation theory and the practices it examines such as IT management and systems development.

Much recent writing on technological and organisational change focuses on the rise of the knowledge or information worker (see *Journal of Management Studies*, 1993). Often this also discusses the increasing importance of information as a strategic resource and information-based, analytical and brokering abilities as strategic skills (Reich, 1990). This literature on 'new organisational forms' also stresses the growing need to share information and skills both between managerial specialisms and between organisations. And it foresees radical changes in managerial practice: delayering and the withering away of hierarchy; business process re-engineering; the empowerment of managers and employees and the rise of network organisations (Zuboff, 1988; Peters, 1992; Quinn, 1992).

These researchers predict that information gathering, analysis and communication will be central strategic features of future organisations and that strength in these areas will become more important than the ability to produce 'things' or material commodities (see especially, Reich, 1990). Information and communications technologies and systems will have a key role to play in providing the infrastructure to realise these predicted changes.

We are sceptical of many of the claims made by this literature. However, it highlights the growing importance of information and information systems in contemporary organisations. Often though it treats information and organisation with a surprising naivety. This literature calls for a new era of open and trusting relationships in organisations combined with rapid and radical change but it fails to enquire into the basis on which such openness and trust is to be based (Webber, 1993).

The argument we have presented in this book suggests two problems that this literature will have to confront. Firstly, information cannot be treated in an innocent way. In particular, as information becomes strategically more important so the politics of information will intensify both within and between organisations. Information is not pumped out of the ground like oil. Rather, it is socially constructed to convey politically charged messages to politically motivated people.

Secondly, the new 'trusting' organisation looks like being born dead in the water unless organisational commentators and practitioners begin to consider the realms of power and politics with greater care and insight. If this literature is to contribute to its task of revitalising and changing Western capitalism, it must begin to take more seriously the very real constraints on organisational change and the complexity of the organisational politics and identity issues that are central features of any living organisation. It may be, however, that organisations have to be radically reorganised to encompass truly democratic and trust relations of the kind promoted by Semler (1993) at Semco in São Paulo.

With particular regard to the systems development arena it is clear that the issue of user relations will continue to be central to the development of effective systems. It remains to be seen if organisations can move beyond the forms of conflictual user relations generated in the companies we studied. In part, we have argued, these conflicts are endemic to organisations, where competition and insecurity are such overriding conditions of possibility. However, the confrontation and clarification of power and politics in organisations, instead of their concealment, might prove interesting. Whether or not this might make 'better' or 'more successful' systems can only be a matter of, often conflicting, managerial and observer judgements for, as we have argued, 'success' itself is an issue of politics and conflict.

The concerns expressed here clearly have implications for the training of IS specialists. Specifically, MIS degrees and training should address and explore issues of organisational politics in some depth. IS specialists need to understand the social and political complexities of organisational life and the manner in which technology choices and processes are socially constructed. This might then allow IS specialists to appreciate the genesis and contextual specificity of the technical rational outlook they are so often inclined, or encouraged, to adopt.

We have stressed the importance of identity and links between organisational and gender identities to show the deeply embedded character of organisational process and politics. In particular, we have suggested that organisational politics, the politics of technology, systems development, and a dominant masculinity mutually interact to generate practices that are self-contradictory and counter-productive to the potential that information systems can offer an organisation. If we want to take the issue of organisational change seriously and predict 'progressive' forms of organisation and technology use that are more equitable and democratic than those current, these linkages and the power relations of class and race that underlie so much organisational politics must be subject to greater critical scrutiny at local and global sites of enquiry.

As it stands, systems development has to be seen as a particularly 'masculinised' area of endeavour. It needs uncoupling from dominant masculinities, so as to be open to new possibilities and less fearful of the uncertain and often uncontrollable flux and flow of organisational life. While such change is neither easy nor painless, since technology systems supplement change as well as replace certain organisational practices and relations in unpredictable ways, it is surely just and necessary to draw upon the full repertoire of masculine and feminine skills, abilities, ideas and emotions that men and women can muster.

It is all very well for us as academics to cajole practitioners to change while we remain firmly committed to our own masculine projects and career systems. Hopefully, however, the analysis also carries implications for the study of organisations and information systems particularly with respect to relations of power, knowledge, gender and identity. If, as we argued in Chapter 1, we cannot simply attribute the way things are to capitalist or patriarchal interest at a global level, the study of particular organisations and the way in which global and local conditions interact and feed back become an important site of enquiry. For it also suggests that change takes place, and can be influenced, at many different levels and in different ways. For the academic studying technological change and wishing for a (problematically defined) 'better world', engagement with, and exposure to, particular organisations, their members and their politics, may be a fruitful path to follow. Of course, to become self-consciously part of organisational change processes exposes the academic to challenges and commitments that may threaten identities that are grounded in strict demarcations between academia and the business world.

Nevertheless, the all pervasiveness of information technology and the rapid shifts associated with changing markets and technologies suggest we will all be faced with important change issues over the years to come. These change processes may be highly constrained by their conditions of possibility but this book has argued that individual and collective actions, unintended consequence and accident can all shift the direction of these processes at a multiplicity of levels. The potential gains to be derived from the approach of this book relate to what has been our attempt to understand the political terrain of IT growth and development, in terms of a gender-informed analysis of power and identity and their conditions of possibility in contemporary organisations and management.

References

Abrahams, P. (1989) 'Throwing away the paper-based system', *The Financial Times*, 24 April.

Allison, G. (1971) *The Essence of Decision: Explaining the Cuban Missile Crisis*, Boston, Massachussets: Little, Brown & Co.

Armstrong, P. (1985) 'Changing management control strategies: the role of competition between accountancy and other professions', *Accounting, Organizations and Society*, **10**(2), 129–48.

Armstrong, P. (1987) 'The Rise of accounting controls in British capitalist enterprises', *Accounting, Organizations and Society*, **12**(5), 415–36.

Aroronovitz, S (1978) 'Marx, Braverman and the logic of capital', *Insurgent Sociologist*, **8**(2,3), 126–46.

Association of British Insurers (1992) *Statistics*, London: ABI.

Attewell, P. (1987) 'The deskilling controversy', *Work and Occupations*, **14**, 323–46.

Auerbach, P. (1988) *Competition: The Economics of Industrial Change*, Oxford: Blackwell.

Avner, E. (1993) 'Trade unions , IT and equal opportunities in Sweden', in Green, E., Owen, J. and Pain, D. (eds), *Gendered by Design: Information Technology and Office Systems*, London: Taylor.

Bacharach, S.B. and Lawler, E.J. (1980) *Power and Politics in Organizations*, London: Jossey-Bass.

Bariff, M.L. and Galbraith, J.R. (1978) 'Intraorganizational power considerations for designing information systems', *Accounting, Organizations and Society*, **3**, 15–27.

Barker, J. and Downing, H. (1980) 'Word Processing and the Transformation of the patriarchal relations of control in the office', *Capital and Class*, **10**, 64–99.

Barras, R. and Swann, J. (1983) *The Adoption and Impact of Information Technology in the UK Insurance Industry*, London: Technical Change Centre.

Batten, J.D. and Swab, J.L. (1965) 'How to crack down on company politics', *Personnel* **42**, 8–20.

Beech, C. (1990) *Women and WIT*, London: British Computer Society.

Benjamin, R.I., de Long, D. W. and Scott Morton, M.S. (1990) 'Electronic data interchange: how much competitive advantage?', *Long Range Planning*, **23**(1), 29–40.

Bertrand, O. and Noyelle, T. (1988) *Human Resources and Corporate Strategy: Technological Change in Banks and Insurance Companies*, Paris: OECD.

Bessant, J., Guy, K., Miles, I. and Rusk, N. (1985) *IT Futures*, London: NEDO.

Bhaskar, R. (1989) *Reclaiming Reality: A Critical Introduction to Contemporary Philosophy*, London: Verso.

Bijker, W., Hughes, T. and Pinch, T. (eds) (1987) *The Social Construction of Technological Systems*, Cambridge, Mass.: MIT Press.

Bijker, W. and Law. J. (1992) *Shaping Technology, Building Society: Studies in Socio-Technical Change*, Cambridge, Mass: MIT Press.

Blau, P. M. (1964) *Exchange and Power in Social Life*, New York: Wiley.

Blauner, R. (1964) *Alienation*. Chicago: University of Chicago Press.

Bloomfield, B. and Best, A. (1992), 'Management consultants: systems development, power and the translation of problems', *The Sociological Review*, **41**(3), 533–60.

Boguslaw, R. (1982) *Systems Analysis and Social Planning: Human Problems of Post-industrial Society*, New York: Irvington.

Boland, R.J. and Pondy, L. (1983) 'Accounting in organizations; a union of rational and natural perspectives', *Accounting, Organizations and Society*, **8**, 223–4.

Boland, R.J. (1979) 'Control, causality and information systems requirements', *Accounting Organizations and Society*, **4**(4), 259–72.

Borum, F. (1987) 'Beyond Taylorism: The IT-Specialists and the deskilling hypothesis', CHIPS Working paper, Institute of Organisation and Industrial Sociology, Copenhagen School of Economics and Social Science.

Braverman, H. (1974) *Labour and Monopoly Capital: The Degradation of Work in the Twentieth Century*, London: Monthly Review Press.

Brittan, A. (1989) *Masculinity and Power*, Oxford: Blackwell.

Buckroyd, B. and Cornford, D. (1988) *The IT Skills Crisis: The Way Ahead*, Manchester: NCC Publications.

Burawoy, M. (1979) *Manufacturing Consent: Change in the Labour Process under Monopoly Capitalism*, Chicago: Chicago University Press.

Burawoy, M. (1985) *The Politics of Production: Factory Regimes under Capitalism and Socialism*, London: Verso.

Burns, T. (1969) *Industrial View: Selected Readings*, Harmondsworth: Penguin.

Burns, T. and Stalker, G. M. (1961) *The Management of Innovation*, London: Pergamon.

Burns, T. (1977) *The BBC: Public Institution and Private World*, London: Macmillan.

Burrell, G. and Morgan, G. (1979) *Sociological Paradigms and Organisational Analysis* London: Heinemann.

Butler, J. (1991) *Gender Trouble*, New York: Routledge.

Button, G. (1993) *Technology in Working Order: Studies of Work Interaction and Technology*, London, Routledge.

Callon, M. (1986) 'Some elements of a sociology of translation: domestication of the scallops and the fishermen of St Brieuc's Bay', in J. Law (ed.), *Power, Action and Belief: A New Sociology of Knowledge?*, Sociological Review Monograph, No. 32, London: Routledge and Kegan Paul.

Callon, M. (1987) 'Society in the making: the study of technology as a tool for sociological analysis in Bijker, Wiebe, E., Hughes, Thomas P. and Pinch, Trevor, J. (eds), *The Social Construction of Technological Systems: New Directions in the Sociology and History of Technology*, Cambridge, Mass: MIT Press, pp. 83–106.

Callon, M. (1991) 'Techno-economic networks and irreversibility', paper delivered at the International Conference on the Economics and Sociology of Technology, UMIST.

Callon, M., Law, J. and Rip, A. (1986) *Mapping the Dynamics of Science and Technology: Sociology of Science in the Real World*, London: Macmillan.

Camus, A. (1960) *The Collected Fiction of Albert Camus*, London: Hamish Hamilton.

Cane, A. (1988) 'Advisers at board level', *The Financial Times*, 5 October.

Cane, A. (1992) 'New search for value', *The Financial Times Survey: Computers in Finance*, 10 November p.1.

Cash, J.I. and Konsynski, B.R. (1985), 'IS redraws competitive boundaries', *Harvard Business Review*, March–April, 134–42.

Child, J. (1973) 'Organisation, structure and environment: the role of strategic choice' in Salaman, G. and Thompson, K. (eds), *People and Organisations*, London: Longman.

Child, J. (1985) 'Managerial Strategies, New Technology and the Labour Process', in Knights, D., Willmott, H. and Collinson, D. (eds), *Job Redesign*, London: Gower.

Child, J. and Loveridge, R. (1990) *Information Technology in European Services: Towards a Microelectronic Future*, Oxford: Blackwell.

Child, J., Rowlinson, M. and Smith, C. (1990), *Reshaping Work: The Cadbury Experience*; Cambridge University Press.

Child, J. and Smith, C. (1987) 'The context and process of organisational transformation—Cadbury Limited in its sector', *Journal of Management Studies*, 24, 565–93.

Clegg, S. (1975) *Power Rule and Domination: A Critical and Empirical Understanding of Power in Sociological Theory and Organizational Life*, London: Routledge and Kegan Paul.

Clegg, S. (1979) *The Theory of Power and Organizations*, London: Routledge and Kegan Paul.

Cockburn, C. (1983) *Brothers: Male Dominance and Technological Change*, London: Pluto.

Cockburn, C. (1985) *Machinery of Dominance: Women, Men and Technical Know-How*, London: Pluto.

Cockburn, C. (1991) *Men's Resistance to Sex Equality in Organisations*, Basingstoke: Macmillan.

Cohen, M.D., March, J.G. and Olsen, J.P. (1972) 'A garbage can model of organizational choice', *Administrative Science Quarterly*, 17, 1–25.

Collinson, D. and Hearn, J. (eds) (1995) *Management and Masculinity*, London: Sage.

Collinson, D. and Knights, D. (1986) 'Men only: theories and practices of job segregation', in *The Gendered Labour Process*, Aldershot: Gower.

Collinson, D., Knights, D. and Collinson, M. (1990) *Managing to Discriminate*, London: Routledge.

Connell, R.W. (1987) *Gender and Power*, Cambridge: Polity.

Coombs, R. (1993) 'Information technology: a challenge to organisation theory', paper presented at the PICT National Conference, Kenilworth, Warwickshire, 19–21 May 1993.

Coopers and Lybrand (1988) *IT in Insurance*, London: Coopers and Lybrand.

Corneau, G. (1991) *Absent Fathers Lost Sons: The Search for Masculine Identity*, Boston: Shambhala.

Couger, J.D. and Zawacki, R.A. (1980), *Motivating and Managing Computer Personnel*, New York: Wiley.

Crompton, R. and Jones, G. (1984) *White Collar Proletariat: Deskilling and Gender in Clerical Work*, London: Macmillan.

Crozier, M. (1964) *The Bureaucratic Phenomena*, Chicago: University of Chicago Press.

Crozier, M. (1974) *The Bureaucratic Phenomena*, Chicago: University of Chicago Press.

Crozier, M. and Friedberg, E. (1980) *Actors and Systems*, Chicago: University of Chicago Press.

Cyert, R.M. and March, J.G. (1963) *A Behavioral Theory of the Firm*, Englewood Cliffs: Prentice-Hall.

Daft, R.L. (1989) *Organisation Theory and Design*, New York: West.

Dahl, R. (1957) 'The concept of power', *Behavioural Sciences*, 2, 201–15.

Dahl, R.A. (1961) *Who Governs?*, New Haven: Yale University Press.

Dalton, M. (1959) *Men Who Manage*, New York: Wiley.

Day, R. A. and Day, J. V. (1977) 'A Review of the Current State of Negotiated Order Theory: An Appreciation and a Crituque', *Sociological Quarterly*, 18 (Winter): 126–42.

Dearden, J. (1987) 'The withering away of the IS organization', *Sloan Management Review*, Summer, 87–91.

Derber, C. (1982) 'Towards a new theory of professionals as workers: advanced capitalism and postindustrial labour', in Derber, C. (ed.), *Professionals as Workers: Mental Labor in Advanced Capitalism*, Boston: G.K.Hall pp. 193–208.

Dixon, P. J. and John, D. A. (1989) 'Technology issues facing corporate management in the 1990s', *MIS Quarterly*, 13, September, 247–55.

Dosi, G. (1982) 'Technological paradigms and technological trajectories', *Research Policy*, 147–62.

Drory, A. and Romm, T. (1990) 'The definition of organizational politics: a review', *Human Relations* 43(11), 1133–54.

Dudman, J. (1989) 'Norwich Union puts £4m in case to fill skills gap', *Computing*, 19, January.

Duffy, N.M. and Assad, M.G. (1980) *Information Management: An Executive Approach*, Cape Town: Oxford University Press.

Durkheim, E. (1947) *The Division of Labour in Society*, trans. G. Simpson, Glencoe, Ill: Free Press.

Durkheim, E. (1951) *Suicide*, trans. J.A. Spalding and G. Simpson, Glencoe, Ill: Free Press.

Easlea, B. (1983) *Fathering the Unthinkable: Masculinity, Scientists and the Nuclear Arms Race*, London: Pluto.

Edwards, R. (1979) *Contested Terrain: The Transformation of the Workplace in the Twentieth Century*. New York: Basic Books.

Ehn, P. (1989) *Work Oriented Design of Computer Artifacts*, Hillsdale,NJ: Erlbaum.

Ehn, P. and Sandberg, A. (1986) 'Local union influence on technology and work organization', in J. Fry (ed.) *Towards a Democratic Rationality*, Aldershot: Gower.

Eldridge, J. E. T. (1967) *Industrial Disputes*, London: Routledge & Kegan Paul.

Elger, T. (1978) 'Valorisation and deskilling: a critique of Braverman', *Capital and Class*, 7, 58–99.

Featherstone, M. (1991) *Consumer Culture and Postmodernism*, London: Sage.

Financial Adviser, October 15th 1989.

Fleck, J., Webster, J. and Williams, R. (1989) 'The dynamics of IT implementation: a reassessment of paradigms and trajectories of development', University of Edinburgh: PICT Working Paper Series.

Foucault, M. (1977) *Discipline and Punish*, Harmondsworth: Penguin.

Foucault, M. (1980) *Power/Knowledge* Gordon, C. (ed.), Brighton, England: Harvester Press.

Foucault, M. (1982) 'The subject and power', in Dreyfus, H.L. and Rabinow, P. (eds), *Beyond Structuralism and Hermeneutics*, Brighton, Sussex: Harvester Press.

Foucault, M. (1984) *The Foucault Reader*, Rabinow, P. (ed.), Harmondsworth: Penguin.

Fox, A. (1971) *A Sociology of Work in Industry*, London: Collier Macmillan.

Fox, A. (1974) *Beyond Contract: Work, Power and Trust Relations*, London: Faber.

Franz, C.R. and Robey, D. (1984) 'An investigation of user-led system design: rational and political perspectives, *Communications of the ACM*, **27**(12), 1202–9.

Friedman, A. (1977) *Industry and Labour*, London: Macmillan.

Friedman, A. (1987a) 'Strategies for Computer People', Copenhagen: Institute of Organisation and Industrial Sociology, School of Economics and Social Science, CHIPS Working Paper.

Friedman, A. (1987b) 'Understanding the employment position of computer programmers: a managerial strategies approach', Copenhagen: Institute of Organisation and Industrial Sociology, School of Economics and Social Science, CHIPS Working Paper.

Friedman, A. and Cornford, D. (1987) 'Strategies for meeting user demands: an international perspective', *International Journal of Information Management*, No. 7.

Friedman, A.L. and Cornford, D.S. (1989) *Computer Systems Development: History Organization and Implementation*. London: Wiley.

Game, A. (1990) *Undoing the Social*, Milton Keynes: Open University Press.

Giddens, A. (1971) *Capitalism and Modern Social Theory*, Cambridge University Press.

Giddens, A. (1976) *New Rules of Sociological Method*, London: Hutchinson.

Giddens, A. (1979), *Central Problems in Social Theory*, London: Macmillan.

Gide, A. (1960) *The Immoralist*, Harmondsworth: Penguin.

Goodrich (1975) *The Frontier of Control*, London: Pluto Press.

Gouldner, A. W. (1954a) *Patterns of Industrial Bureaucracy*. Glencoe, Ill: Free Press.

Gouldner, A. W. (1954b) *Wildcat Strike*. New York: Antioch Press.

Gouldner, A. (1976) *The Dialectic of Ideology and Technology*, London: Macmillan.

Gouldner, A.W. (1986) *The Coming Crisis of Western Sociology*, London: Heinemann.

Gramsci, A. (1971) *Selections from the Prison Notebooks of Antonio Gramsci*, Hoare, Q. and Nowell-Smith, G. London: Lawrence and Wishart.

Green, E., Owen, J. and Pain, D. (1993) '"City Libraries": Human-centred opportunities for women', in Green, E., Owen, J. and Pain. D. (eds), *Gendered by Design: Information Technology and Office Systems*, London: Taylor.

Guinan P. J. (1988) *Patterns of Excellence for IS Professionals: An Analysis of Communication Behaviour*, Washington DC: ICIT Press.

Habermas, J. (1973) *Towards a Rational Society*, London: Heinemann.

Hacker, S. (1990) *Doing It the Hard Way: Investigations of Gender and Technology*, Boston: Unwin Hyman.

Hage, J. (1980) *Theories of Organizations: Forms, Process and Transformation*, New York: Wiley.

Hage, J. and Aiken, M. (1970) *Social Change in Complex Organizations*, New York: Random House.

Hammer, M. (1990) 'Reengineering work: don't automate, obliterate', *Harvard Business Review*, July/August, 104–12.

Harding, S. (1986) *The Science Question in Feminism*, Milton Keynes: Oxford Univerity Press.

Harper, R.H.R. and Hughes, J. (1993) 'What an F.ing System! Send 'Em All to the Same Place and Then Expect Us to Stop 'Em Hitting': Making Technology Work in Air Traffic Control in Button, G. (ed.) *Technology in Working Order: Studies of Work Interaction, and Technology*, London: Routledge, 127–144.

Hebden, J.E. (1975) 'Patterns of work identification', *Sociology of Work and Occupations*, 2(2), 107–33.

Hedberg, B. and Mumford, E. (1975) 'The design of computer systems: man's vision of man as an integral part of the systems design process', in E. Mumford and H. Sackman (eds) *Human Choice and Computers*, Amsterdam: North Holland, pp. 31–59.

Hekman, S. (1990) *Gender and Knowledge*, Oxford: Polity Press.

Henderson, J. C. and Sifonis, J. G. (1988) 'The value of strategic IS planning: understanding consistency, validity and IS markets', *MIS Quarterly*, 12, June, 187–99.

Henwood, F. (1993) 'Establishing gender perspectives on information technology: problems, issues and opportunities', in Green, E., Owen, J. and Pain, D. (eds), *Gendered by Design: Information Technology and Office Systems*, London: Taylor, pp.31–52.

Hickson, D.J., Hinings, C.R., Lee, C.A., Schneck, R.E. and Pennings, J.M. (1971) 'A strategic contingencies theory of intra-organisational power', *Administrative Science Quarterly*, 16, 216–29.

Hickson, J.H., Butler, R.J., Gray, D., Mallory, G.R. and Wilson, D.C. (1986) *Top Decisions: Strategic Decision Making in Organisations* Oxford: Blackwell.

Holti, R. W. (1989) 'The Nature of the Control of Work in Computer Software Production', unpublished PhD Thesis, Imperial College of Science and Technology, London.

Hoskins, K. (1990) 'Using history to understand theory: a re-consideration of the historical genesis of "strategy"', paper delivered at the EIASM Workshop on Strategy, Accounting and Control, Venice.

Hughes, T.P. (1987) 'The evolution of large technological systems', in Bijker et al 1987 (eds), *The Social Construction of Technological Systems*, Cambridge, Mass: MIT Press, pp. 51–82.

Hyman, R. (1987) 'Strategy or structure: capital, labour and control.' *Work, Employment and Society*, 1(1), 25–56.

Income Data Services (1988) *Computer Staff Pay*, IDS Study, No. 404.

Isaac, J.C. (1987) *Power and Marxist Theory: A Realist View*, Ithaca: Cornell University Press.

Ives, B. and Olson, M.H. (1984) 'User involvement and MIS success: a review of research', *Management Science*, 30, 586–603.

Jackal, R. (1988) *Moral Mazes: The World of Corporate Managers*, New York: Oxford University Press.

Jameson, F. (1984) 'Postmodernism, or the cultural logic of late capitalism', *New Left Review*, 146, 53–93.

Jameson, F. (1991) *Postmodernism*, London: Verso.

Johnson, J. (1987) *Professions and Power*, London: Macmillan.

Jones, I. (l985) 'Trade union influence over systems development: opportunities and constraints in the case of a British Civil Service union', Paper to Development and Use of Computer-Based Systems and Tools, Aarhus University, August l985.

Jordanova, L. J., (1987) 'Gender, science and creativity', in McNeil, M. (ed.) *Gender and Expertise*, London: Free Association Books.

Journal of Management Studies (1993) Special Edition on Knowledge Workers, *Journal of Management Studies*, **30**(6).

Kerfoot, D. and Knights, D. (1995) 'The gendered terrains of paternalism', in Wright, S. and Roper, M. (eds), *Anthropology of Organizations*, London: Routledge.

Kerfoot, D. and Knights, D. (1994) 'Management, masculinity and manipulation', *Journal of Management Studies*, **30**(4), pp. 659–678.

Kidder, T. (1981) *The Soul of the New Machine*, Harmondsworth: Penguin.

Klein, H. and Hirschheim, R. (1987) 'Social change and the future of information systems', in Boland, R. and Hirschheim, R. (eds), *Critical Issues in Information Systems Research*, Chichester: Wiley.

Kling, R. (1980), 'Social analyses of computing: theoretical perspectives in recent empirical research', *Computing Surveys*, **12**(1), 61–110.

Kling, R. (1991) 'Computerization and social transformations', *Science, Technology and Human Values*, **16**(3), 342–67.

Kling, R. and Iacono, S. (1984) 'The control of information systems development after implementation', *Communications of the ACM*, **27**(12), 1218–26.

Kling, R. and Scachi, W. (1982), 'The web of computing: computer technology as social organization', in Yovits, M.C. (ed.), *Advances in Computers, Number 21*, New York: Academic Press.

Knights, D. (1990) 'Subjectivity, power and the labour process', in Knights, D. and Willmott, H. (eds), *Labour Process Theory*, London: Macmillan.

Knights, D. (1992), 'Changing spaces: the disruptive impact of a new epistemological location for the study of management', *Academy of Management Review*, **17**(3): 514–36.

Knights, D. (1995) 'Refocusing the case study: researching the politics of IT and the politics of IT research', *Technology Studies*, **3**.

Knights, D. and Morgan, G. (1991) 'Corporate strategy, organizations and subjectivity: a critique', *Organization Studies*, **12**(9), 251–73.

Knights, D., and Murray, F. (1990) 'Competition and control: the strategic use of IT in a life insurance company', forthcoming in Legge, K., Clegg, C.W and Kemp, N.J. (eds), *Case Studies in Information Technology*, Oxford: Blackwell.

Knights, D. and Murray, F. (1992) 'Politics and pain in managing information technology', *Organization Studies*, **13**(2) 211–28.

Knights, D. and Willmott, H. (1983) 'Dualism and domination: an analysis of Marxian, Weberian and existentialist perspectives', *Australian and New Zealand Journal of Sociology*, **19**(1), 33–49.

Knights, D. and Willmott, H. (1985) 'Power and identity in theory and practice', *Sociological Review*, **33**(1).

Knights, D. and Willmott, H. (1987) 'Organisational culture as management strategy: a critique and illustration from the financial services industry', *International Studies of Management and Organisation*, **17**(3).

Knights, D. and Willmott, H. (1987) 'The executive fix; strategic decision making in the financial services industry', in McGoldrick, J. (ed.), *Teaching Studies in Behavioural Management*, London: Van Nostrand.

Knights, D. and Willmott, H. (eds) (1988), *New Technology and the Labour Process*, London: Macmillan.

Knights, D. and Willmott, H. (eds) (1990) 'Labour Process Theory', London: Macmillan.

Knights, D. and Willmott, H., 'Power and subjectivity at work: from degradation to subjugation in social relations', *Sociology*, **23**(4), 535–58.

Knights, D. and Willmott, H., (1993) 'A very foreign discipline: the genesis of expenses control in a mutual life insurance company', *The British Journal of Management*, **4**(1), 1–18.

Knights, D., Murray, F. and Willmott, H. (1993) 'Networking as knowledge work: a study of strategic inter-organisational development in the financial services industry', *Journal of Management Studies*, **30**(6).

Knights, D. and Vurdubakis, T. (1994), 'Foucault, power, resitance and all that', in Jermier, J., Knights, D. and Nord, W. (eds), *Resistance and Power in Organisations: Agency, Subjectivity and the Labour Process*, London: Routledge.

Kraft, P. (1977) *Programmers and Managers: the Routinization of Computer Programming in the United States*, New York: Springer-Verlag.

Kraft, P. (1979) 'The industrialisation of computer programming: from programming to 'software production', in Zimbalist, A. (ed.) *Case Studies in the Labour Process* London: Monthly Review Press, pp.1–17.

Kraft, P. and Dubnoff, S. (1986) 'Job content, fragmentation and control in computer software work', *Industrial Relations*, **25**(2), 185–96.

Latour, B. (1987), *Science in Action*, Milton Keynes: Open University Press.

Latour, B. (1988a) 'How to write *The Prince* for machines as well as machinations', in Elliot, B. (ed.), *Technology and Social Change*. Edinburgh: Edinburgh University Press, pp. 20–63.

Latour, B. (1988b) 'Mixing humans and nonhumans together: the sociology of the door closer', *Social Problems*, **35**(3), 298–310.

Lederer, A. L. and Mendelow, A.L. (1988) 'Convincing top management of the strategic potential of information systems ', *MIS Quarterly*, **12**, 525–34.

Lederer, A. L. and Sethi, V. (1988) 'The Implentation of Strategic Information Systems Planning Methodologies' MIS Quarterly, **12**(3), 445–461.

Lipietz, A. (1987) *Miracles and Mirages: The Crisis of Global Fordism*, London: Verso.

Lipietz, A. (1992) *Towards a New Economic Order; Postfordism, Ecology and Democracy*. Oxford: Polity Press.

Littler, C. (1982) *The Development of the Labour Process in Capitalist Societies*, London: Heinemann.

Littler, C. (1990) 'The labour process debate: a theoretical review 1974-88', in Knights, D. and Willmott, H. (eds), *Labour Process Theory*, Basingstoke: Macmillan, pp. 46–94.

Lucas, H.C. (1984) 'Organizational power and the information services department', *Communications of the ACM*, **27**(1), 58–64.

Lukes, S. (1974) *Power: a Radical View*, London: Macmillan.

Lyotard, J. F. (1984) *The Postmodern Condition*. Manchester: Manchester University Press.

Lyytinen, K. (1993) 'Information systems and critical theory', in Willmott H. and Alvesson, M. (eds), *Critical Management Studies*, London: Sage.

Mackay, H. and Lane, S. (1989) 'Towards a sociology of systems analysts', paper for the ESRC/PICT Software Workshop, Manchester, July, 1989.

MacKenzie, D. (1990) 'Economic and sociological explanation of technical change', paper to the Conference on Firm Strategy and Technical Change: Micro Economics or Micro Sociology ? Manchester, 27–28 September.

MacKenzie, D. and Wajcman, J. (eds) (1989) *The Social Shaping of Technology*, Milton Keynes: Open University Press.

Mandel, E. (1975) *Late Capitalism*, London: Verso.

March, J. G. (1965) *Handbook of Organizations*, Chicago: Rand McNally.

March, J. G. (1981) 'Decision making perspectives: Decisions in organizations and theories of choice', in Van de Ven, A.H. and Joyce, W.F. (eds), *Perspectives on Organization Design and Behaviour*, New York: Wiley.

Markus, M. (1984) *Systems in Organizations: Bugs and Features*, Boston: Pitman.

Markus, M. L. and Bjorn-Andersen, N. (1987), 'Power over users: its exercise by systems professionals', *Communications of the ACM*, **30**(6), 498–504.

Markus, M. and Pfeffer, J. (1983) 'Power and design and implementation of accounting and control systems', *Accounting Organizations and Society*, **8**(2/3), 205–218.

Marsden, R. (1993) 'The politics of organizational analysis', *Organization Studies*, **14**(1), 93–124.

Massey, J. (1988) 'I don't want a cowboy, just somebody to love', *Computing*, 10 November.

McFarlan, F. W. and McKenney J. L. (1983) *Corporate Information Systems Management: The Issues Facing Senior Executives*, Homewood, Illinois: Richard Irwin.

Miles. I., Rush, H. , Turner, K. and Bessant, J. (1988) *Information Horizons: The Long-term Implications of New Information Technologies*, Aldershot: Edward Elgar.

Miliband, R. (1973) *The State in Capitalist Society*, London: Quartet.

Mill, J. (1989) 'Room at the top', *Computing*, 5 January.

Miller, E. and Rice, A. (1967) *Systems of Organisations*, London: Tavistock.

Mills C. Wright (1956) *White Collar*, New York: OUP.

Mintzberg, H. (1973) *The Nature of Managerial Work*, Englewood Cliffs, New York: Prentice Hall.

Mintzberg, H. (1978) 'Patterns in Strategy Formation', *Management Science*, 14 pp 934–948.

Mintzberg, H. (1983) *Power in and Around Organisations*, Englewood Cliffs, NJ: Prentice Hall.

Morgan, G. and Knights, D. (1991) 'Gendering jobs: Corporate Strategy, Managerial Control and the Dynamics of Job Segregation', *Work, Employment and Society*, **5**(2) 181–200.

Mumford, E. (1972) *Job Satisfaction: A Study of Computer Specialists*, London: Longman.

Mumford, E. (1979) 'Systems design and human needs', in Bjorn Andersen, N., Hedberg, B., Mumford, E. and Sole, A. (eds), *The Impact of Systems Change in Organizations*, Alphen aan den Rijn: Sijthoff and Noordhoff, pp. 1–6.

Mumford, E. and Henshall, D. (1979) *The Participative Design of Computer Systems*, London: Associated Business Press.

Mumford, E. and Ward, T.B. (1968) *Computers: Planning for People*, London: Batsford.

Murray, F. (1989a) 'Beyond the negation of gender: technology bargaining and equal opportunities', *Economic and Industrial Democracy*, **10**, 517–42.

Murray, F. (1989b) 'The organisational politics of information technology: studies from the UK financial services industry', *Technology Analysis and Strategic Management*, **1**(3), 285–97.

Murray, F. (1991) 'Technical rationality and the IS specialist: power, discourse and identity', *Critical Perspectives on Accounting*, **2**(1), 59–81.

Murray, F. (1993) 'A separate reality: science, technology and masculinity', in Green, E., Owen, J. and Pain, D. (eds), *Gendered by Design: Information Technology and Office Systems*, London: Taylor and Francis, pp.64–80.

Murray, F. and Knights, D. (1990) 'Inter-managerial competition and capital accumulation: IT specialists, accountants and executive control', *Critical Perspectives in Accounting*, **1**(2), 167–190.

Murray, F. and Knights, D. (1990) 'Inter-managerial competition and the use of information technology: the case of the UK insurance industry', Final Project Report to the Economic and Social Research Council.

Murray, F. and Willmott, H. (1991) 'The communications problem in informations systems development: towards a relational approach', in *Proceedings of the Twelfth International Conference on Information Systems*, New York, 16–18 December 1991, pp. 83–92.

Murray, F. and Woolgar, S. (1991) 'Social perspectives on software: a preliminary report', Mimeo CICT, Brunel University.

Murray, F., O'Reilly, J. and Knights, D. (1992) *IFAs Networks and Technology: Who Benefits?* Manchester: UMIST.

Nelson, P. R. and Winter, S. G. (1977) 'In search of a useful theory of innovation', *Research Policy*, 36–76.

Nelson, P. R. and Winter, S. G. (1982) *An Evolutionary Theory of Economic Change*, Cambridge, Mass: Belknap Press.

Newman, M. and Rosenberg, D. (1985) 'Systems analysts and the politics of organizational control', *Omega International Journal of Management Science*, **13**(5), 393–406.

Nichols, T. and Armstrong, P. (1976) *Workers Divided*, Glasgow: Fontana.

Noble, D. F. (1977) *America by Design: Science, Technology and the Rise of Corporate Capitalism*. New York: Alfred A. Knopf.

Noble, D. (1984) *Forces of Production: a Social History of Industrial Automation*. New York: Alfred A. Knopf.

Orlikowski, W. J. (1988) 'The data processing occupation: professionalization or proletarianization?', *Research in the Sociology of Work*, **4**, 95–124.

Parker, T. and Udundun, M. (1988) 'Managing Information Systems in 1987: the top issues for IS managers', *Journal of Information Technology*, **3**(1), 34–42.

Parsons, T. (1951) *The Social System*, London: Tavistock.

Parsons, T. (1963) 'On the concept of power', *Proceedings of the American Philosophical Society*, **107**, 232–62.

Parsons, T. (1959) *Economy and Society*, London: Routledge.

Peat Marwick Mclintock/Bristol Business School (1988) *The Management Development Dimension: Information Technology in Insurance*, Bristol: Bristol Business School.

Peters. T. (1992) *Liberation Management*, London: Macmillan.

Pettigrew, A. (1973) *The Politics of Organisational Decision-Making*, London: Tavistock.

Pettigrew, A. (1985) *The Awakening Giant: Continuity and Change at ICI*, Oxford: Blackwell.

Pettigrew, A. M. (1980) 'The politics of organisational change', in Anderson, A.B. (ed.), *The Human Side of Information Processing*, Amsterdam: North Holland.

Pfeffer, J. (1981) *Power in Organizations*. Boston: Pitman.

Pfeffer, J. and Salincik, G. R. (1978) *The External Control of Organizations: A Resource Dependency Perspective*, New York: Harper & Row.

Pinch, T. and Bijker, W. E. (1987) 'The social construction of facts and artifacts: or how the sociology of science and the sociology of technology might benefit each other', in Bijker, W.E., Hughes, T.P. and Pinch, T.J. (eds), *The Social Construction of Technological Systems*, Cambridge, Mass: MIT Press.

Piore, M. and Sabel, C. (1984) *The Second Industrial Divide*, New York: Basic Books.

Porter, M. (1980) *Competitive Strategy*, New York: Free Press.

Poster, M. (1984) *Foucault, Marxism and History; Mode of Production v. Mode of Information*, Cambridge: Polity.

Poster, M. (1990) *The Mode of Information: Poststructuralism and Social Content*, Cambridge: Polity Press.

Poulantzas, N. (1973) *Political Power and Social Classes*, London: New Left Books.

Quinn, J. B. (1992) *Intelligent Enterprise: A Knowledge and Service Based Paradigm for Industry*, New York: Free Press.

Quinton, A. (1966) 'Excerpt from "Contemporary British Philosophy"', in Pitcher, G. (ed.), *Wittgenstein: The Philosophical Investigations*, London: Macmillan.

Rajan, A. (1984) *New Technology and Employment in Insurance, Banking and Building Societies*, Aldershot: Gower.

Rajan, A. (1987) *Services—The Second Industrial Revolution?*, London: Butterworths.

Reich, R. B. (1990) *The Work of Nations: Preparing Ourselves for 21st Century Capitalism*, New York: Simon & Schuster.

Rice, A. K. (1963) *The Enterprise and its Environment*, London: Tavistock Publications.

Robey, D. and Farrow, D. (1982) 'User involvement in information system development: a conflict model and empirical test', *Management Science*, **28**(1), 73–85.

Robey, D. and Markus, L. (1984) 'Rituals in information systems design', *MIS Quarterly*, March, 5–15.

Rose, M. (1969) *Computers, Managers and Society*. Harmondsworth: Penguin.

Rossiter, M. (1982) *Women Scientists in America: Struggles and Strategies to 1940*, Baltimore: Johns Hopkins University Press.

Russell, S. (1986) 'The Social Construction of Artefacts: A Response to Pinch and Bijker', *Social Studies of Science*, **16**, 331–46.

Sabel, C. (1982) *Work and Politics*, Cambridge: Cambridge University Press.

Sartre, J. P. (1962) *Nausea*, London: Hamish Hamilton.

Sartre, J. P. (1966) *Being and Nothingness*, New York: Washington Square Press.

Sayles, L. R. (1958) *Behaviour of Industrial Work Groups: Prediction and Control*, New York: John Wiley.

Scarbrough, H. and Corbett, J. M. (1992) *Technology and Organization: Power, Meaning and Design*. London: Routledge.

Scarborough, H. and Lannon, R. (1988) 'The successful implementation of new technology in banking', *Journal of General Management*, **13**(3), Spring, 38–51.

Scase, R. and Goffee, R. (1989) *Reluctant Managers: Their Work and Lifestyles*, London: Unwin Hyman.

Scott Morton, M. S. (ed.) (1991) *The Corporation of the 1990s: Information Technology and Organizational Transformation*, New York: Oxford University Press.

Seidler, V. J. (1989) *Rediscovering Masculinity: Reason, Language and Sexuality*, London: Routledge.

Selznick, P. (1949) *T.V.A. and the Grass Roots*, California: University of California Press.

Selznick, P. (1957) *Leadership in Administration*. New York: Harper and Row.

Semler, R. (1993) *Maverick! The Success Story Behind the World's Most Unusual Workplace*, London: Century.

Shaiken, H. (1986) *Work Transformed: Automation and Labor in the Computer Age*, Lexington, Mass.: Lexington Books.

Sharpe, R. (1989) 'Increasing DP's sphere of influence', *Computing*, 13 May.

Sharrock, W. and Anderson, B. (1993) 'Working Towards Agreement' in G. Button (ed.) *Technology in Working Order*, London: Routledge pp. 149–161.

Smith, C. (1987) *Technical Workers: Class, Labour and Trade Unionism*, London: Macmillan.

Smith, S. L. and Wield, D. (1987) 'New Technology and bank work: banking on IT as an 'organisation technology' in L. Harris (ed.) *New Perspectives on the Financial System*, London: Croom Helm.

Storey, J. (1987) 'The management of new office technology: choice, control and social structure in the insurance industry', *Journal of Management Studies*, **24**(1).

Strassman, P. A. (1985) *Information Payoff: The Transformation of Work in the Electronic Age*, London: Collier Macmillan.

Strauss, A. and Glaser, B. (1980) *Discovery of Grounded Theory*, Chicago: Aldine.

Strauss, A. et al (1963) 'The Hospital and its negotiated order', in Friedson, E. (ed.), *The Hospital in Modern Society*, New York: Macmillan, pp. 125–47.

Sturdy, A. (ed.) (1989) *Managing Information Technology in Insurance: A Guide to the Key Issues*, Harlow: Longman.

Sturdy, A. (1990) 'Clerical Consent: An Analysis of Social Relations in Insurance Work', unpublished PhD Manchester School of Management, UMIST, UK.

Sturdy, A. (1992) 'Clerical Consent: "Shifting" Work in the Insurance Office' in Sturdy, A., Knights, D. and Willmott, H. (ed.) *Skill and Consent*, London: Routledge, pp. 115–148.

Sturdy, A. and Heery, M. (1989) 'Introduction', in Sturdy, A. (ed.), *Managing Information Technology in Insurance: A Guide to the Key Issues*, Harlow: Longman, pp. 1–15.

Sutherland, E. and Morieux, Y. (1988) 'Effectiveness and competition—linking business strategy, organizational culture and the use of information technology', *Journal of Information Technology*, **3**(1), 43–7.

Taylor, P. (1992) 'Paperless dream still tantalises', *The Financial Times Survey: Technology in the Office*, 5 October, p.1.

Tierney, M. and Wickham, J. (1989) 'Controlling software labour: professional ideologies and the problem of control', paper for the ESRC/PICT Software Workshop, Manchester, July 1989.

Touche Ross (1985), *The Impact of Technology on Banking: World Summary*, London: Touche Ross.

Trist, A., Higgin, G. and Murray, H. (1963) *Organisational Choice*, London: Tavistock.

Wajcman, J. (1991) *Feminism Confronts Technology*, Oxford: Polity Press.

Watkins, J. (1989) 'The existing technology', in Sturdy, A. (ed.), *Managing Information Technology in Insurance: A guide to the Key Issues*, Harlow: Longman, pp. 19–38.

Webber, A.M. (1993) 'What's so new about the new economy?' *Harvard Business Review*, January–Febuary, 24–42.

Webster, J. (1989), *Office Automation: The Labour Process and Women's Work in Britain*, Hemel Hempstead: Wheatsheaf.

Whyte, W. H. (1961) *The Organization Man*, Harmondsworth: Penguin.

Wightman, D. (1987) 'Competitive advantage through information technology', *Journal of General Management*, **12**(4) 36–45.

Wilkinson, B. (1983) *The Shopfloor Politics of New Technology*, London: Heinemann.

Willcocks, L. and Mason, D. (1987) *Computerising Work: People, Systems Design and Workplace Relations*, London: Paradigm Publishing.

Williams, R. (1985) 'Democratising system development', paper to Development and Use of Computer-Based Systems and Tools, Aarhus University, August 1985.

Williams, R. and Steward, F. (1984) *The Role of the Parties Concerned in the Introduction of New Technology—Case Studies on the Implementation of Collective Agreements on New Technology in Britain*, Dublin European Foundation for the Improvement of Living and Working Conditions.

Winkler, C. (1986) 'Battling for new roles', *Datamation*, 15 October, 82–7.

Woodward, J. (1958) *Management and Technology*, London: HMSO.

Woodward, J. (1965) *Industrial Organization: Theory and Practice*, Oxford: Oxford University Press.

Woodward, J. (ed.) (1970) *Industrial Organization: Behaviour and Control* Oxford: Oxford University Press.

Woolgar, S. and Grint, K. (1991) 'Computers and the transformation of social analysis', *Science, Technology and Human Values*, **16**(3), 368–78.

Zaltman, G., Duncan, R. and Holbek, J. (1973) *Innovations and Organizations*, New York: Wiley.

Zimbalist, A. (ed.) (1979) *Case Studies on the Labour Process*, London: Monthly Review Press.

Zuboff, S. (1988) *In the Age of the Smart Machine*. London: Heinemann.

Zussman, R. (1984) 'The middle levels: engineers and the "Working Middle Class"', *Politics & Society*, **13**(3), 217–38.

Index

Note: page references in *italics* refer to figures; those in **bold** refer to tables

Index compiled by Annette J. Musker